English Sentence Structure

An Intensive Course in English
English Language Institute

English Sentence Structure

Robert Krohn
And the Staff of the
English Language Institute

Ann Arbor   The University of Michigan Press

Copyright © by The University of Michigan 1971
All rights reserved
ISBN 0-472-08307-4
Library of Congress Catalog Card No. 73-142589
Published in the United States of America by
The University of Michigan Press and simultaneously
in Rexdale, Canada, by John Wiley & Sons Canada, Limited
Manufactured in the United States of America

1984   1983   1982   1981   26   25   24   23   22   21   20   19   18

Inquiries concerning tapes should be addressed to:
The English Language Institute
2001 North University Building
The University of Michigan
Ann Arbor, Michigan 48109

Preface

ENGLISH SENTENCE STRUCTURE is the central volume in the textbook series developed in the Intensive Course at the English Language Institute of the University of Michigan. Each lesson in this book is coordinated with a lesson in a pattern practice book, which provides additional exercises. The Intensive Course series also includes books in pronunciation, vocabulary, and conversation practice. Although designed primarily for students at an intermediate level, the series can be used in elementary classes and in advanced classes for remedial oral work. Absolute beginners in English may require preparatory lead-in materials before the early lessons of this volume can be used.

The history of ENGLISH SENTENCE STRUCTURE goes back more than a quarter of a century to the early 1940's, when the staff of the English Language Institute, under the direction of Charles C. Fries, began to produce materials to teach English as a foreign language. Over the years, these materials have been expanded and have undergone several major revisions. During that time the major contributors to the previous editions of the grammar materials were Charles C. Fries, who provided the original inspiration, and Robert Lado and Gerald Dykstra, who developed the exercises and the form of the materials. In addition, William H. Buell and Edward T. Erazmus contributed portions of the third edition, ENGLISH SENTENCE PATTERNS, which appeared in 1958.

In 1967, the English Language Institute and the University of Michigan Press decided to revise ENGLISH SENTENCE PATTERNS. Robert Krohn, who was thoroughly familiar with the book, having used it in a variety of classes, was put in charge of the revision.

Quite early it was decided that the new grammar materials should cover the same topics as the previous edition and in approximately the same order. Consequently, the new lessons are comparable with the previous edition and with the other books in the Intensive Course series. Because of this compatibility, each new lesson could be used by teachers as soon as it was written. In this way the new material was classroom tested by Dr. Krohn and the staff of the English Language Insitute over a period of two and a half years. Although much material was incorporated from the 1958 book, nearly every lesson has been completely rewritten, and new grammatical explanations and exercises have been developed.

In all stages of the revision, Dr. Krohn worked very closely with Professor Harold V. King, who helped revise each one of the first drafts of the new lessons and initiated the drafts of Lessons 21 and 22. Professor King helped guide the project from beginning to end, and much of the credit for its success must be given to him.

The English Language Institute
July 1970

Acknowledgments

Many people have contributed to this book. I wish to express my gratitude to all the teachers of the English Language Institute for their comments and suggestions. In particular, I owe thanks to Joyce Zuck for many valuable ideas on presenting structure and practicing English, and to Nancy Hewett for a large number of detailed suggestions for improving the text. I would also like to express my thanks to William H. Buell, who provided original material for Lessons 11 and 14. Others who were especially helpful include John Chandler, Robert Dakin, Ruth Hok, Marvin Kierstead, John T. Lamendella, Penny Larson, John Rohsenow, Judy Sabine, Randee Sorscher and Jack Wilson. My thanks also go to Charles H. Blatchford for his invaluable assistance in proofreading.

I owe a great debt to Professor Ronald Wardhaugh, who in his capacity as the Director of the English Language Institute, has encouraged experimentation and innovation in the teaching of English as a foreign language. He first suggested this project to me in 1967 and has closely followed its development. I am thankful to him for his help and advice.

Finally, I would like to express my thanks to Professor Harold V. King, who spent countless hours improving each lesson. He has been a constant source of ideas and encouragement, and his insights into the structure of English appear throughout the book.

R.K.

Suggestions for the Teacher

The teacher may use the following procedures to present the various parts of a lesson.

THE GRAMMAR FRAME

The frame is a box enclosing examples and COMMENTS. Put example sentences from the frame on the blackboard. Using the COMMENTS as a guide, discuss briefly the grammar point being illustrated, or ask the students to supply the comments. At the conclusion of this brief introduction, begin the exercises.

THE ORAL CLASSROOM EXERCISES

Ask the class to respond in unison. After doing an exercise with the entire class, do it again, calling on students individually. Students usually do not need their books during the exercises; the books can remain closed. However, with older students, in more advanced classes, or when the sentences being practiced are rather long, open books may be appropriate. Vary the procedures to determine which techniques are best for a particular class.

THE TEACHER'S EXPLANATIONS

In general, any remarks about structure preceding the exercises should be kept as short as possible. It is not necessary to explain everything in detail. Some potential questions will be answered by the exercise material. Some questions can be answered after an exercise, when the class has had an opportunity to go through a number of examples. Answers to students' questions should be simple and confined to the point. As a general rule, keep discussions about structure brief, and intersperse them with appropriate examples and exercises. Examples are very important in the learning process.

THE NOTES

Some explanations about structure are given outside the frames, under the heading of NOTES. It is not necessary to discuss all the NOTES in class. The amount of discussion depends on the needs of the class. Intermediate and advanced students can profit by reading this material at home.

HOMEWORK

It may be helpful to assign some of the exercises or parts of the exercises as written homework. Substitution drills, which are too repetitious for written work, might well be avoided. Instead, one can assign exercises that require students to answer questions, or to transpose parts of sentences, or to paraphrase sentences.

MEANING-ORIENTED PRACTICE

Probably the best way to practice a foreign language is to use it in com municating with others. Thus, teachers should provide time for meaning-oriented practice. For example, teachers can ask the students questions or initiate a class discussion that will force the students to use the grammar that has been presented that hour. Such question and discussion periods provide the members of the class with an occasion to use English structure to express their thoughts. This meaningful use of English provides an excellent opportunity for a student to improve his speaking ability, and it is one of the best tests of whether the grammatical principles have been assimilated.

Contents

Contents

Contents

Contents

Lesson 1

A.   *Be: am, are, is.*
        Statements and questions: It is green. Is it green?
        Contractions: *It's* green. It *isn't* green.
        Short answers: Yes, it is.

B.   Singular and plural noun phrases.

A.1 Notice the position of *is* in statements and questions.

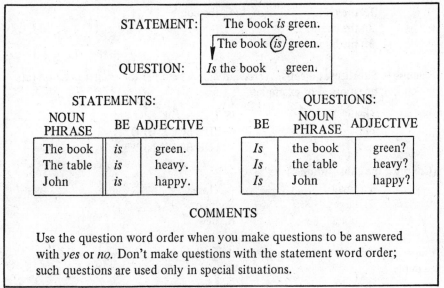

| STATEMENT: | The book *is* green. |
| QUESTION: | *Is* the book   green. |

STATEMENTS:

NOUN PHRASE	BE	ADJECTIVE
The book	*is*	green.
The table	*is*	heavy.
John	*is*	happy.

QUESTIONS:

BE	NOUN PHRASE	ADJECTIVE
Is	the book	green?
Is	the table	heavy?
Is	John	happy?

COMMENTS

Use the question word order when you make questions to be answered with *yes* or *no.* Don't make questions with the statement word order; such questions are used only in special situations.

NOTE: Words like *book, table, pencil, John, Mary,* etc., are nouns. *The book, the table, John, Mary,* etc. are noun phrases.

INSTRUCTIONS TO THE TEACHER: The students' exercises begin below. The words in small letters are the teacher's part. The words in CAPITAL LETTERS are the students' part. In the examples, the teacher says both parts, and the students repeat their part after the teacher. The teacher then continues the exercise, saying only the teacher's part. The students continue by producing the students' part on the pattern of the examples.

Exercise 1. Let's practice some statements. Substitute adjectives (*green, old, new,* etc.) in the proper position. For example:

green	THE BOOK IS GREEN.
old	THE BOOK IS OLD.
new	THE BOOK IS NEW.

(Continue the substitutions:)

1. small	4. closed
2. large	5. blue
3. open	6. new

Exercise 2. Substitute noun phrases in the proper position in statements. For example:

the pencil	THE PENCIL IS NEW.
the watch	THE WATCH IS NEW.

(Continue the substitutions:)

1. the table	4. the comb
2. the chair	5. the key
3. the book	6. the pen

Exercise 3. Substitute adjectives (*green, old, new,* etc.) in the proper position (at the end) in questions. For example:

green	IS THE BOOK GREEN?
old	IS THE BOOK OLD?
new	IS THE BOOK NEW?

(Continue the substitutions:)

1. small	4. closed
2. large	5. blue
3. open	6. new

Exercise 4. Substitute noun phrases in the proper position in questions. For example:

the pencil	IS THE PENCIL NEW?
the watch	IS THE WATCH NEW?

(Continue:)

1. the table	4. the comb
2. the chair	5. the key
3. the book	6. the pen

Exercise 5. Change the teacher's statement into a question. For example:

The book is new.	IS THE BOOK NEW?
The table is heavy.	IS THE TABLE HEAVY?

1. The pencil is red.	7. The table is large.
2. The book is green.	8. The key is small.
3. The chair is new.	9. The comb is black.
4. The book is open.	10. The book is old.
5. The door is closed.	11. The student is busy.
6. The chair is heavy.	12. The exercise is easy.

A.2 Notice the correlation of *am, are,* and *is* with the subject noun phrase:

NOUN PHRASE	*BE*			NOUN PHRASE (PRONOUN)	*BE*	
			sg.			
			1	I	*am*	happy.
			2	You	*are*	happy.
John	*is*	happy.	3	He	*is*	happy.
Mary	*is*	happy.	3	She	*is*	happy.
The book	*is*	green.	3	It	*is*	green.
			pl.			
You and I	*are*	happy.	1	We	*are*	happy.
John and I	*are*	happy.	1	We	*are*	happy.
You and John	*are*	happy.	2	You	*are*	happy.
Mary and John	*are*	happy.	3	They	*are*	happy.
The books	*are*	green.	3	They	*are*	green.

COMMENT

Be has three forms in the simple present tense: *am, are,* and *is.*

NOTE: Sg. and pl. are abbreviations for singular and plural. The numbers 1, 2, and 3 mean first person, second person, and third person.

Exercise 6. Change the teacher's statement into a question. Substitute a pronoun for the teacher's noun phrase. For example:

The book is new.	IS IT NEW?
John is happy.	IS HE HAPPY?
The students are busy.	ARE THEY BUSY?

1. The book is open.
2. Mary is tired.
3. The pencils are red.
4. John and Mary are busy.
5. The window is open.
6. The table is heavy.
7. The pencil is long.
8. The pencils are long.
9. Mary is happy.
10. John is busy.
11. The dog is hungry.
12. The dogs are hungry.

A.3   Notice the contractions which are made with *am, are,* and *is:*

CONTRACTIONS:

I	*am*	busy.	1	*I'm*	busy.
You	*are*	busy.	2	*You're*	busy.
He	*is*	busy.	3	*He's*	busy.
She	*is*	busy.	3	*She's*	busy.
It	*is*	green.	3	*It's*	green.
We	*are*	busy.	1	*We're*	busy.
You	*are*	busy.	2	*You're*	busy.
They	*are*	busy.	3	*They're*	busy.
John	*is*	busy.	3	*John's*	busy.
Mary	*is*	busy.	3	*Mary's*	busy.

COMMENTS

(1)   Contractions are commonly used in speaking.

(2)   Contractions are often written in notes and letters to friends and relatives. However, full forms are usually used in formal writing, such as papers which students write in college.

Exercise 7. Practice the contractions which are made with *be.* Make substitutions in the proper places. For example:

I'm	I'M HUNGRY.
Mary's	MARY'S HUNGRY.
She's	SHE'S HUNGRY.
You're	YOU'RE HUNGRY.

1. they're	4. I'm
2. John's	5. you're
3. he's	6. we're

(Continue with the following forms:)

7. we	12. you
8. I	13. the teacher
9. he	14. we
10. she	15. I
11. we	

4

A.4 Observe the patterns with *be*.

NOUN PHRASE	BE	ADJECTIVE PHRASE
The book	is	green.
John	is	twenty years old.
He	is	hungry.

NOUN PHRASE	BE	NOUN PHRASE
Mr. Allen	is	a lawyer.
Mary	is	a student.

NOUN PHRASE	BE	ADVERBIAL
Mary	is	from Mexico.
She	is	in class.
She	is	in the room.

COMMENTS

Be is used in all these patterns. (Some other adjectives which are used with *be* are *thirsty, right, wrong, warm, cold, tired,* and *sleepy.* We do not use the verb *have* in this pattern.)

Exercise 8. Substitute the words in the proper position.

John is hungry.

cold	JOHN IS COLD.
a student	JOHN IS A STUDENT.
in class	JOHN IS IN CLASS.
John and Mary	JOHN AND MARY ARE IN CLASS.

1. tired	8. in class	15. thirsty
2. cold	9. a student	16. you
3. hungry	10. in the United States	17. tired
4. from California	11. I	18. Mary
5. from San Francisco	12. right	19. sleepy
6. John	13. busy	20. hungry
7. happy	14. a doctor	21. twenty years old

Exercise 9. Practice the use of *be* in questions. Substitute the words in the proper position.

Is John hungry?

cold	IS JOHN COLD?
a student	IS JOHN A STUDENT?
in class	IS JOHN IN CLASS?
John and Mary	ARE JOHN AND MARY IN CLASS?

(Continue with the substitutions of Exercise 8.)

A.5   Notice the use of a short answer.

QUESTION	SHORT ANSWER
Is John busy?	Yes, he is.

COMMENT

Yes, he is means 'Yes, John is busy' or 'Yes, he's busy.'

AFFIRMATIVE SHORT ANSWERS

Yes, I am.	Yes, we are.
Yes, you are.	Yes, you are.
Yes, he is.	Yes, they are.
Yes, she is.	
Yes, it is.	

COMMENT

Be is not contracted when it is the last word in a sentence.

Exercise 10.   Practice the use of short answers.   Answer the teacher's question with an affirmative short answer.

Is the book green?	YES, IT IS.
Is Mary a student?	YES, SHE IS.
Is she busy?	YES, SHE IS.

1. Are the pencils red?
2. Is Mr. Miller tired?
3. Is Mr. Allen a lawyer?
4. Is Mrs. Allen a teacher?
5. Is Mary twenty years old?
6. Is Mary from Mexico?

7. Are John and Mary hungry?
8. Is Mary sleepy?
9. Is the book open?
10. Is Mr. Miller in the room?
11. Is the teacher busy?
12. Are the students busy?

A.6 Notice the negative short answers.

QUESTION	SHORT ANSWER
Is the book blue?	No, it isn't.

NEGATIVE SHORT ANSWERS

No, I'm not.
No, you aren't.
No, he isn't.
No, she isn't.
No, it isn't.

No, we aren't.
No, you aren't.
No, they aren't.

COMMENTS

I'm not is the contraction of *I am not.*
Isn't is the contraction of *is not.*
Aren't is the contraction of *are not.*

NOTE: The following forms of negative short answers are equally acceptable:

No, you're not.
No, he's not.
No, she's not.
No, it's not.

No, we're not.
No, you're not.
No, they're not.

Exercise 11. Practice the negative short answers.

Is Mary a doctor?	NO, SHE ISN'T.
Is she a lawyer?	NO, SHE ISN'T.
Are the books black?	NO, THEY AREN'T.

1. Is the key large?
2. Is the key green?
3. Is the teacher from England?
4. Is the teacher a lawyer?
5. Is the table red?
6. Are the pencils heavy?

7. Is Mary a teacher?
8. Is John hungry?
9. Is John ten years old?
10. Are John and Mary from England?
11. Is the comb heavy?
12. Is the comb red?

Exercise 12. Practice both affirmative and negative short answers. Answer the teacher's questions (individually). Give a true answer.

Are you a student?	YES, I AM.
Are you from the United States?	NO, I'M NOT.
Is the book blue?	NO, IT ISN'T.

1. Are you from England?
2. Is the book twenty-nine years old?

3. Are you hungry?
4. Am I from England?
5. Are you a doctor?

6. Is the door open?
7. Are you from Japan?
8. Are the students in the room?
9. Are they busy?
10. Is the book new?
11. Are you a teacher?
12. Is the table heavy?
13. Is the watch heavy?
14. Is the door closed?

15. Are you a lawyer?
16. Am I a teacher?
17. Is Mr. A. from New York?
    (Use the name of a student.)
18. Is Miss B. from Chicago?
    (Use the name of a student.)
19. Are Mr. C. and Mr. D. students?
    (Use the names of students.)
20. Are we in the United States?

A.7 Notice the use of pronouns.

John's from Chicago. *He's* a student.
Is the book closed? No, *it* isn't. *It's* open.

COMMENTS

The noun phrase cannot be entirely suppressed in such sentences. To avoid repeating or emphasizing the noun phrase, you may use in its place one of the pronouns *he, she, it, they.*

Exercise 13. Answer the teacher's questions. Be sure to use pronouns. Give true answers.

Is the book red?   NO, IT ISN'T. IT'S GREEN.
Am I a doctor?   NO, YOU AREN'T. YOU'RE A TEACHER.
Are you a teacher?   NO, I'M NOT. I'M A STUDENT.

1. Are you from England?
2. Are you from the United States?
3. Are you a lawyer?
4. Is Mr. A. a teacher?
   (Use the name of a student.)
5. Is the comb red?
6. Is Miss B. from England?
   (Use the name of a student.)

7. Is the table new?
8. Is Mr. C. a doctor?
   (Use the name of a student.)
9. Am I a businessman?
10. Is the pencil heavy?
11. Are the books blue?
12. Are the books in Mexico?

B.1 Notice the singular and plural forms of the nouns and the use of *a* or *an* with the singular.

I'm	*a*	student.	sg.
We're		students.	pl.
You're	*a*	student.	sg.
You're		students.	pl.
It's	*a*	book.	sg.
They're		books.	pl.
He's	*an*	architect.	sg.
He's	*a*	doctor.	sg.
They're		architects.	pl.
They're		doctors.	pl.
John's	*a*	student.	sg.
Mary's	*a*	student.	sg.
John and Mary are		students.	pl.
They're		students.	pl.

COMMENTS

In this pattern, use *a* or *an* with the singular forms of nouns (*student, book,* etc.) but not with the plural forms (*students, books,* etc.) Use the form *an* only if the word after it begins with a vowel sound.

Exercise 14. Practice singular nouns with *a* and plural nouns without *a*. Substitute the teacher's words and change the rest of the statement if necessary.

I'm a student.

doctor	I'M A DOCTOR.
lawyer	I'M A LAWYER.
he	HE'S A LAWYER.
they	THEY'RE LAWYERS.
teachers	THEY'RE TEACHERS.
Mary	MARY'S A TEACHER.

1. student	5. he	9. she	13. I
2. I	6. they	10. we	14. they
3. doctor	7. students	11. he	15. John
4. lawyer	8. Mary	12. you	16. I

B.2 Notice the form of the adjectives and the article *the*.

sg.	*The* book is *new.*
pl.	*The* books are *new.*
sg.	*The* student is *busy.*
pl.	*The* students are *busy.*

COMMENT

Adjectives and the article *the* have the same form with both singular and plural nouns.

Exercise 15. Change the teacher's statement from the singular to the plural. For example:

The book is green.	THE BOOKS ARE GREEN.
The book is closed.	THE BOOKS ARE CLOSED.
The chair is old.	THE CHAIRS ARE OLD.

1. The book is new.
2. The student is busy.
3. The window is open.
4. The comb is black.
5. The pen is black.
6. The student is hungry.
7. The book is closed.
8. The pen is new.
9. The student is tired.
10. The chair is heavy.
11. The shoe is black.
12. The shirt is white.

Exercise 16. This is a review exercise. Change the teacher's statement into a question. Another student will give a true answer.

The book is green.	Student A: IS THE BOOK GREEN?
	Student B: YES, IT IS.
The students are hungry.	Student B: ARE THE STUDENTS HUNGRY?
	Student C: YES, THEY ARE.
	(NO, THEY AREN'T.)
You're a doctor.	Student C: ARE YOU A DOCTOR?
	Student D: NO, I'M NOT. I'M A STUDENT.

1. The books are new.
2. You're from England.
3. The pencil is heavy.
4. The students are busy.
5. You're a businessman.
6. The door is open.
7. The windows are open.
8. The table is heavy.
9. The book is black.
10. Mr. A. is from Mexico.
    (Use the name of a student.)
11. The comb is heavy.
12. The teacher is busy.
13. You're hungry.
14. The exercise is easy.
15. Miss B. is from Japan.
    (Use the name of a student.)
16. Are Mr. C. and Mr. D. in the room?
    (Use the names of students.)

10

Lesson 2

A. Simple present tense with verbs other than *be*.
    Statements: He works.
    Questions with *do, does:* Does he work?
    Short answers: Yes, he does.

B. Single-word adverbs of frequency: *always, usually, often,* etc.
    Position in statements and questions.

A.1 Notice the form of the verb.

Sg.		VERB	
1	I	work	every morning.
2	You	work	every morning.
3	He	works	every morning.
Pl.			
1	We	work	every morning.
2	You	work	every morning.
3	They	work	every morning.

COMMENTS

(1) Verbs other than *be* have two forms in the simple present tense: a simple form and an *-s* form.

(2) The *-s* form is used with third person singular subjects (*he, she, it, John, Mary, the book*, etc.) Otherwise, the simple form is used.

NOTE: The pronunciation of the −s form is treated in the pronunciation book.

Exercise 1. Practice the two forms of the following verbs by substituting as shown in the examples.

reads   JOHN READS IN THE MORNING, AND WE READ IN
               THE AFTERNOON.

writes   JOHN WRITES IN THE MORNING, AND WE WRITE
               IN THE AFTERNOON.

practices JOHN PRACTICES IN THE MORNING, AND WE
               PRACTICE IN THE AFTERNOON.

1. reads	3. studies	5. arrives	7. practices
2. sings	4. works	6. leaves	8. writes

11

Exercise 2. *Has* is the third person singular form of *have*. Practice these two forms by substituting the teacher's words. Change the rest of the statement if necessary.

We	WE HAVE COFFEE HERE IN THE MORNING.
John	JOHN HAS COFFEE HERE IN THE MORNING.

1. he	6. Mary	11. he
2. John and Mary	7. she	12. you
3. they	8. the students	13. I
4. Mr. Allen	9. they	14. you and I
5. he	10. Mr. Miller	15. we

A.2 Notice the use of *does* in questions.

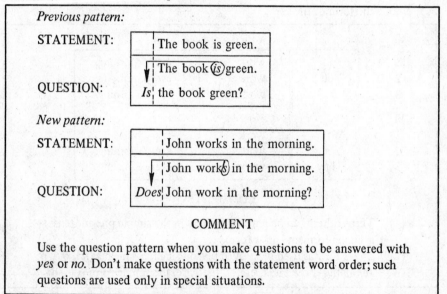

Previous pattern:

STATEMENT: The book is green.

QUESTION: The book *is* green.
Is the book green?

New pattern:

STATEMENT: John works in the morning.

QUESTION: John work*s* in the morning.
Does John work in the morning?

COMMENT

Use the question pattern when you make questions to be answered with *yes* or *no*. Don't make questions with the statement word order; such questions are used only in special situations.

NOTE: In American English, the question which corresponds to *John has a book* is usually *Does John have a book? Has John a book?* is another possible form.

ADDITIONAL EXAMPLES

Does Mr. Smith practice in class?
Does the student study?
Does Mary read Spanish?

Exercise 3. Change the teacher's statement into a question.

John studies at night.	DOES JOHN STUDY AT NIGHT?
Mary studies in the afternoon.	DOES MARY STUDY IN THE AFTERNOON?

1. John studies the lessons.
2. He understands the lessons.
3. He has coffee at 11 o'clock.
4. He has lunch at noon.
5. Mary practices in the after-noon.
6. She eats supper at 6 o'clock.
7. She writes letters at night.
8. Mr. Allen works in the afternoon.
9. He reads at night.
10. John comes to class every morning.
11. Mr. Miller comes here in the afternoon.
12. He leaves at night.

A.3 Compare the use of *does* and *do* in questions.

STATEMENT:	He works in the morning.
QUESTION:	*Does* he work in the morning?

STATEMENT:	They work every day.
QUESTION:	*Do* they work every day?

COMMENTS

Do and *does* are used to make questions. Use *does* for the third person singular, *do* for the other persons.

ADDITIONAL EXAMPLES

Do I speak well?
Do you read Spanish?
Does Mary work?
Do we begin in the morning?
Do you come here every day?
Do Mr. and Mrs. Allen eat dinner at 7 o'clock?

Exercise 4. Change the teacher's statement into a question. Use *do* or *does*.

John and Mary study English.	DO JOHN AND MARY STUDY ENGLISH?
John studies in the morning.	DOES JOHN STUDY IN THE MORNING?
Mr. and Mrs. Allen teach Spanish.	DO MR. AND MRS. ALLEN TEACH SPANISH?

1. John and Mary have coffee at 10 o'clock.
2. Mrs. Allen has coffee at 11 o'clock.
3. The students understand English.
4. They practice every day.
5. John has a coke in the afternoon.
6. He studies at night.
7. The students study here.
8. They understand the lessons.
9. John has a book.
10. John and Mary speak English.

13

Exercise 5. Change the teacher's statement into a question. Use either *do, does,* or a form of *be.* Substitute a pronoun for the subject noun phrase.

John and Mary study here.	DO THEY STUDY HERE?
Mr. Allen reads at night.	DOES HE READ AT NIGHT?
The book is open.	IS IT OPEN?

1. John likes coffee.
2. John and Bill practice in the morning.
3. Mr. Miller is from New York.
4. The books are in the room.
5. Mary eats lunch at noon.
6. Mr. Green is very hungry.
7. The teachers arrive in the morning.
8. Mr. Allen and Mr. Miller leave in the afternoon.
9. Mary writes letters every week.
10. The teachers have coffee in the afternoon.
11. John is a student.
12. Mrs. Taylor eats breakfast at 7 o'clock.

A.4 Notice the use of affirmative short answers.

Previous pattern (Lesson 1):

QUESTION:	Is John busy?
SHORT ANSWER:	Yes, he *is.*

New pattern:

QUESTION:	Does John like coffee?
SHORT ANSWER:	Yes, he *does.*
QUESTION:	Do Mr. and Mrs. Allen like tea?
SHORT ANSWER:	Yes, they *do.*

COMMENTS

In the short answers above, *Yes, he does* means *Yes, John likes coffee,* and *Yes, they do* means *Yes, Mr. and Mrs. Allen like tea.* Notice that *do* and *does* are substitutes for the verb phrases. In the examples, *does* replaces *likes coffee,* and *do* replaces *like tea.*

AFFIRMATIVE SHORT ANSWERS:

sg.		pl.
Yes, I do.	1	Yes, we do.
Yes, you do.	2	Yes, you do.
Yes, he does.	3	Yes, they do.

ADDITIONAL EXAMPLES

Do you like coffee?   Yes, I do.
Do the students study at night?   Yes, they do.
Do I pronounce well?   Yes, you do.

Does the new student like the class?   Yes, he does.
Does Mary drink coffee?   Yes, she does.

Exercise 6. Answer the teacher's question with an affirmative short answer.

Does Mary study at night?   YES, SHE DOES.
Do Mr. and Mrs. Allen drink tea?   YES, THEY DO.

1. Does Mr. Allen study in the morning?
2. Do John and Mary study in the afternoon?
3. Do they have class in the morning?
4. Do they understand the lessons?
5. Does Mary understand English?
6. Do the students understand it?
7. Does Mr. Miller sing well?
8. Does Mrs. Miller work?
9. Does John pronounce well?
10. Does he practice at home?
11. Do John and Mary study at night?
12. Do they write letters every week?

A.5 Notice the use of negative short answers.

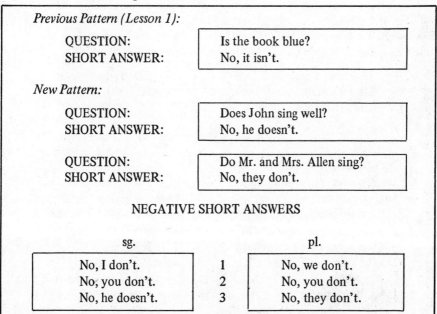

Previous Pattern (Lesson 1):

| QUESTION: | Is the book blue? |
| SHORT ANSWER: | No, it isn't. |

New Pattern:

| QUESTION: | Does John sing well? |
| SHORT ANSWER: | No, he doesn't. |

| QUESTION: | Do Mr. and Mrs. Allen sing? |
| SHORT ANSWER: | No, they don't. |

NEGATIVE SHORT ANSWERS

sg.		pl.
No, I don't.	1	No, we don't.
No, you don't.	2	No, you don't.
No, he doesn't.	3	No, they don't.

15

ADDITIONAL EXAMPLES

Do the classes begin at 7 A.M.?	No, they don't.
Do they begin at 5 P.M.?	No, they don't.
Does Mary eat lunch here?	No, she doesn't.
Does the class begin at 7 A.M.?	No, it doesn't.
Does it begin at 6 A.M.?	No, it doesn't.

Exercise 7. Answer the teacher's question with a negative short answer.

Does John eat lunch here?	NO, HE DOESN'T.
Do classes begin at 6 A.M.?	NO, THEY DON'T.

1. Does John have tea in the morning?
2. Do Mr. and Mrs. Miller have tea in the morning?
3. Does Mary have class at noon?
4. Does she eat lunch here?
5. Does John have eggs and toast for breakfast?
6. Does he have a sandwich for lunch?
7. Do classes begin at 6 A.M.?
8. Do Mr. and Mrs. Miller study at noon?
9. Does Mr. Miller arrive at 6 A.M.?
10. Do John and Mary leave at 4 P.M.?

Exercise 8. Practice the use of affirmative and negative answers. Answer the teacher's question individually. Give a true answer.

Is the book green?	YES, IT IS.
Do I understand English?	YES, YOU DO.
Does the class begin at 7 A.M.?	NO, IT DOESN'T.

1. Is the door closed?
2. Is the door open?
3. Do you have tea for dinner?
4. Do you like coffee?
5. Do you speak Spanish?
6. Does Mr. A. speak Spanish? (Use the name of a student.)
7. Do you drink milk in the morning?
8. Is Mr. B. in class? (Use the name of a student.)
9. Do Mr. C. and Mr. D. speak Spanish? (Use the names of students.)
10. Are we in class?
11. Do I live in the United States?
12. Does Mr. E. teach English? (Use the name of a student.)
13. Is Miss F. a teacher? (Use the name of a student.)
14. Do you study in the afternoon?

B.1   Notice the position of words like *always* and compare their meanings.

	SINGLE-WORD ADVERB OF FREQUENCY	MAIN VERB	
John	*always*	studies	at night.
Mary	*usually*	studies	at night.
Bob	*often*	studies	at night.
Bill	*sometimes*	studies	at night.
Alice	*seldom*	studies	at night.
Tom	*never*	studies	at night.

always	⌐	100% ...	all of the time
usually		...	most of the time
often		50% ...	much of the time
sometimes		...	some of the time
seldom		...	almost never
never	⌐	0% ...	not at any time

COMMENTS

Adverbs like *always* (single-word adverbs of frequency) come *before* the main verb of a sentence. (See section B.2 for sentences with *be*.)

NOTE: Some of these adverbs are also used in other positions, as in the sentence *Sometimes I study at night.*

Exercise 9. Substitute a word like *always* for the multi-word adverbials of frequency.

Mary drinks milk all of the time.   MARY ALWAYS DRINKS MILK.
John drinks milk most of the time.   JOHN USUALLY DRINKS MILK.

1. John drinks coffee some of the time.
2. He almost never drinks tea.
3. Mr. Allen drinks coffee much of the time.
4. Mrs. Allen almost never drinks coffee.
5. She drinks tea most of the time.
6. Mr. Miller has coffee at 10 A.M. all of the time.
7. Mrs. Miller has coffee at 10 A.M. some of the time.
8. Mrs. Miller almost never drinks milk in the morning.
9. She has coffee in the morning most of the time.
10. Mr. and Mrs. Miller eat in a restaurant some of the time.
11. John eats in restaurants all of the time.
12. Mary almost never eats in a restaurant.
13. She eats at home most of the time.
14. Mr. and Mrs. Allen eat in a restaurant much of the time.

B.2 Compare the positions of *always*.

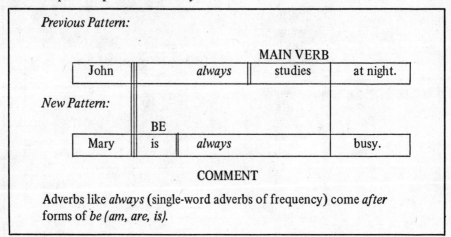

Previous Pattern:

		MAIN VERB	
John	*always*	studies	at night.

New Pattern:

	BE		
Mary	is	*always*	busy.

COMMENT

Adverbs like *always* (single-word adverbs of frequency) come *after* forms of *be (am, are, is)*.

Exercise 10. Substitute a word like *always* for the multi-word adverbials of frequency.

John is busy all of the time.　　　　JOHN IS ALWAYS BUSY.
Mr. Allen is busy most of the time.　　MR. ALLEN IS USUALLY BUSY.

   1. Mrs. Allen is busy much of the time.
   2. She is tired some of the time.
   3. Mr. Miller is almost never tired.
   4. Mr. Miller is thirsty most of the time.
   5. He is hungry some of the time.
   6. John is hungry much of the time.
   7. He is thirsty most of the time.
   8. He is almost never in the room.
   9. He is at home most of the time.
 10. Mr. Allen is at home some of the time.
 11. Mr. Allen is right most of the time.
 12. He is almost never wrong.
 13. Mr. and Mrs. Allen are happy most of the time.
 14. They are almost never sad.

Exercise 11. Summary exercise.

John drinks milk much of the time.　　HE OFTEN DRINKS MILK.
He is thirsty much of the time.　　　　HE IS OFTEN THIRSTY.

   1. He has cornflakes for breakfast all of the time.
   2. He is sleepy at breakfast all of the time.
   3. He is late to class some of the time.
   4. He studies at night all of the time.
   5. Mrs. Miller almost never drinks coffee.

6. She drinks tea most of the time.
7. She is at home much of the time.
8. She eats at home most of the time.
9. She is busy most of the time.
10. She sings at home some of the time.

B.3 Notice the position of *always* in questions.

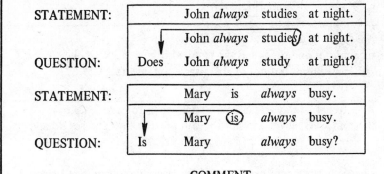

STATEMENT:		John *always*	studies	at night.
QUESTION:	Does	John *always*	study	at night?

STATEMENT:		Mary	is	*always*	busy.
QUESTION:	Is	Mary		*always*	busy?

COMMENT

Adverbs like *always* come before the main verb (*study, arrive,* etc.)
in questions as well as in statements. With forms of *be (am, are, is)*
the adverb of frequency remains with the rest of the predicate when
the verb is put before the subject to make a question.

Exercise 12. Change the teacher's statement into a question. The next student will
answer the question.

The teacher is usually busy.   Student A: IS THE TEACHER USUALLY
                                                          BUSY?
                                       Student B: YES, HE IS.

You are often busy.   Student B: ARE YOU OFTEN BUSY?
                                       Student C: YES, I AM. or
                                                          NO, I'M NOT.

1. You are sometimes tired.
2. You are sometimes hungry.
3. You always eat breakfast in
   the morning.
4. The windows are always open.
5. The teacher is usually in the room.
6. You usually have coffee for
   breakfast.

7. You usually eat lunch at noon.
8. The door is sometimes open.
9. The windows are often closed.
10. You sometimes read at night.
11. You usually understand the
    lesson.
12. Pencils are usually light.
13. Shoes are always white.
14. Shirts are often white.

B.4 Notice the questions with *ever* and the short answers.

QUESTIONS:

> Do you *ever* have cornflakes for breakfast?
> Are you *ever* sleepy?

SOME POSSIBLE
SHORT ANSWERS:

> Yes, always.
> Yes, usually.
> Yes, often.
> Yes, sometimes.
> No, never.

COMMENTS

Ever, meaning 'at any time,' has the same position as adverbs like *always.*
It is used in questions but not in affirmative statements.

NOTES:

(1) An alternative way to make short answers is to include *do* or *be.* In
these answers, adverbs such as *always* precede the forms of *do* and *be.*
> Yes, I always do.
> Yes, I always am.

(2) There is a statement pattern in which *ever* does occur. See Lesson 17
for examples.

(3) The following short answers with *but* are also appropriate replies to
questions with *ever:*
> *Yes, but seldom.*
> *Yes, but rarely.*
> *Yes, but not often.*
> etc.

Exercise 13. This is a review exercise. Change the teacher's statement into a question. Include *ever* in the question. Another student will give a true answer.

You study at night.   Student A: DO YOU EVER STUDY AT NIGHT?
                        Student B: YES, USUALLY. (NO, NEVER, etc.)

You are tired.   Student B: ARE YOU EVER TIRED?
                        Student C: NO, SELDOM. (YES, OFTEN, etc.)

You eat fish.   Student C: DO YOU EVER EAT FISH?
                        Student D: YES, SOMETIMES. (NO, SELDOM, etc.)

1. You eat soup.
2. You have toast for breakfast.
3. You have coffee after dinner.
4. You are hungry in the morning.
5. We practice.
6. You have cornflakes for
   breakfast.
7. You have coffee at 10 A.M.
8. You are busy.
9. You drink tea in the afternoon.
10. We learn new words in class.
11. You have orange juice for
    breakfast.
12. You write letters at night.
13. You sing in the morning.
14. You have a coke in the afternoon.

Lesson 3

A. Adverbials of place and time.

B. Past tense of *be* in statements, questions, and short answers.
   He *was* here. *Was* he here? Yes, he *was.*

C. Past tense of regular verbs.
   Regular past tense ending: He work*ed.*
   Questions and short answers with *did:*
   Did he work? Yes, he *did.*

A. Notice the position of the adverbial expressions.

	ADVERBIAL OF PLACE	ADVERBIAL OF TIME
He studies English	*here.*	
He studies		*in the morning.*
He studies English	*here*	*in the morning.*
He comes	*to class*	*at 9:00 A.M.*
He practices	*in class*	*every day.*

COMMENTS

(1) Adverbials of place (location or direction) and of time, including multi-word adverbials of frequency, come after the verb and its object, if any.

(2) Expressions of place come before expressions of time.

Exercise 1. Practice using adverbials of place. Substitute the words in the correct position.

I study in the library.	I STUDY IN THE LIBRARY.
here	I STUDY HERE.
we	WE STUDY HERE.
in the library	WE STUDY IN THE LIBRARY.

1. read	5. at the restaurant	9. in that building
2. I	6. John	10. we
3. here	7. there	11. have coffee
4. eat	8. studies	12. at the restaurant

Exercise 2. Practice using adverbials of time. Substitute the words in the proper positions.

We usually have lunch at noon.	WE USUALLY HAVE LUNCH AT NOON.
at 1 o'clock	WE USUALLY HAVE LUNCH AT 1 O'CLOCK.
coffee	WE USUALLY HAVE COFFEE AT 1 O'CLOCK.
in the morning	WE USUALLY HAVE COFFEE IN THE MORNING.
always	WE ALWAYS HAVE COFFEE IN THE MORNING.

1. at noon	5. coffee	9. dinner
2. lunch	6. in the evening	10. always
3. at 12 o'clock	7. in the afternoon	11. tea
4. usually	8. at night	12. in the morning

Exercise 3. Practice the position of adverbials of place and time. Substitute the words in the proper positions.

The teacher has breakfast at a restaurant in the morning.

at 7 A.M.	THE TEACHER HAS BREAKFAST AT A RESTAURANT AT 7 A.M.
at home	THE TEACHER HAS BREAKFAST AT HOME AT 7 A.M.
every day	THE TEACHER HAS BREAKFAST AT HOME EVERY DAY.

1. at a restaurant	5. in that building	9. at noon
2. coffee	6. in the afternoon	10. lunch
3. at noon	7. every day	11. there
4. here	8. we	12. at 1 o'clock

NOTES:

(1) When several adverbials of place or of time are used in the same sentence, those which refer to small units are usually placed before those which refer to larger units. For example:

He goes to class in that building.
He went to school in a small town in California.
He came to class at 2:00 o'clock every day last week.
He had coffee at 10:00 o'clock in the morning every day last week.

(2) Some of these adverbials are also used at the beginning of sentences. See Lesson 29 for examples.

B.1 Notice the use of *was* and *were*.

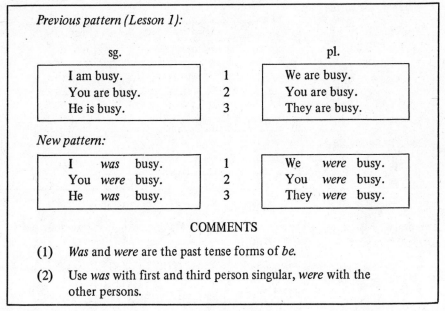

Previous pattern (Lesson 1):

	sg.			pl.
	I am busy. You are busy. He is busy.	1 2 3		We are busy. You are busy. They are busy.

New pattern:

I *was* busy. You *were* busy. He *was* busy.	1 2 3		We *were* busy. You *were* busy. They *were* busy.

COMMENTS

(1)   *Was* and *were* are the past tense forms of *be.*

(2)   Use *was* with first and third person singular, *were* with the other persons.

Exercise 4. Substitute the teacher's words and change *was* or *were* only if necessary.

The boys were busy.	THE BOYS WERE BUSY.
John	JOHN WAS BUSY.
the students	THE STUDENTS WERE BUSY.
I	I WAS BUSY.

1. the teacher	5. I	9. the class
2. the boys	6. you	10. the doctor
3. John	7. we	11. John and Mary
4. the students	8. Mary	12. they

Exercise 5. Practice the correlation of forms of *be* with adverbials of time. Substitute the words and change the forms of *be* if necessary.

We were here yesterday.	WE WERE HERE YESTERDAY.
John	JOHN WAS HERE YESTERDAY.
now	JOHN IS HERE NOW.
the students	THE STUDENTS ARE HERE NOW.
yesterday	THE STUDENTS WERE HERE YESTERDAY.

1. Mary	5. they	9. now
2. now	6. now	10. last night
3. last night	7. yesterday	11. the books
4. I	8. the teacher	12. now

B.2 Notice the position of *was* and *were* in questions.

Previous pattern:

STATEMENT		John	is	busy.
QUESTION	*Is*	John		busy?

New pattern:

STATEMENT		John	was	busy.
QUESTION	*Was*	John		busy?
STATEMENT		You	were	busy.
QUESTION	*Were*	You		busy?

Exercise 6. Listen to the statement with *today*. Make a corresponding question using *yesterday*. Change the form of *be* to the past tense.

Mary is tired today.   WAS SHE TIRED YESTERDAY?
She is sad today.   WAS SHE SAD YESTERDAY?
The students are here today.   WERE THEY HERE YESTERDAY?

1. John is busy today.
2. Mr. Allen is sleepy today.
3. Mr. and Mrs. Miller are hungry today.
4. The book is open today.
5. The coffee is hot today.
6. Mr. and Mrs. Allen are early today.
7. Mrs. Miller is late today.
8. John is right today.
9. Mary is wrong today.
10. The teacher is here today.

B.3 Notice the use of short answers.

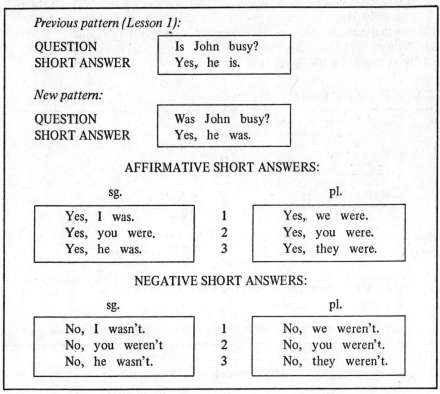

Previous pattern (Lesson 1):

| QUESTION | Is John busy? |
| SHORT ANSWER | Yes, he is. |

New pattern:

| QUESTION | Was John busy? |
| SHORT ANSWER | Yes, he was. |

AFFIRMATIVE SHORT ANSWERS:

sg.   pl.

Yes, I was.	1	Yes, we were.
Yes, you were.	2	Yes, you were.
Yes, he was.	3	Yes, they were.

NEGATIVE SHORT ANSWERS:

sg.   pl.

No, I wasn't.	1	No, we weren't.
No, you weren't	2	No, you weren't.
No, he wasn't.	3	No, they weren't.

ADDITIONAL EXAMPLES

Were you busy last night?	Yes, I was.
Was I right yesterday?	Yes, you were.
Were the students here yesterday?	Yes, they were.
Was John tired on Monday?	No, he wasn't.
Were the lessons difficult?	No, they weren't.

Exercise 7. Answer the question with an appropriate short answer. (Use the names of students for Mr. A., Mr. B., etc.)

Was the table here yesterday?	YES, IT WAS.
Was Mr. A. in New York yesterday?	NO, HE WASN'T.
Is Mr. A. in class today?	YES, HE IS.

1. Was Mr. B. in class yesterday?
2. Was the teacher here yesterday?
3. Were Mr. C. and Mr. D. in class yesterday?
4. Was the green book here yesterday?

(Continue the exercise, calling on students individually.)

5. Were you tired yesterday?
6. Was the lesson easy yesterday?
7. Is it easy today?
8. Was Mr. E. in class yesterday?

25

9. Were Miss F. and Miss G. here
    yesterday?
10. Are they here today?
11. Were you in Chicago last night?
12. Was the lesson difficult yesterday?

13. Were you here yesterday?
14. Was I here yesterday?
15. Are you from Japan?
16. Am I from the United States?

C.1 Notice the past tense form of the verbs.

Previous pattern (Lesson 2):

I	study	English	every	day.
John	studies	English	every	day.

New pattern:

I	*studied*	English	yesterday.
John	*studied*	English	yesterday.

COMMENTS

(1) Verbs other than *be* have one form in the past tense, that is, one
form for all persons.

(2) For most verbs, an *-ed* ending is used to indicate the past tense.

ADDITIONAL EXAMPLES

I walked.
You walked.
He walked.

We walked.
You walked.
They walked.

He arrived at nine o'clock.
He watched a television program.
He wanted a glass of milk.

Exercise 8. Change the adverbial from *every day* to *yesterday* and make the necessary change in the verb.

I study every day.
The doctor works here every day.

He waits for John every day.

I STUDIED YESTERDAY.
THE DOCTOR WORKED HERE
    YESTERDAY.
HE WAITED FOR JOHN
    YESTERDAY.

1. John walks home every day.
2. Mary wants coffee after dinner every day.
3. John wants a glass of milk every day.
4. John visits Mr. Allen every day.
5. Mr. Allen watches a television program
    every day.

6. Mary listens to the radio every
    day.
7. We study every day.
8. We practice every day.
9. We learn new words every day.
10. The students study every day.

C.2 Notice the use of *did* in questions.

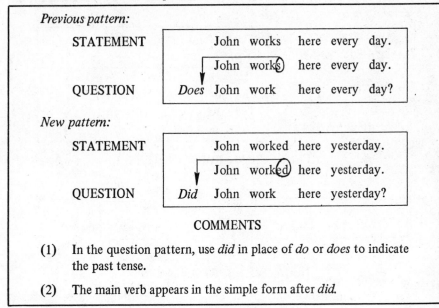

Previous pattern:

STATEMENT   John works here every day.

             John works here every day.

QUESTION   *Does* John work here every day?

New pattern:

STATEMENT   John worked here yesterday.

             John worked here yesterday.

QUESTION   *Did* John work here yesterday?

COMMENTS

(1)   In the question pattern, use *did* in place of *do* or *does* to indicate the past tense.

(2)   The main verb appears in the simple form after *did.*

Exercise 9. Change the statements into questions.

The teacher presented the lesson yesterday.	DID THE TEACHER PRESENT THE LESSON YESTERDAY?
The teacher pronounced the sentences.	DID THE TEACHER PRONOUNCE THE SENTENCES?
The students repeated the new words.	DID THE STUDENTS REPEAT THE NEW WORDS?

1. Mr. and Mrs. Allen practiced the conversation yesterday.
2. They studied the lesson in the afternoon.
3. They learned the new words.
4. They walked home yesterday.
5. Mr. Allen wanted hot dogs for dinner.
6. Mrs. Allen wanted fish.
7. Mr. Allen waited for Mrs. Allen.
8. They visited Mr. Miller last night.
9. They arrived at 8 o'clock.
10. They talked about the lesson.
11. They watched television last night.

C.3 Notice the use of short answers.

Previous pattern:

QUESTION	Does John study every day?
SHORT ANSWER	Yes, he does.

New pattern:

QUESTION	Did John study yesterday?
SHORT ANSWER	Yes, he did.

AFFIRMATIVE SHORT ANSWERS

Singular		Plural
Yes, I did.	1	Yes, we did.
Yes, you did.	2	Yes, you did.
Yes, he did.	3	Yes, they did.

NEGATIVE SHORT ANSWERS

Singular		Plural
No, I didn't.	1	No, we didn't.
No, you didn't.	2	No, you didn't.
No, he didn't.	3	No, they didn't.

ADDITIONAL EXAMPLES

Did you study grammar yesterday?	Yes, I did.
Did I answer the question?	Yes, you did.
Did Mary want the book?	Yes, she did.
Did you study last night?	No, I didn't.

Exercise 10. Answer the question with an appropriate short answer. (Use the names of students for Mr. A., Mr. B., etc.)

Did we study lesson two yesterday?	YES, WE DID.
Did we study lesson one yesterday?	NO, WE DIDN'T.

1. Did Mr. A. come to class yesterday?
2. Did we practice in class yesterday?
3. Did Mr. B. attend class yesterday?
4. Did Miss C. go to Chicago yesterday?
5. Did we talk in class yesterday?

(Continue, calling on students individually.)

6 Did you study the lesson yesterday?
7. Did you watch television last night?

8. Did you eat dinner yesterday?
9. Did you write a letter last night?
10. Did you read a book last night?
11. Did you speak English yesterday?
12. Did you speak Japanese yesterday?
13. Did you speak French yesterday?
14. Did Mr. D. and Mr. E. speak German last night?
15. Did you eat soup yesterday?
16. Did we practice in class yesterday?
17. Did you sleep in class yesterday?
18. Did we eat breakfast in class yesterday?

Exercise 11. This is a review exercise. Listen to the statement with *every day*. Make a corresponding statement with *yesterday*. Then convert the statement into a question. Use the pronoun *you* in the question. The next student will give a true answer.

We study English every day.   Student A:
      WE STUDIED ENGLISH YESTERDAY.
      DID YOU STUDY ENGLISH YESTERDAY?

    Student B:
      YES, I DID.

We watch television every day.   Student B:
      WE WATCHED TELEVISION YESTERDAY.
      DID YOU WATCH TELEVISION YESTERDAY?

    Student C:
      NO, I DIDN'T.

1. We learn new words every day.
2. We practice pronunciation every day.
3. We walk to class every day.
4. We attend class every day.
5. We repeat the new words every day.
6. We talk about the lesson every day.
7. We listen to the radio every day.
8. We answer the teacher's questions every day.
9. We talk to the teacher every day.
10. We study grammar every day.
11. We repeat the exercises every day.

Exercise 12. This is a review exercise. Answer the teacher's questions individually. Use short answers.

Were you in New York last night?   NO, I WASN'T.
Were you ever in New York?   YES, I WAS.
      (NO, I WASN'T.)
      (NO, NEVER.)

1. Do you like New York?
2. Did you ever visit the Empire State Building in New York?
3. Did you ever visit California?
4. Were you in California last night?
5. Do you like California?
6. Is San Francisco in California?
7. Is Chicago in California?
8. Is Caracas in Venezuela?
9. Is Paris in Italy?
10. Is London in England?
11. Did Shakespeare live in England?
12. Did Shakespeare write plays?
13. Was Shakespeare here yesterday?

29

Lesson 4

A. *Wh*-questions: *who, what, where, when.*

B. Present progressive: He *is* writ*ing.*

C. Using adjectives and nouns to modify nouns: *small* class, *grammar* class.

A.1 Compare the word order of *yes/no* questions and *wh*-questions.

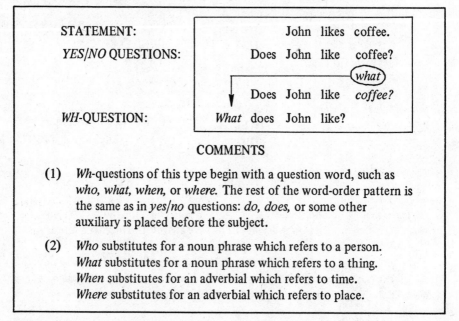

STATEMENT:	John likes coffee.
YES/NO QUESTIONS:	Does John like coffee?
	Does John like *coffee?* ← *what*
WH-QUESTION:	*What* does John like?

COMMENTS

(1) *Wh*-questions of this type begin with a question word, such as *who, what, when,* or *where.* The rest of the word-order pattern is the same as in *yes/no* questions: *do, does,* or some other auxiliary is placed before the subject.

(2) *Who* substitutes for a noun phrase which refers to a person. *What* substitutes for a noun phrase which refers to a thing. *When* substitutes for an adverbial which refers to time. *Where* substitutes for an adverbial which refers to place.

NOTE: In this pattern, the *wh*-words are substitutes for parts of the predicate phrase. The use of *wh*-words as substitutes for the subject is treated in Lesson 9.

ADDITIONAL EXAMPLES

QUESTIONS	SHORT ANSWERS
What does John like?	Coffee.
What does he study?	English.
What did he study yesterday?	Grammar.
Where does he study at night?	In the library.
Where did he study last night?	At home.
When does he usually study?	In the morning.
When did he study yesterday?	In the morning.
Who does he visit every day?	Mary.
Whom does he visit every day?	Mary.

NOTE: *Who* in this pattern is informal standard English. It is used in conversation and in notes and letters to friends and relatives. *Whom* is formal standard English and is used in speeches and formal writing, such as papers which students write in college.

Exercise 1. Change the statement into a *yes/no* question. Then make a *wh*-question beginning with the word *what*.

John likes milk.

Does	DOES JOHN LIKE MILK?
What	WHAT DOES JOHN LIKE?

Paul likes water.

Does	DOES PAUL LIKE WATER?
What	WHAT DOES PAUL LIKE?

1. Mary likes coffee.   Does/What
2. Mr. Miller likes beer.   Does/What
3. Mrs. Miller likes wine.
4. Mrs. Allen usually has tea.
5. John likes tomato juice.
6. Mary usually likes orange juice.

(Continue, using the PAST tense.)

7. Paul practiced pronunciation.
8. John studied grammar.
9. Mary repeated the exercises.
10. Mr. Miller repeated the new words.
11. Mr. Miller learned the new words.
12. Mr. Allen studied the exercises.

Exercise 2. Practice the use of *what* in questions. Substitute the words into the question.

What does big mean?

intelligent	WHAT DOES INTELLIGENT MEAN?
exist	WHAT DOES EXIST MEAN?
actual	WHAT DOES ACTUAL MEAN?

1. difficult
2. tiny
3. simple
4. penny
5. dime
6. quarter
7. tooth
8. entire
9. funny
10. assist

Exercise 3. Ask for the meaning of words. Change the statement into a question beginning with *what*. Another student will answer.

Smart means intelligent.	Student A: What does smart mean?
	Student B: It means intelligent.
Big means large.	Student A: What does big mean?
	Student B: It means large.

1. Huge means very large.
2. Tiny means very small.
3. Assist means help.
4. Hard often means difficult.

5. Right often means correct.
6. Noon means twelve o'clock.
7. Rarely means seldom.
8. Dozen means twelve.

Exercise 4. Practice the use of *when* in questions. Listen to the information about Paul. Ask a corresponding question about John.

Paul arrived in June.   WHEN DID JOHN ARRIVE?
Paul studied a year ago.   WHEN DID JOHN STUDY?
Paul telephoned yesterday.   WHEN DID JOHN TELEPHONE?

1. Paul studied a month ago.
2. Paul telephoned yesterday.
3. Paul studied a year ago.
4. Paul arrived yesterday.
5. Paul called two hours ago.
6. Paul arrived a year ago.

7. Paul practiced a year ago.
8. Paul telephoned at 8 o'clock.
9. Paul returned a week ago.
10. Paul worked yesterday.
11. Paul called on Wednesday.
12. Paul practiced in the morning.

Exercise 5. Practice the use of *where* in questions. Listen to the information about Paul. Ask a corresponding question about John and Mary.

Paul lives in New York.   WHERE DO JOHN AND MARY LIVE?

Paul studies in the library.   WHERE DO JOHN AND MARY STUDY?

1. Paul eats dinner at a restaurant.
2. Paul lives on Main Street.
3. Paul plays tennis in the park.
4. Paul reads books in the library.
5. Paul studies at home.
6. Paul has coffee at a restaurant.

7. Paul practices in class.
8. Paul learns new words in class.
9. Paul lives in New York.
10. He usually reads in the library.
11. He usually eats lunch at a restaurant.

Exercise 6. Change the teacher's statement into a question beginning with *who*.

The teacher knows John.   WHO DOES THE TEACHER KNOW?

Mary visited her father.   WHO DID MARY VISIT?

1. Mary telephoned Paul.
2. Mary assisted the new student.
3. John called Paul.
4. John visited Mr. Miller.
5. The teacher asked Mary.

6. The teacher knows Mary.
7. John sees Mary.
8. The students see the teacher.
9. The students hear the teacher.
10. The students understand the teacher.

A.2 Observe the word order of questions with the verb *be*.

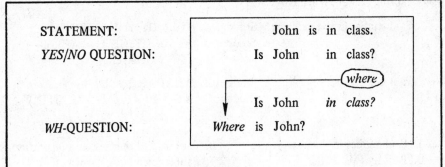

COMMENT

(1)   The *wh*-word which replaces a part of the predicate phrase is put at the beginning of the question.

(2)   The rest of the pattern is the same as for *yes/no* questions: the form of *be (am, are, is, was,* or *were)* is placed before the subject.

ADDITIONAL EXAMPLES

Who was that man?	My father.
What is he?	An architect.
What are you?	A student.
Where is John?	In class.
When is he here?	In the morning.

Exercise 7. Change the statement into a question with *where* or *when*. Another student will answer. The answer should be like the expression of time or place in the teacher's statement.

John is in class.	Student A: WHERE IS JOHN?
	Student B: IN CLASS.
John is tired at night.	Student A: WHEN IS JOHN TIRED?
	Student B: AT NIGHT.

1. Mary is sleepy in the morning.
2. Mary was in Chicago.
3. Mr. Miller was hungry at noon.
4. The children were quiet on the bus.
5. George was at the library.
6. Betty was in New York.
7. George was sick last week.
8. George was twenty years old last week.
9. George and Betty were at the movies.
10. George and Betty are in class.
11. Suits are expensive in New York.

Exercise 8. Listen to the statement about Paul. Make a *wh*-question with the word *you*. Another student will answer.

Paul studies in the morning.   Student A: WHEN DO YOU STUDY?
                                     Student B: AT NIGHT. (IN THE AFTER-
                                                     NOON, etc.)

Paul is a doctor.   Student B: WHAT ARE YOU?
                                     Student C: A STUDENT. (AN ARCHITECT,
                                                     etc.)

1. Paul studies in the library.
2. Paul sees Mr. Miller.
3. Paul is a lawyer.
4. Paul studied grammar yesterday.
   (Two possibilities)
5. Paul was in New York last year.
   (Two possibilities)
6. Paul studied business administration.
7. Paul studied in Chicago.
8. Paul arrived last week.
9. Paul studies at night.
10. Paul was at the library last
    night.
    (Two possibilities)

A.3 Notice the use of the expression *do what.*

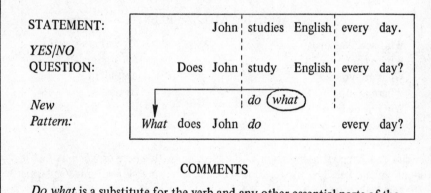

STATEMENT: John ¦ studies English ¦ every day.

YES/NO
QUESTION: Does John ¦ study   English ¦ every day?

                              ¦ *do* (what)

New
Pattern: *What* does John *do*   every day?

COMMENTS

Do what is a substitute for the verb and any other essential parts of the verb phrase. In the example, *do what* corresponds to the verb phrase *study English.*

Exercise 9. Make *wh*-questions using the expression *do what.*

John eats breakfast at   WHAT DOES JOHN DO AT 7 O'CLOCK?
  7 o'clock.

John goes to class at   WHAT DOES JOHN DO AT 8 O'CLOCK?
  8 o'clock.

1. John has coffee at 10 o'clock.
2. John eats lunch at noon.
3. John studies in the afternoon.
4. John studies English in the library.

5. John has dinner at 6 P.M.
6. John usually watches television in the evening.
7. Mr. and Mrs. Miller have dinner at 6:30.
8. Mr. Miller usually studies in the evening.
9. Mrs. Miller often reads in the evening.
10. Mr. and Mrs. Miller sometimes visit friends in the evening.

(Continue, using the PAST tense.)

11. They visited friends yesterday.
12. They talked.
13. They played cards after dinner.
14. They watched television at nine o'clock.

A.4 Notice the position of the prepositions.

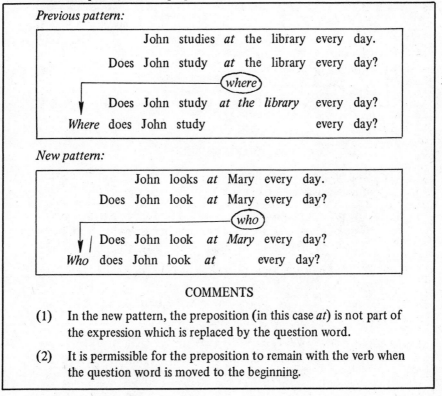

Previous pattern:

	John	studies	*at*	the	library	every	day.
Does	John	study	*at*	the	library	every	day?
			where				
Does	John	study	*at the library*			every	day?
Where	does	John	study			every	day?

New pattern:

	John	looks	*at*	Mary	every	day.
Does	John	look	*at*	Mary	every	day?
			who			
Does	John	look	*at*	*Mary*	every	day?
Who	does	John	look	*at*	every	day?

COMMENTS

(1) In the new pattern, the preposition (in this case *at*) is not part of the expression which is replaced by the question word.

(2) It is permissible for the preposition to remain with the verb when the question word is moved to the beginning.

Exercise 10. Make *wh*-questions which correspond to the teacher's statements.

John waits for *Mary* every day.
WHO DOES JOHN WAIT FOR
EVERY DAY?

John works *on Wednesday.*
WHEN DOES JOHN WORK?

John is from *Canada.*
WHERE IS JOHN FROM?

1. John arrived *in September*.
2. Alice waited for *her friend*.
3. John lives *on Main Street*.
4. John visited *the museum*.
5. He looked at *a new painting*.
6. The painting was from *Spain*.
7. Mary looked at *the painting*.
8. John waited for *Mary*.
9. He waited *in the museum*.
10. John talked to *Mr. Miller*.
11. Mr. Miller is from *New York*.
12. John and Mary waited for *the bus*.
13. They were hungry *at 5 o'clock*.
14. They watched television *in the evening*.

B.1 Observe the new notation, and compare the simple present tense with the present progressive.

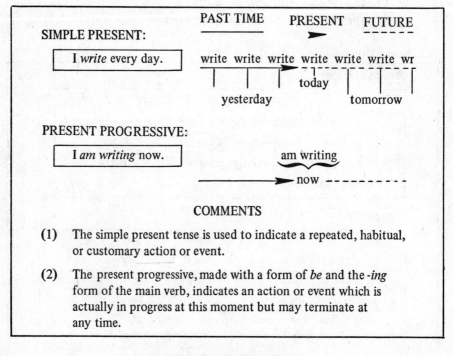

COMMENTS

(1) The simple present tense is used to indicate a repeated, habitual, or customary action or event.

(2) The present progressive, made with a form of *be* and the *-ing* form of the main verb, indicates an action or event which is actually in progress at this moment but may terminate at any time.

ADDITIONAL EXAMPLES

We are studying lesson four now.
We are studying verbs today.
We are studying grammar this semester.
We are studying English this year.

(Note that the idea of present time may refer to the present moment, today, this week, or this century.)

Exercise 11. Watch the teacher and listen to his statement. Make a statement in the simple present tense with the phrase *every day*.

I'm walking now.   THE TEACHER WALKS EVERY DAY.

I'm writing now.   THE TEACHER WRITES EVERY DAY.

1. I'm using the eraser.
2. I'm talking.
3. I'm speaking English.
4. I'm moving the chair.
5. I'm sitting.
6. I'm using a pencil.
7. I'm writing.
8. I'm looking at the book.
9. I am sitting.
10. I am standing.
11. I am speaking slowly.
12. I am looking at Mr. A.
13. I am going to the door.
14. I am opening the door.
15. I am leaving the room.

Exercise 12. Listen to the teacher's statement. Make a statement using the present progressive.

I walk every day.   YOU'RE WALKING NOW.

I write every day.   YOU'RE WRITING NOW.

1. I use the eraser every day.
2. I move my chair every day.
3. I sit every day.
4. I use a pencil every day.
5. I use the book every day.
6. I look at the book every day.
7. I stand every day.
8. I look at Mr. A. every day.
9. I go to the door every day.
10. I open the door every day.

Exercise 13. Practice the use of the simple present, the present progressive, and the past tense. Substitute the words and change the verb if necessary.

Mary is watching a movie.   MARY IS WATCHING A MOVIE.

she   SHE IS WATCHING A MOVIE.
yesterday   SHE WATCHED A MOVIE YESTERDAY.
every day   SHE WATCHES A MOVIE EVERY DAY.
now   SHE IS WATCHING A MOVIE NOW.

1. John
2. we
3. studying a lesson
4. every day
5. he
6. now
7. last week
8. they
9. now
10. watching a movie
11. last night
12. we
13. now
14. you

37

B.2 Notice the use of the simple present tense of verbs which indicate situations or states rather than actions or events.

> He *likes* milk.
> He *wants* the book now.
> He *is* here.
> He *has* a new bicycle.

COMMENT

(1) Verbs such as *like, want, be, have* (=possess), *know, mean, see,* and *understand* indicate situations or states rather than actions or events.

(2) Such verbs are seldom used in the progressive form. The simple present tense of these verbs indicates an actual present-time situation.

ADDITIONAL EXAMPLES

I see Mary.	I like apples.	I live in Florida.
I hear John.	I prefer bananas.	I need a book.

(Note that "I am *looking at* an apple" is a voluntary action. "I see an apple" is a state. Similarly, "I am *listening to* John" is a voluntary action, but "I hear John" is a state.)

Exercise 14. Practice the use of two kinds of verbs: those which require the progressive form to express action in progress and those which use the simple form expressing an actual situation.

They are waiting for John.	THEY ARE WAITING FOR JOHN.
like	THEY LIKE JOHN.
help	THEY ARE HELPING JOHN.

(In all cases, keep in mind the meaning of "right now.")

1. understand	5. study	9. want
2. visit	6. the book	10. see
3. know	7. read	11. study
4. the history of California	8. like	12. know

B.3 Notice the position of the verb *be* in *yes/no* questions.

STATEMENT:	John is studying grammar.
	John (is) studying grammar.
YES/NO QUESTION:	*Is* John studying grammar?

SHORT ANSWERS:
> Yes, he is.
> No, he isn't.

COMMENT

Put the verb *be* at the beginning of a sentence to make a *yes/no* question.

Exercise 15. Change the statement into a question. Another student will give a true answer.

> The teacher is standing.   Student A: IS THE TEACHER STANDING?
>   Student B: YES, HE IS.
>
> You are sitting.   Student A: ARE YOU SITTING?
>   Student B: YES, I AM.

1. We are speaking English.
2. We are speaking Japanese.
3. You are studying in the United States.
4. We are practicing English.
5. The teacher is sitting.
6. You are standing.
7. The teacher is looking at his book.
8. You are studying English this semester.
9. We are speaking slowly.
10. The teacher is walking.
11. Mr. A. is writing.
12. Miss B. is reading.
13. We are watching television.
14. We are eating dinner.

B.4 Compare the word order of *yes/no* questions and *wh*-questions.

STATEMENT:	John is studying grammar.
YES/NO QUESTION:	Is John studying grammar.
	(what)
	Is John studying grammar.
WH-QUESTION:	What is John studying ?

ADDITIONAL EXAMPLES

WH-QUESTIONS	SHORT ANSWERS
Where are you studying?	In the United States.
What is John learning?	English.
Who is John visiting?	A friend.

Exercise 16. Listen to the statement about Mary. Ask a corresponding question about John. Use *who, what,* or *where.*

    Mary is studying grammar.   WHAT IS JOHN STUDYING?
    Mary is studying here.   WHERE IS JOHN STUDYING?

1. Mary is drinking coffee.
2. Mary is studying medicine.
3. Mary is telephoning Paul.
4. Mary is watching the teacher.
5. Mary is eating a sandwich.
6. Mary is visiting Mrs. Miller.
7. Mary is buying a book.
8. Mary is eating an apple.
9. Mary is helping Mr. Allen.
10. Mary is working in the library.
11. Mary is studying grammar.
12. Mary is playing tennis.
13. Mary is drinking milk.
14. Mary is reading in the library.

Exercise 17. Listen to the statement. Ask the next student a corresponding *wh*-question. He will give a true answer.

    Paul is practicing Spanish.   Student A: WHAT ARE YOU
                                          PRACTICING?
                                Student B: ENGLISH.

    Paul is studying in Mexico.   Student B: WHERE ARE YOU
                                          STUDYING?
                              Student C: IN THE UNITED STATES.

1. Paul is sitting in the classroom.
2. Paul is looking at the teacher.
3. Paul is studying Japanese.
4. Paul is watching Mr. Allen.
5. Paul is talking to Mr. Miller.
6. Paul is practicing in the classroom.
7. Paul is looking at Mr. Miller.

(Continue, reviewing the simple present and past tenses.)

8. Paul likes coffee.
9. Paul studies in the library.
10. Paul studies at night.
11. Paul sees the teacher.
12. Paul is from Canada.
13. Paul was in Mexico last year.
14. Paul studied English.
15. Paul studied in New York.

C. Notice the form and position of the modifiers.

				ADJEC-TIVE	NOUN
Sg.	The store is new.	It	is a	*new*	store.
Pl.	The stores are new.	They	are	*new*	stores.

				NOUN	NOUN
Sg.	The store sells books.	It	is a	*book*	store.
Pl.	The stores sell books.	They	are	*book*	stores.

COMMENTS

(1) The modifier of a noun can be either an adjective (*new, small,* etc.) or another noun (*book, shoe,* etc.).

(2) Such modifiers are placed *before* the main noun.

(3) Modifiers that precede plural nouns have the same form as those that precede singular nouns.

(4) In the noun + noun pattern discussed here, the strongest stress is on the modifying noun, not on the main noun: *bookstore.* In the adjective + noun pattern, the main stress is on the noun: *new store* (unless the adjective is being emphasized).

NOTE: *Bookstore, shoestore, drugstore* are usually written as single words, that is, without a space between the two nouns. However, in general, most modifiers are separated from the following noun: *furniture store, grocery store, grammar book,* etc.

ADDITIONAL EXAMPLES

A *milk bottle* is a bottle for milk.
A *law school* is a school where you can study law.
A *school bus* is a bus that takes children to school.
A *coffee cup* is a cup that you can use for coffee.

Exercise 18. Listen to the two sentences. Repeat the first one and include an appropriate modifier.

It's a class. It's small.	IT'S A SMALL CLASS.
They're classes. They're large.	THEY'RE LARGE CLASSES.
It's a class. We learn grammar here.	IT'S A GRAMMAR CLASS.
It's a watch. I carry the watch in my pocket.	IT'S A POCKET WATCH.
It's a pocket. I carry my watch in the pocket.	IT'S A WATCH POCKET.

41

1. It's a book. It's green.
2. They're books. They're green.
3. It's a book. It presents grammar.
4. They're books. They present grammar.
5. It's a watch. It's small.
6. It's a watch. I wear the watch on my wrist.
7. They're pencils. They're long.
8. It's an egg. It's fried.
9. They're eggs. They're fried.
10. It's a table. It's for cards.
11. It's cream. It's for coffee.
12. It's soup. It's hot.
13. It's a spoon. It's for soup.
14. It's a store. It sells books.
15. It's a store. It's large.
16. It's a cover. It's large.
17. It's a cover. It's on a magazine.
18. They're stores. They sell books.
19. It's a cup. It's for coffee.
20. They're cups. They're for coffee.
21. It's a lamp. It's on a desk.
22. They're lamps. They're on desks.
23. It's a bottle. It's for milk.
24. It's a bottle. It's small.
25. It's a tree. It has apples.
26. They're trees. They have apples.
27. It's a room. It's for classes.
28. It's a room. It's large.

Exercise 19. Answer the questions.

What's a bus station?	IT'S A STATION.
What's a telephone book?	IT'S A BOOK.
What's fruit juice?	IT'S JUICE.

1. What's a milk bottle?
2. What's a pocket watch?
3. What's a watch pocket?
4. What's a car factory?
5. What's a flower garden?
6. What's a garden flower?
7. What's a soup spoon?
8. What's a table lamp?
9. What's a train ticket?
10. What's an apple tree?
11. What's a card table?
12. What's a coffee cup?

Lesson 5

   A.   *Be + going to* to indicate future time:
         He *is going to* sing.

   B.   Negative statements: He isn't here. He didn't come.

   C.   Negative statements with single-word adverbs of frequency:
         He isn't *always* here. He doesn't *always* study.

   D.   *Some* and *any*.

A.1 Notice the use of *be* and *going to* when referring to future time.

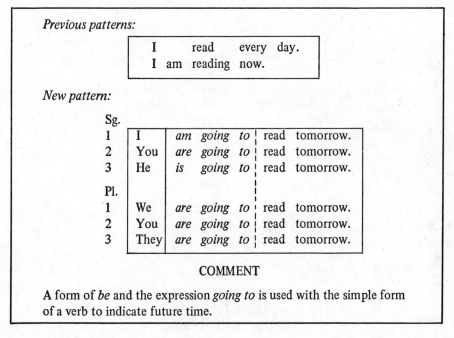

Previous patterns:

I		read	every	day.
I	am	reading	now.	

New pattern:

Sg.

1	I	*am*	*going*	*to*	read	tomorrow.
2	You	*are*	*going*	*to*	read	tomorrow.
3	He	*is*	*going*	*to*	read	tomorrow.

Pl.

1	We	*are*	*going*	*to*	read	tomorrow.
2	You	*are*	*going*	*to*	read	tomorrow.
3	They	*are*	*going*	*to*	read	tomorrow.

COMMENT

A form of *be* and the expression *going to* is used with the simple form of a verb to indicate future time.

NOTES:
   (1)   The forms of *be* in the above pattern are usually contracted in speaking and in informal writing. For example:
         I'm going to read tomorrow.
   (2)   The auxiliary *will*, which is also commonly used to indicate future time, will be treated in Lesson 11.

Exercise 1. Substitute the words and make the necessary changes.

I'm going to study tomorrow.

    he   HE'S GOING TO STUDY TOMORROW.
    we   WE'RE GOING TO STUDY TOMORROW.
    I   I'M GOING TO STUDY TOMORROW.

1. he	5. I	9. you
2. we	6. she	10. the man
3. the students	7. John	11. the doctor
4. they	8. John and Mary	12. I

Exercise 2. Answer "no" to the question and add a statement using the word *tomorrow.*

Did George study yesterday?   NO, HE'S GOING TO STUDY
                                       TOMORROW.

Did Mary read the book?   NO, SHE'S GOING TO READ THE
                                       BOOK TOMORROW.

1. Did Mr. Miller play tennis yesterday?
2. Did John write a letter?
3. Did Mary work in the garden?
4. Did John eat fish for dinner yesterday?
5. Did Mr. Allen eat dinner at a restaurant?
6. Did Mary learn the new words?
7. Did George buy a wrist watch?
8. Did Mr. and Mrs. Miller visit the museum?
9. Did George move the table?
10. Did Mary repeat the words?

Exercise 3. Contrast the present progressive with the forms used with future time. Substitute the words and make the necessary changes.

I'm going to practice tomorrow.

    now   I'M PRACTICING NOW.
    next week   I'M GOING TO PRACTICE NEXT WEEK.
    we   WE'RE GOING TO PRACTICE NEXT WEEK.
    tomorrow   WE'RE GOING TO PRACTICE TOMORROW.
    now   WE'RE PRACTICING NOW.

1. he	6. next year	11. they
2. they	7. we	12. now (at the present moment)
3. she	8. I	13. he
4. tomorrow	9. study	14. I
5. next week	10. he	15. tomorrow

A.2 Compare the word order of statements and questions.

STATEMENT: George *is going to* read a book.

George *is* *going to* read a book.

YES/NO QUESTION: *Is* George *going to* read a book?

what

Is George *going to* read *a book?*

WH-QUESTION: *What* *is* George *going to* read?

ADDITIONAL EXAMPLES

Are they going to study tomorrow?	Yes, they are.
Are we going to play baseball tomorrow?	Yes, we are.
Is John going to study engineering?	Yes, he is.
Is David going to be a dentist?	Yes, he is.
What is Tom going to study?	Engineering.
When is he going to visit us?	Next year.

Exercise 4. Listen to the statement. Form a corresponding question.

They're going to study.	ARE THEY GOING TO STUDY?
John's going to play baseball.	IS HE GOING TO PLAY BASEBALL?
The boys are going to be late.	ARE THEY GOING TO BE LATE?

1. John's going to study engineering.
2. He is going to be an engineer.
3. He's going to be here next week.
4. The students are going to eat lunch.
5. They're going to study English.
6. The girl is going to learn English.
7. She's going to visit the museum.
8. She's going to attend the university.
9. Mr. Miller is going to study Japanese.
10. Mr. Allen is going to eat dinner at a restaurant.
11. George is going to be busy.
12. Mary is going to arrive at 9 o'clock.

Exercise 5. Listen to the statement. Make a *yes/no* question with *you*. Another student will give a true short answer.

George is going to play baseball tomorrow.

Student A: Are you going to play baseball tomorrow?
Student B: Yes, I am. (No, I'm not.)

George is going to study tonight.

Student B: Are you going to study tonight?
Student C: Yes, I am.

1. George is going to work at home tonight.
2. George is going to get up early tomorrow.
3. George is going to go to San Francisco.
4. George is going to have a vacation this summer.
5. George is going to have a cup of coffee.
6. George is going to buy a wrist watch tomorrow.
7. George is going to study Japanese.
8. George is going to visit the museum.
9. George is going to drink a cup of coffee.
10. Mary is going to drink a glass of milk.

Exercise 6. Listen to the statements. Form corresponding questions with *what* at the beginning and *tomorrow* at the end. A second student will answer.

He's studying grammar today.

Student A: What is he going to study tomorrow?
Student B: He's going to study vocabulary.

He's drinking coffee today.

Student B: What is he going to drink tomorrow?
Student C: He's going to drink milk.

1. John is eating ice cream today.
2. Mr. Miller is having tomato juice today.
3. Mary is reading an American newspaper today.
4. John is buying a red shirt today.
5. Mary is buying a new umbrella today.
6. Mr. Miller is visiting a large city today.
7. Mrs. Miller is studying Spanish today.
8. Mary is reading a history book today.
9. John is using a blue pencil today.
10. George and Mary are playing tennis today.
11. Paul is selling apples today.
12. Mr. and Mrs. Allen are drinking coffee today.
13. John is repeating the easy words today.
14. We are studying lesson five today.

B.1   Notice the negative forms.

Previous pattern:

SHORT ANSWERS

(Lesson 1 — A.6)

| No, I'm not. |
| No, you aren't. |
| No, he isn't. |
| etc. |

(Lesson 3 — B.3)

| No, I wasn't. |
| No, you weren't. |
| etc. |

New pattern:

FULL FORMS				CONTRACTIONS		
be + not						
I	*am*	*not*	tired.	*I'm*	*not*	tired.
You	*are*	*not*	tired.	You	*aren't*	tired.
We	*are*	*not*	tired.	We	*aren't*	tired.
They	*are*	*not*	tired.	They	*aren't*	tired.
He	*is*	*not*	tired.	He	*isn't*	tired.
I	*was*	*not*	tired.	I	*wasn't*	tired.
He	*was*	*not*	tired.	He	*wasn't*	tired.
You	*were*	*not*	tired.	You	*weren't*	tired.
We	*were*	*not*	tired.	We	*weren't*	tired.
They	*were*	*not*	tired.	They	*weren't*	tired.

COMMENT

These contractions are the same as those which were introduced as parts of short answers.

NOTE: The contractions in the following sentences are equally acceptable:

You're not busy.
He's not busy.

ADDITIONAL EXAMPLES

I'm not studying.
I'm not going to study.

He isn't studying.
They aren't going to study.

Exercise 7. Substitute the words and make the necessary changes.

I'm not in Detroit now.

he	HE ISN'T IN DETROIT NOW.
last week	HE WASN'T IN DETROIT LAST WEEK.
next week	HE ISN'T GOING TO BE IN DETROIT NEXT WEEK.
here	HE ISN'T GOING TO BE HERE NEXT WEEK.
now	HE ISN'T HERE NOW.
they	THEY AREN'T HERE NOW.

1. Mary	7. they	13. he	19. you
2. she	8. now	14. at home	20. they
3. in Detroit	9. tomorrow	15. Mary	21. last week
4. yesterday	10. we	16. now	22. I
5. you	11. I	17. yesterday	23. they
6. I	12. you	18. we	24. we

B.2 Notice the negative forms used with verbs other than *be*.

Previous pattern:

SHORT ANSWERS

(Lesson 2 — A.5)

> No, you don't.
> No, he doesn't.

(Lesson 3 — C.3)

> No, they didn't.

New pattern:

FULL FORMS   CONTRACTIONS
do + *not*

You	*do*	*not*	study.
He	*does*	*not*	study.
They	*did*	*not*	study.

You	*don't*	study.
He	*doesn't*	study.
They	*didn't*	study.

COMMENT

These contractions are the same as those which were introduced as parts of short answers.

Exercise 8. Substitute the words and make the necessary changes.

He doesn't study engineering.

they	THEY DON'T STUDY ENGINEERING.
last year	THEY DIDN'T STUDY ENGINEERING LAST YEAR.
I	I DIDN'T STUDY ENGINEERING LAST YEAR.
don't	I DON'T STUDY ENGINEERING.

1. we	6. she	11. Mr. and Mrs. Miller	16. they
2. John	7. a year ago	12. you	17. Mary
3. he	8. Paul	13. don't	18. Mary and Alice
4. they	9. we	14. I	19. Paul
5. you	10. I	15. he	20. we

Exercise 9. Listen to the statement about Paul. Make a negative statement about George.

Paul is happy.   GEORGE ISN'T HAPPY.
Paul has a car.   GEORGE DOESN'T HAVE A CAR.

1. Paul is tired.
2. Paul studied last night.
3. Paul is a student.
4. Paul was hungry last night.
5. Paul reads in the morning.
6. Paul is often busy.
7. Paul wanted fish for dinner.
8. Paul walked home yesterday.
9. Paul is writing a letter.
10. Paul is usually tired.
11. Paul likes ice cream.
12. Paul is sick.
13. Paul is at the library.
14. Paul likes beer.
15. Paul has a new car.
16. Paul was sick yesterday.
17. Paul was absent yesterday.
18. Paul studied in the library yesterday.
19. Paul is going to go to New York.
20. Paul is studying now.
21. Paul has coffee in the morning.

C.   Notice the position of *doesn't* and *isn't*.

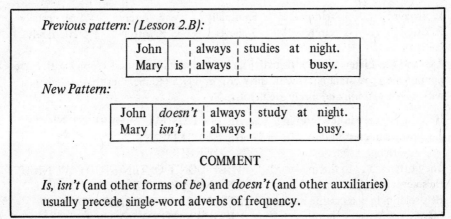

Previous pattern: (Lesson 2.B):

John		always	studies at night.
Mary	is	always	busy.

New Pattern:

John	*doesn't*	always	study at night.
Mary	*isn't*	always	busy.

COMMENT

Is, isn't (and other forms of *be*) and *doesn't* (and other auxiliaries) usually precede single-word adverbs of frequency.

NOTES:

(1) Auxiliaries are words such as *do, don't, does, doesn't, can,* and *must. Have* in the sentence *They have always worked at night,* is also an auxiliary.

(2) The word *sometimes* is an exception to the above comment. It precedes negative auxiliaries and negative forms of *be.*

> He sometimes doesn't know the answers.
> He sometimes isn't here.

Exercise 10. Listen to the statement about Paul. Make a negative statement about George.

Paul is always happy.	GEORGE ISN'T ALWAYS HAPPY.
Paul always studies at night.	GEORGE DOESN'T ALWAYS STUDY AT NIGHT.

1. Paul usually drinks milk in the morning.
2. Paul often eats in a restaurant.
3. Paul is often busy.
4. Paul is usually hungry.
5. Paul often reads at night.
6. Paul is often tired.
7. Paul always has coffee for breakfast.
8. Paul usually studies in the morning.

Exercise 11. The adverbs *never, rarely,* and *seldom* are negative. (Do not use these words with other negative words such as *don't* and *isn't.*) Make negative statements in this exercise. Substitute the words and make the necessary changes.

He doesn't usually smoke.

often	HE DOESN'T OFTEN SMOKE.
never	HE NEVER SMOKES.
rarely	HE RARELY SMOKES.
always	HE DOESN'T ALWAYS SMOKE.
seldom	HE SELDOM SMOKES.

1. always	3. seldom	5. usually	7. rarely	9. usually
2. often	4. rarely	6. never	8. often	10. rarely

Exercise 12. Listen to the affirmative and negative statements. Respond with corresponding negative statements with the words *at night.* (Remember that statements with *never, seldom,* and *rarely* are negative.)

He's usually here in the morning.	HE ISN'T USUALLY HERE AT NIGHT.
He's always in class in the morning.	HE ISN'T ALWAYS IN CLASS AT NIGHT.
They often study in the morning.	THEY DON'T OFTEN STUDY AT NIGHT.
He's never here in the morning.	HE'S NEVER HERE AT NIGHT.
He's seldom in class in the morning.	HE'S SELDOM IN CLASS AT NIGHT.
I rarely study in the morning.	I RARELY STUDY AT NIGHT.

1. I often study in the morning.
2. I never study in the morning.
3. I usually sing in the morning.
4. He usually sings in the morning.
5. I never run to class in the morning.
6. I always study grammar in the morning.
7. She never eats in the morning.
8. She's usually absent in the morning.
9. Mary's often hungry in the morning.
10. John's never hungry in the morning.
11. He rarely smokes in the morning.
12. He seldom runs in the morning.
13. He's seldom late in the morning.
14. He's never busy in the morning.
15. He's rarely absent in the morning.

Exercise 13. Listen carefully to the teacher's statement and question. Answer the question using the same adverb of frequency that the teacher uses in the question.

John often wears blue shirts. Does he always wear blue shirts?   NO, HE DOESN'T ALWAYS WEAR BLUE SHIRTS.

Mrs. Miller seldom drinks tea. Does she usually drink tea?   NO, SHE DOESN'T USUALLY DRINK TEA.

1. Mr. Miller seldom has water with dinner. Does he usually have water with dinner?
2. Bob sometimes watches television at night. Does he always watch television at night?
3. John sometimes listens to the radio at 8 P.M. Does he always listen to the radio at 8 P.M.?
4. Paul does his homework every night. Does he always do his homework?
5. Mr. Allen usually has milk with dinner. Does he usually have beer with dinner?
6. Mary eats at a restaurant at noon every day. Does she always eat lunch at a restaurant?
7. Mr. Miller eats breakfast every day. Does he always eat breakfast?
8. Mr. Miller often eats sandwiches for lunch. Does he always eat sandwiches for lunch?
9. Mr. Allen usually studies at home. Does he usually study in the library?
10. John sometimes eats apple pie. Does he usually eat apple pie?

D.   Notice the use of *some* and *any*.

| QUESTIONS: | Do you need | *some* | pencils? |
| | Do you need | *any* | pencils? |

| AFFIRMATIVE STATEMENT: | I need | *some* | pencils. |
| NEGATIVE STATEMENT: | I don't need | *any* | pencils. |

COMMENTS

(1)   The word *some,* usually unstressed, means an indefinite number of countable things (*some pencils, some books, some students*) or an indefinite quantity of something not countable (*some milk, some bread, some fruit*).

(2)   After negative expressions, *any* is used in place of *some.*

(3)   Both *some* and *any* are used in questions.

Exercise 14. Listen to the affirmative statement about John. Make a negative statement about Paul.

John needs some pencils.   PAUL DOESN'T NEED ANY PENCILS.
John is buying some books.   PAUL ISN'T BUYING ANY BOOKS.

1. John is buying some apples.
2. John is singing some songs.
3. John is repeating some words.
4. John is looking at some pictures.
5. John is moving some chairs.
6. John is making some sandwiches.
7. John is eating some apples.
8. John needs some books.
9. John wants some sandwiches.
10. John has some stamps.
11. John sees some flowers.
12. John wants some magazines.
13. John needs some new shirts.
14. John has some letters.
15. John sees some grammar books.
16. John needs some red ink.
17. John is going to buy some ink.
18. John is going to write some letters.
19. John is going to read some books.
20. John is going to drink some coffee.
21. John is going to make some sandwiches.
22. John is going to have some milk.
23. John is going to eat some fruit.

Exercise 15. Substitute the words and make the necessary changes. (Use *any* in the questions.)

I have some potatoes.

I don't have   I DON'T HAVE ANY POTATOES.
do you have   DO YOU HAVE ANY POTATOES?
bread   DO YOU HAVE ANY BREAD?
he doesn't have   HE DOESN'T HAVE ANY BREAD.

1. did he have
2. he has
3. coffee
4. do they have
5. do you need
6. I need
7. she needed
8. John doesn't need
9. Mrs. Miller doesn't have
10. I don't need
11. we want
12. bread
13. the dog is eating
14. John didn't eat
15. Mrs. Miller has
16. does she have
17. she doesn't have
18. coffee
19. shoes
20. stamps
21. she needs
22. fruit
23. does she need

NOTE: *Some* and *any* are also substitutes for noun phrases like *some stamps, any stamps*, etc.

Do you have any stamps?   Did Mary buy any fruit?

Yes, I do.   Yes, she did.
Yes, I have SOME.   Yes, she bought SOME.
No, I don't.   No, she didn't.
No, I don't have ANY.   No, she didn't buy ANY.

Exercise 16. Practice short answers with *some* and *any*. Answer the teacher's questions individually.

Do you see any books?   YES, I SEE SOME.

Do you know any engineers?   NO, I DON'T KNOW ANY.
(YES, I KNOW SOME.)

1. Do you see any students?
2. Do you know any American songs?
3. Do you need any pens?
4. Do you have any stamps?
5. Do you see any stamps?
6. Are you going to buy some stamps today?
7. Did you learn any new words yesterday?
8. Do you see any books?
9. Do you see any pencils?
10. Do you have any pens?

Lesson 6

A.   The articles: *the, a, an.*
B.   Count and noncount nouns: a *pencil;* some *ink.*
C.   Quantity expressions: *much, many, a few,* etc.
D.   Demonstratives: *this, that, these, those.*
E.   Possessives: *my, your, his,* etc.

A.   Notice the use of the articles *a* and *the.*

> I bought *a* comb and *a* pencil yesterday.
> *The* comb is black and
> *the* pencil is red.

COMMENTS

(1)   The article *a* is used in the first sentence to indicate that the *comb* and the *pencil* which the speaker is talking about are being mentioned for the first time and that they are not identified.

(2)   In the second sentence, the article *the* is used to indicate that the nouns *comb* and *pencil* have been identified; that is, the hearer knows which particular comb the speaker is talking about.

A NOTE ON THE ARTICLE IN ENGLISH:

The words *a, an,* and *the* are called articles. In general, we use the definite article *the* when the noun which follows names an identified specimen; that is, when we believe that the hearer knows which person, place, or thing the noun refers to.

There are three important ways of establishing this identification: (1) Frame A shows that a noun can be identified in a previous sentence. (2) In the sentences below, the noun is identified by the phrase which follows:

> The book *on Mr. Allen's desk* is yellow.
> The philosophy *of Aristotle* is interesting.
> I like the hat *that you are wearing.*

(Such phrases are often sufficient to establish identification, but not always.)
(3) Sometimes the things referred to are understood from the situation and are therefore identified. For example, when the teacher asks, "Is the door open?", you know the teacher is asking about the door of the classroom.

The indefinite article *a/an* can be used when an unidentified specimen is introduced, as in Frame A. Another important use of *a/an* is in sentences of description or classification (Lesson 1):

> John is *a student.*
> Paris is *a city.*

A and *an* are weak (unstressed) forms of *one.* We use the full form *one* when we emphasize the number. For example:

> *One* boy arrived late, not *two.*

Compare:

> *A boy* arrived late, not *a girl.*

Exercise 1. Contrast the use of definite and indefinite articles. The teacher will use the article *a/an* to introduce a topic. Give a short answer to the question.

> I bought a pencil and a book. What did I read?   THE BOOK.
> I bought a pen and a comb. What did I write with?   THE PEN.

1. John bought a pencil and an apple. What did he eat?
2. Mary bought a newspaper and a key. What did she read?
3. Mr. Allen bought a knife and an umbrella. What did he cut the apple with?
4. Mrs. Allen bought a chair and a watch. What did she sit on?
5. Mr. Miller bought a chair and a car. What did he drive?
6. Robert bought a pen and a spoon. What did he eat ice cream with?
7. Paul bought a shirt and a comb. What did he wear?
8. George bought a toothbrush and an apple. What did he eat?
9. Mary bought a pencil and a book. What did she write with?
10. Mr. Miller bought a newspaper and an orange. What did he read?

NOTE: *The* is not used with the names of persons, languages, *most* countries, streets, or the time of day.

EXAMPLES

> *Mr. Smith* is a teacher.
> We are going to visit *Dr. Brown.*
> We are speaking *English.*
> *Spanish* is an important language.
> Mary is going to *Argentina.*
> The Amazon River is in *Brazil.*
> John lives on *State Street.*
> He goes to class at *eight o'clock.*

SOME EXCEPTIONS

The Mississippi River is in *the United States.*
The Dominican Republic is in Latin America.
The Netherlands is in Europe.

Exercise 2. Substitute the words which are given. Use the article *the* where an article is necessary.

I am going to see the professor.

Professor Miller   I AM GOING TO SEE PROFESSOR MILLER.
doctor   I AM GOING TO SEE THE DOCTOR.

1. Doctor Allen   5. Pacific Ocean   9. South America
2. Miss Smith   6. Pennsylvania Avenue   10. Colombia
3. United States   7. Fifth Avenue   11. professor
4. Canada   8. New York City   12. Professor Taylor

NOTE: In English the article *the* is usually not used when the noun phrase refers to something in a very general way. For example, "John likes *milk*.", "Mary is studying *history*." However, *the* is often required if the noun phrase is followed by an identifying phrase. (See the note following Frame A.) Example: Mary is studying *the history* of the United States.

Exercise 3. Substitute the words which are given. Use the article *the* when necessary.

John is studying music.
music of Mozart   JOHN IS STUDYING THE MUSIC
                             OF MOZART.

philosophy   JOHN IS STUDYING PHILOSOPHY.

1. philosophy of Aristotle   9. art of the Netherlands
2. history   10. architecture
3. history of Thailand   11. architecture of Greece
4. music   12. Greek architecture
5. music of Mexico   (no following identifying
6. Mexican music   phrase)
   (no following identifying   13. architecture of Greece
   phrase)   14. English
7. algebra   15. Japanese
8. art

Exercise 4.

Mary likes television.

milk   MARY LIKES MILK.
history   MARY LIKES HISTORY.

              1. American history
              2. history of the United States
              3. coffee

(Continue, using the items of Exercise 3.)

NOTE: The article *the* is generally a part of the name of a university or college when that name also includes a phrase beginning with the preposition *of.*

> The University of Illinois
> The University of Michigan
> The University of California

but:

> Harvard University
> Cornell University
> Western Michigan University
> Jackson Junior College

B. Compare the count and noncount nouns.

Count nouns	Noncount nouns
1 pencil, 2 pencils, 3 pencils, . . .	ink
1 table, 2 tables, 3 tables, . . .	water
1 chair, 2 chairs, 3 chairs, . . .	air
1 apple, 2 apples, 3 apples, . . .	coffee
. . .	. . .

COMMENTS

In general, we cannot put numbers in front of noncount nouns. Furthermore, they do not have a plural form.

NOTE: In certain special situations, noncount nouns are sometimes used as count nouns (or count nouns as noncount nouns). In a restaurant, for example, it is possible that you will hear someone say, "Two coffees, please."

Exercise 5. In this exercise, the words preceded by *some* are noncount nouns. The words preceded by *a/an* are count nouns. ("Would you like an apple?" is a polite way of asking "Do you want an apple?")

> an apple   Student A: WOULD YOU LIKE AN APPLE?
>   Student B: YES, PLEASE. (or NO, THANK YOU.)
>
> some bread   Student B: WOULD YOU LIKE SOME BREAD?
>   Student C: YES, PLEASE. (or NO, THANK YOU.)

1. an orange
2. some orange juice
3. some coffee
4. a sandwich
5. some tomato juice
6. some soup
7. a hot dog
8. a banana
9. some tea
10. some sugar
11. an egg
12. some fruit
13. some milk

(Repeat the above exercise leaving out *a/an* and *some* in the cue.)

NOTE: *Some* can also be used with the plural form of count nouns.

COUNT: a pencil, some pencils
NONCOUNT: some ink

Exercise 6. Practice the use of *a, an,* and *some* with nouns. Substitute the words into the statement and make the necessary changes.

He's going to buy a car tomorrow.

house   HE'S GOING TO BUY A HOUSE TOMORROW.
apples   HE'S GOING TO BUY SOME APPLES TOMORROW.
fruit   HE'S GOING TO BUY SOME FRUIT TOMORROW.

1. table	6. bananas	11. soap	16. milk
2. chairs	7. bread	12. toothbrush	17. sandwich
3. furniture	8. cheese	13. toothpaste	18. butter
4. tomatoes	9. book	14. orange juice	19. car
5. tomato soup	10. books	15. coffee	20. chalk

Exercise 7. Words such as *cup, slice, piece* are often used with noncount nouns. For example: *a cup of coffee, a slice of bread, a piece of paper, a bit of news.*

I need some paper. I need   I NEED TWO PIECES OF PAPER.
    two pieces.

I'm going to eat some bread.   I'M GOING TO EAT TWO SLICES
    I'm going to eat two   OF BREAD.
    slices.

John needs some ink. He   JOHN NEEDS A BOTTLE OF INK.
    needs one bottle.

1. Mary is going to buy some ink. She is going to buy two bottles.
2. Mary wants some chalk. She wants two pieces.
3. Mr. Miller bought some milk. He bought two bottles.
4. Mr. Miller is going to drink some milk. He is going to drink two glasses.
5. John drank some water. He drank two glasses.
6. Mary drank some coffee. She drank four cups.
7. Mrs. Miller bought some bread. She bought one loaf.
8. Mr. Miller is going to eat some bread. He is going to eat three slices.
9. John is going to eat some toast. He is going to eat two slices.
10. Mary bought some soap. She bought three bars.
11. Mary bought some butter. She bought one pound.
12. John bought some toothpaste. He bought one tube.

NOTE: The use of the articles *the, a/an,* and *some* with nouns is summarized in the following table:

	COUNT CONSTRUCTIONS		NONCOUNT CONSTRUCTIONS
	Singular	Plural	
Indefinite	an apple	some apples	some coffee
Definite	the apple	the apples	the coffee

In addition, when nouns do not refer to particular specimens, but refer to a category in a general way, no article is used.	apples	coffee

Apples grow in Michigan.   I like apples.
Coffee grows in Hawaii.   I like coffee.

Exercise 8. Practice the use of count nouns and noncount nouns. Substitute the words into the statement. Use the plural form of count nouns. (This exercise can be simplified if the teacher gives the plural forms of count nouns, e.g., *pencils* instead of *pencil.*)

That store sells pens.

pencil	THAT STORE SELLS PENCILS.
ink	THAT STORE SELLS INK.

1. apple
2. coffee
3. milk
4. banana
5. bread
6. orange

7. fruit
8. soap
9. apple
10. butter
11. tea
12. radio

13. chair
14. table
15. furniture
16. tomato
17. tomato juice
18. fruit

C. Notice the quantity expressions which are used with the count noun *apple* and the noncount noun *water*.

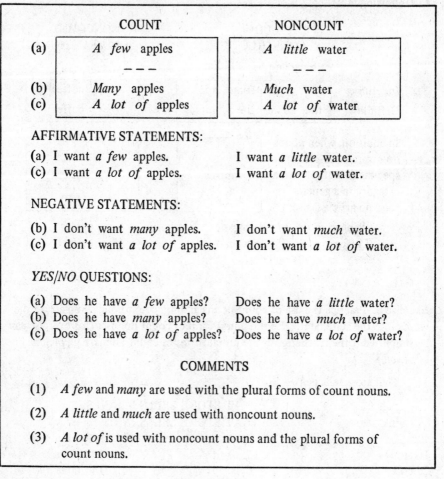

	COUNT	NONCOUNT
(a)	*A few* apples	*A little* water
	– – –	– – –
(b)	*Many* apples	*Much* water
(c)	*A lot of* apples	*A lot of* water

AFFIRMATIVE STATEMENTS:

(a) I want *a few* apples.   I want *a little* water.
(c) I want *a lot of* apples.   I want *a lot of* water.

NEGATIVE STATEMENTS:

(b) I don't want *many* apples.   I don't want *much* water.
(c) I don't want *a lot of* apples.   I don't want *a lot of* water.

YES/NO QUESTIONS:

(a) Does he have *a few* apples?   Does he have *a little* water?
(b) Does he have *many* apples?   Does he have *much* water?
(c) Does he have *a lot of* apples?   Does he have *a lot of* water?

COMMENTS

(1) *A few* and *many* are used with the plural forms of count nouns.

(2) *A little* and *much* are used with noncount nouns.

(3) *A lot of* is used with noncount nouns and the plural forms of count nouns.

NOTES:

(1) The quantity expressions *much* and *many* are not generally used in object noun phrases of affirmative statements. These quantity expressions are used chiefly in questions and negative statements and in the subject noun phrases of affirmative sentences. (See the note which follows Exercise 11.)

In the object noun phrases of affirmative statements, *a lot of, a great deal of, a large amount of,* and similar expressions are regularly used in place of *much* and *many*, especially in informal situations.

(2) *Few* and *a few, little* and *a little* are slightly different. *A few* and *a little* mean "a small number" and "a small quantity," respectively. *Few* and *little* mean "not . . . many" and "not . . . much."

John has a few good friends.
John has few good friends. (He does*n't* have *many* good friends.)

You made a few mistakes.
You made few mistakes. (You did*n't* make *many* mistakes.)

I have a little time.
I have little time (I do*n't* have *much* time.)

Exercise 9. Practice the use of *a little* and *a few.*

Do you need any ink?   YES, JUST A LITTLE, PLEASE.
Do you need any tomatoes?   YES, JUST A FEW, PLEASE.

1. butter	6. bread	11. stamps
2. pencils	7. chairs	12. envelopes
3. water	8. sugar	13. information
4. bananas	9. gasoline	14. time
5. money	10. eggs	15. help

Exercise 10. Substitute *a few,* and *a little* in place of *a small number* or *a small quantity.* Substitute *a lot of* in place of *a large number* or *a large quantity.* (When students respond individually, *much* and *many* may also be used.)

John drinks a large quantity of   JOHN DRINKS A LOT OF COFFEE.
    coffee.

I need a small quantity of sugar.   I NEED A LITTLE SUGAR.

Mary has a small number of   MARY HAS A FEW GOOD FRIENDS.
    good friends.

I didn't see a large number of   I DIDN'T SEE A LOT OF STUDENTS.
    students.   (I DIDN'T SEE MANY STUDENTS.)

1. They have a small quantity of money.
2. He has a small number of apples.
3. We don't have a large number of classes today.
4. We need a large quantity of bread.
5. Do you drink a large quantity of milk?
6. Does John have a large number of ties?
7. Mary drinks a small quantity of coffee.
8. We usually buy a small quantity of soap.
9. We usually buy a small number of bars of soap.
10. He doesn't usually buy a large number of pencils.
11. John doesn't eat a large quantity of fruit.
12. Americans don't drink a large quantity of tea.
13. Mary doesn't have a large number of books.
14. Children need a large quantity of milk.
15. John doesn't drink a large quantity of fruit juice in the morning.
16. This newspaper doesn't give a great deal of news.

Exercise 11. Practice the use of *how much* and *how many* in questions and *a little* and *a few* in answers.

    ink   Student A: HOW MUCH INK DID YOU BUY?
                      Student B: ONLY A LITTLE. (ONLY A FEW BOTTLES.)

    apples   Student A: HOW MANY APPLES DID YOU BUY?
                      Student B: ONLY A FEW.

1. books	7. ice cream	13. orange juice	19. pencils
2. coffee	8. lamps	14. bread	20. shirts
3. combs	9. wine	15. soap	21. stamps
4. eggs	10. magazines	16. butter	22. tomato juice
5. beer	11. milk	17. pens	23. tooth paste
6. hot dogs	12. newspapers	18. tea	24. tooth brushes

NOTE: Negative expressions such as *not many, not much, not all,* and *none (= not any)* can be used in subject position in sentences:

COUNT
    Not many of the apples are good. Only a few of them are good.
    Not all of the books are good. Only some of them are good.
    None of the apples are good. All of them are bad.

NONCOUNT
    Not much of the bread is good. Only a little of it is good.
    Not all of the news is good. Only some of it is good.
    None of the coffee is good. All of it is bad.

Both singular and plural forms of verbs are used with *all* and *none: not all . . . are, not all . . . is,* etc. The noun phrase following the *of* determines whether the verb is singular or plural.

Exercise 12. Listen to the questions, which contain quantity expressions. Answer the questions with the negative forms.

QUANTITY EXPRESSIONS	NEGATIVE QUANTITY EXPRESSIONS
many	not many
much	not much
all	not all
any	none (not any)

Do many of the students write letters?	NO, NOT MANY OF THE STUDENTS WRITE LETTERS.
Are any of the students sick?	NO, NONE OF THE STUDENTS ARE SICK.

1. Are all of the books here?
2. Was much of the coffee hot?
3. Do any of the students want a ticket?
4. Do all of the students speak Spanish?
5. Is any of the food ready?
6. Are any of the exercises difficult?
7. Do many of the students live in apartments?
8. Was much of the discussion interesting?
9. Is any of the bread fresh?
10. Are any of the apples good?
11. Were many of the students at the meeting?
12. Is any of the milk good?
13. Are all of the stories interesting?
14. Is any of the chalk broken?
15. Is any of the news important?

Exercise 13. For advanced students. As in the preceding exercise, answer the questions with the negative forms, *not many, not much, not all,* and *none.* Then add an appropriate second statement which contains *a few, a little, some,* or *all.* (The pronouns *them* and *it* may be used in the second sentence.) (Call on students individually.)

Are all of the books here?

NO, NOT ALL OF THE BOOKS ARE HERE. ONLY SOME OF THEM ARE HERE.

Is any of the chalk green?

NO, NONE OF THE CHALK IS GREEN. ALL OF IT IS WHITE.

1. Are any of the questions difficult?
2. Do many of the students live in an apartment?
3. Are any of the students sick?
4. Do many of the students write letters?
5. Was much of the discussion interesting?
6. Are many of the books open?
7. Are any of the apples good?
8. Is any of the ink red?
9. Are all of the pencils long?
10. Do any of the students eat breakfast in class?
11. Is any of the bread soft?
12. Are all of the books green?
13. Is much of the furniture new?
14. Were many of the students at the meeting?
15. Is any of the milk good?
16. Are all of the stories interesting?
17. Is all of the news good?
18. Did the students eat much of the fruit?

D.   Notice the meaning and use of demonstratives.

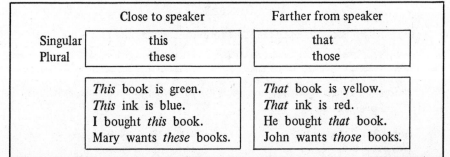

	Close to speaker	Farther from speaker
Singular	this	that
Plural	these	those
	This book is green. *This* ink is blue. I bought *this* book. Mary wants *these* books.	*That* book is yellow. *That* ink is red. He bought *that* book. John wants *those* books.

NOTE: Demonstratives, like articles, adjectives, and other noun modifiers, have the same form whether the noun they modify is in the subject position or in the object position.

Exercise 14. Listen to the statements and the words *here* and *there*. Repeat the statements and use the appropriate demonstrative.

The exercises are easy.	There	THOSE EXERCISES ARE EASY.
The university is large.	Here	THIS UNIVERSITY IS LARGE.
The lessons are easy.	Here	THESE LESSONS ARE EASY.
The book is green.	There	THAT BOOK IS GREEN.

1. The chairs are comfortable.   Here
2. The ideas are new and interesting.   Here
3. The student comes from Peru.   There
4. The students come from Venezuela.   There
5. The book has a green cover.   Here
6. The girl is beautiful.   There
7. The news is exciting.   There
8. I like the dictionary.   Here
9. I like the pencils.   There
10. I like the drug store.   Here
11. I need the books.   Here

E.   Notice the use of possessives.

1	my	our
2	your	your
3	his, her, its	their

My books are in *my* room
My new book is on *her* table.
Your coffee is hot.
John washed *his* face and hands.
George and Paul washed *their* hands.

COMMENTS

(1) The possessives have the same form for singular and plural nouns.

(2) Use possessives with parts of the body. Don't use *the*.

NOTE: Singular count nouns are nearly always preceded by an article, a demonstrative, or a possessive.

John has *a* car.	Where is *the* car?
This car is old.	*My* car is gray.

Exercise 15.

Mary washed her hands.

| I | I WASHED MY HANDS. |
| John | JOHN WASHED HIS HANDS. |

1. Mrs. Miller
2. George and Paul
3. The students
4. We

5. The man
6. Mary
7. Mr. and Mrs. Allen
8. You

9. You and I
10. You and John
11. I
12. Mrs. Smith

Exercise 16.

Mary is leaving.	DOES SHE HAVE HER BOOKS?
John is leaving.	DOES HE HAVE HIS BOOKS?
The students are leaving.	DO THEY HAVE THEIR BOOKS?

1. John and Mary are leaving.
2. Miss Smith is leaving.
3. Bill
4. The man
5. The woman

6. The boy
7. My wife
8. My son
9. Your father
10. George and Paul

11. We
12. Your mother
13. You and I
14. Your friends

NOTES:

(1)   As was pointed out above, the quantity expression *all* can be used with plural count nouns and also with noncount nouns:

1. *All apples* grow on trees.
2. John wanted *all* (of) the *apples*.
3. *All water* contains oxygen.
4. John used *all* (of) our *water*.
5. We need *all* (of) this *coffee*.
6. She invited *all* (of) her *friends*.

Of is optional in sentences 2, 4, 5, and 6, where it is followed by *the, this, my*, or the equivalent.

(2)   In expressions of repeated time, use *every:*

1. I study *every day*.
2. I write to them *every week*.

Do not say, "all the days" or "all the weeks" in sentences of this type.

Lesson 7

A.   Requests: Please read the book. *(Would you; let's)*
B.   Irregular nouns: *man, men; people.*
C.   The noun substitute *one.*
D.   The use of *other* and *another.*
E.   The object forms of pronouns: *me, him, them,* etc.

A.   Notice the request sentences.

POSITIVE	Please open your books.
POLITE POSITIVE	Would you please open your books.
NEGATIVE	Please don't open the door.

INCLUSIVE REQUEST (including speaker):

POSITIVE	Let's watch television.
NEGATIVE	Let's not watch television.

COMMENTS

(1)   The word *please* may be omitted. However, including *please* makes the request sentence more polite. (*Please* may also be inserted at the end, instead of the beginning, of the sentence.)

(2)   The negative word *not* is used in request sentences when *let's* or *would* (or another auxiliary) appears in addition to the main verb. *Don't* is used in the first pattern above.

SOME ADDITIONAL FORMS OF REQUEST SENTENCES

Will you please open the window.
Won't you please open the window.
Could you please open the window.

NOTE: The following patterns are often used to make requests (rather than to ask questions).

Why don't you open the window.
Why don't we go to the movies.

AN INVITATION. This is always a question. It requires an answer like *yes* or *no.*

Would you like to go to the movies?

Exercise 1. Form polite request sentences with the suggested words. A second student will respond with *Yes, I'd be glad to.*

close the window   Student A: WOULD YOU PLEASE CLOSE THE
                                 WINDOW.
                     Student B: YES, I'D BE GLAD TO.

open your book   Student B: WOULD YOU PLEASE OPEN YOUR
                                 BOOK.
                     Student C: YES, I'D BE GLAD TO.

1. read the sentence.
2. write your name.
3. translate the sentence.
4. close the door.
5. go to the store.
6. pass the salt.

7. walk to the blackboard.
8. give me that notebook.
9. cash this check.
10. write with a pen.
11. pass the sugar.
12. lend me your pencil.

Exercise 2. Form negative request sentences.

George speaks rapidly.   PLEASE DON'T SPEAK RAPIDLY.
George is usually late.   PLEASE DON'T BE LATE.

1. George drives fast.
2. George wastes time.
3. George writes with red ink.
4. George often misses class.

5. George often smokes in class.
6. George speaks fast.
7. George often forgets to say, "Thank you."
8. George sometimes sleeps late.

Exercise 3. Form request sentences that include the speaker.

sing some songs   LET'S SING SOME SONGS.
go to the movies   LET'S GO TO THE MOVIES.
write some letters   LET'S WRITE SOME LETTERS.

1. speak English
2. go to class
3. go to the museum
4. go to the new restaurant
5. go to the movies
6. go to Los Angeles

7. sing some songs
8. write some letters
9. play baseball
10. play basketball
11. play tennis
12. play ping pong

Exercise 4. Form a negative request sentence. Then add an affirmative request (individually).

Let's open the window.   NO, LET'S NOT OPEN THE WINDOW.
                              LET'S OPEN THE DOOR.

Let's go to the movies.   NO, LET'S NOT GO TO THE MOVIES.
                              LET'S WATCH TELEVISION.

1. Let's speak rapidly.
2. Let's study in the morning.
3. Let's eat dinner now.
4. Let's walk fast.
5. Let's go to the concert.

6. Let's use red ink.
7. Let's listen to the radio.
8. Let's write letters.
9. Let's sing songs.
10. Let's play tennis.

B.   Notice the irregular nouns.

SG.	PL.
man	men
gentleman	gentlemen
policeman	policemen
businessman	businessmen
woman	women
child	children
wife	wives
knife	knives
loaf	loaves
shelf	shelves
foot	feet
tooth	teeth
mouse	mice
sheep	sheep
fish	fish
	people
	police
	clothes

COMMENTS

(1)   The nouns *people, police,* and *clothes* do not have singular forms.

(2)   There is no difference in the pronunciation of the final syllables of *gentleman* and *gentlemen, policeman* and *policemen,* etc. Thus the singular and plural forms of these words are pronounced the same.

(3)   The difference in the pronunciation of *woman* and *women* is in the first vowel. The difference in the final vowels is an orthographic change only.

NOTE: The noun *news* is a noncount noun. When it is the subject of a sentence, it requires a singular form of the verb:

The news is good.

Exercise 5. Practice irregular plurals.

I see a man.	I SEE TWO MEN.
I see a gentleman.	I SEE TWO GENTLEMEN.
I see a woman.	I SEE TWO WOMEN.

1. child	3. foot	5. mouse	7. fish
2. knife	4. tooth	6. sheep	8. salesman

Exercise 6. Substitute the following words and make the necessary changes.

The man is here.

are	THE MEN ARE HERE.
the child	THE CHILD IS HERE.
the people	THE PEOPLE ARE HERE.
interesting	THE PEOPLE ARE INTERESTING.

1. the news	11. happy	21. here
2. bad	12. are	22. the police
3. the tooth	13. the woman	23. the man
4. are	14. the women	24. were
5. were	15. the children	25. the knife
6. good	16. is	26. the children
7. the knives	17. the wives	27. was
8. is	18. is	28. the woman
9. the news	19. the people	29. the police
10. the man	20. good	30. the people

C.   Notice the use of the word *one* as a noun substitute.

Previous pattern (Lesson 5. D):

> Did you buy *any pencils* yesterday?
>
> No, I'm going to buy *SOME* tomorrow.

New pattern:

> Did you buy *a pencil* yesterday?
>
> No, I'm going to buy *ONE* tomorrow.

COMMENT

In the sentence above, *one* is a substitute for *a pencil.*

NOTE: The substitute for *the pencil* is *it*:

I need *the pencil.* Does John have *it?*

ADDITIONAL EXAMPLES

I need an eraser.   The teacher has *one.*

Did you ever see an elephant?   Yes, I saw *one* yesterday.

Are you going to write a letter to   Yes, I'm going to write *one* tonight.
your parents?

Exercise 7. Practice the use of *one* and *some* as noun substitutes. Use *tomorrow* in your answer.

Did you write a letter today?   NO, I'M GOING TO WRITE ONE
                                          TOMORROW.

Did you buy some apples today?   NO, I'M GOING TO BUY SOME
                                          TOMORROW.

1. Did you buy a pen today?
2. Did you buy some stamps today?
3. Did you read a newspaper today?
4. Did you learn any words today?
5. Did you get some milk today?
6. Did you buy a magazine today?
7. Did you visit a museum today?
8. Did you make any sandwiches today?
9. Did you eat an egg for breakfast today?
10. Did you talk to a lawyer this morning?
11. Did you sing any songs today?
12. Did you bring a book today?

(Continue as above using *one* and *it* in the responses.)

13. Did you buy a pen yesterday?
14. Did you buy that pen yesterday?
15. Did you read a newspaper today?
16. Did you read the New York Times yesterday?
17. Did you visit a museum today?
18. Did you visit the art museum today?
19. Did you bring a book today?
20. Did you bring the grammar book?

D.1   Notice the use of *another one* and *the other one.*

> I have a pen here on the table.
>
> I have *another one* at home.
>
> This one is old, and *the other one* is new.

COMMENTS

(1)   *Other* means "additional" or "different."

(2)   When the article *an* precedes the word *other,* the two words are written as one: *another.*

(3)   In the examples, *another one* means *another pen* and *the other one* means *the other pen.* The noun *pen* can be replaced by the substitute *one* because the context makes it clear which noun is being replaced.

Exercise 8.   Practice the use of *another one.*

John is reading a magazine now.   HE IS GOING TO READ ANOTHER ONE TOMORROW.

Mr. Miller is singing a song now.   HE IS GOING TO SING ANOTHER ONE TOMORROW.

1. Mr. Allen is writing a letter now.
2. George is reading a book now.
3. Tom is visiting a museum now.
4. Bill is attending a concert now.
5. Mr. Ross is eating a sandwich now.
6. Mr. King is drinking a cup of coffee now.
7. Mr. Taylor is painting a picture now.
8. John is studying a lesson in the grammar book now.
9. George is learning a conversation now.
10. Miss Ford is buying a book now.
11. Mrs. Miller is singing a song now.
12. The students are practicing a conversation now.

Exercise 9.   Practice the use of *the other one.*

Mr. Allen is going to write two letters. He's writing one now.   HE'S GOING TO WRITE THE OTHER ONE TOMORROW.

John is going to read two magazines. He's reading one now.   HE'S GOING TO READ THE OTHER ONE TOMORROW.

1. Mrs. Taylor is going to paint two pictures. She's painting one now.
2. George is going to read two books. He's reading one now.
3. John is going to study two grammar lessons. He's studying one now.
4. Tom is going to visit two museums. He's visiting one now.
5. Miss Ford is going to buy two hats. She is buying one now.
6. The students are going to practice two conversations. They're practicing one now.

NOTE: *Other* can also be used in the plural:

> the other pens
> the other ones
> the others

The following sentences illustrate the use of *other* in the plural.

> 1. I have three pens. One is here.
> 2. The other ones are at home.
> 3. The others are at home.

Sentences 2 and 3 mean the same. In the plural, it is very common to use the short form *the others* in place of *the other ones.*

Exercise 10. Listen to the statement about one student. Make a question about the other students, using *who, what,* or *where.* (Do the exercise once with *the other students* in the response. Then repeat it using *the others* or *the other ones.* A second student can answer the question.)

One student is reading a magazine.   A: WHAT ARE THE OTHER
                                          STUDENTS READING?
                                      B: THEY'RE READING SOME
                                          BOOKS.

One student is studying in the   C: WHERE ARE THE OTHER
    library.   STUDENTS STUDYING?
                                      D: THEY'RE STUDYING AT HOME.

1. One student is drinking milk.
2. One student is eating in a restaurant.
3. One student is buying some stamps.
4. One student is learning some words.
5. One student is playing baseball.
6. One student is sitting on a chair.
7. One student is reading the lesson.
8. One student is reading in the library.
9. One student is waiting for Mr. Miller.
10. One student is speaking English.
11. One student is eating a hot dog.
12. One student is walking in the park.

13. One student is waiting for the bus.
14. One student is studying a grammar lesson.
15. One student is standing near the door.
16. One student is eating an apple.
17. One student is talking to Mr. Miller.
18. One student is washing a shirt.

NOTE: *Other* may be followed by adjectives:

    another old book   some other old blue shirt
    the other green bananas   other young American students

In place of the articles (*an-, the, some* and "zero"), *other* may also be preceded by either a demonstrative or a possessive according to the following formula:

$$\left\{ \begin{array}{l} \text{article} \\ \text{demonstrative} \\ \text{possessive} \end{array} \right\} \quad \text{(other) (adjectives) noun}$$

    this other old book   your other old blue shirt
    his other books   those other young American students

In addition, articles, demonstratives, and possessives may be preceded by quantity expressions.

    a lot of the other old books   none of your other old blue shirts
    many other books   three of those other young American
    a few of these other green   students
        bananas   three other young American students

Exercise 11. Listen to the statements. They are descriptions of something that occurs in the morning. The same situation occurs at night. Describe the situation at night using *others.*

    Four men work here in the   FOUR OTHERS WORK HERE
        morning.   AT NIGHT.

    A few students study in the   A FEW OTHERS STUDY AT
        morning.   NIGHT.

1. Several students read a newspaper in the morning.
2. Sixteen people work here in the morning.
3. Three students eat there in the morning.
4. Three people write letters in this room in the morning.
5. Many students study in the morning.
6. Some teachers teach in the morning.
7. Ten students read books here in the morning.
8. Many students sing songs in the morning.
9. Three hundred automobiles leave the factory in the morning.

E.   Observe the personal pronouns.

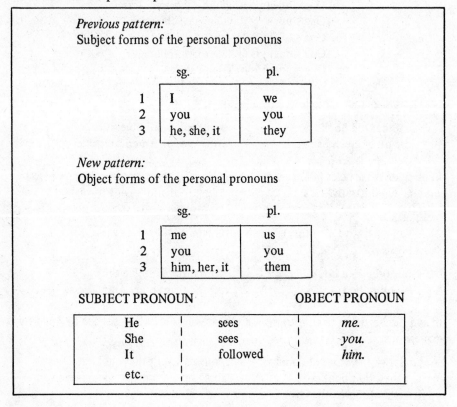

Previous pattern:
Subject forms of the personal pronouns

	sg.	pl.
1	I	we
2	you	you
3	he, she, it	they

New pattern:
Object forms of the personal pronouns

	sg.	pl.
1	me	us
2	you	you
3	him, her, it	them

SUBJECT PRONOUN		OBJECT PRONOUN
He	sees	*me.*
She	sees	*you.*
It	followed	*him.*
etc.		

NOTE: The object forms, but not the subject forms, of the personal pronouns are used after prepositions such as: *to, by, for, with, before, after, from, toward(s), about, near, above, under, beside, between, among,* etc.

He studied *with me.*
She is standing *beside you.*
They are coming *near us.*

Exercise 12.   Practice the object forms of the personal pronouns.

John explained the question.	JOHN EXPLAINED IT.
They asked Mary.	THEY ASKED HER.
We followed John and Mary.	WE FOLLOWED THEM.
The boys attended the class.	THE BOYS ATTENDED IT.

1. The boys helped the girls.
2. They study word order.
3. The teacher is explaining the pattern.
4. Mary answers John.
5. The class learned the word.

6. I received my books yesterday.
7. I helped the new students.
8. I am going to see Mary tonight.
9. He is going to visit John.
10. I followed their car.

74

Exercise 13. Answer the questions affirmatively using the subject and object forms of the personal pronouns. Use the adverb *yesterday* in your answer.

Did Mary learn the new words?   YES, SHE LEARNED THEM
                                                          YESTERDAY.

Did the students practice the   YES, THEY PRACTICED IT
    conversation?   YESTERDAY.

1. Did John help his friends?
2. Did Mary study the lesson?
3. Did Paul listen to the radio?
4. Did the students repeat the new words?
5. Did Mr. and Mrs. Miller look at the painting?
6. Did Mrs. Miller visit Mary?
7. Did John move the table and chairs?
8. Did Paul watch television?
9. Did John pronounce the new words?
10. Did Mary answer the letter?
11. Did Mr. Miller visit Mr. Allen?
12. Did Mrs. Miller talk to Mary?

Exercise 14. Practice the use of the personal pronouns and possessives by asking questions.

John is leaving.   DOES HE HAVE HIS LUGGAGE WITH HIM?

Mary is leaving.   DOES SHE HAVE HER LUGGAGE WITH HER?

John and Mary are leaving.   DO THEY HAVE THEIR LUGGAGE WITH
                                            THEM?

1. Mr. Miller is leaving.
2. My friends are leaving.
3. My brother is leaving.
4. My sister is leaving.
5. Mr. and Mrs. Miller are leaving.
6. Mr. Ross is leaving.
7. Mrs. Ross is leaving.
8. My father is leaving.
9. My parents are leaving.
10. I am leaving.
11. John and I are leaving.

Lesson 8

A. Verb and indirect object: Give *her* a book. Give a book *to her.*

B. Past tense forms of irregular verbs: eat, *ate;* give, *gave.*

A.1 Notice the position of *to Mary* and *Mary.*

A	He is going to give a book *to Mary.*
B	He is going to give *Mary* a book.

COMMENTS

(1) Two patterns are possible when a direct object *(a book)* and an indirect object *(Mary)* follow a verb such as *give.*

     A.   VERB + D.O.   + to I.O.
              give   the object   to the person

     B.   VERB + I.O.   + D.O.
              give   the person   the object

(2) Some other verbs which are like *give* are: *write, read, show, teach, tell, sell, send, lend, bring, take, pass.* These can be used in either pattern A or B.

NOTE: The opposite of *to* is expressed by *from* in sentences like "He borrowed something from us." Verbs like *demand, steal,* and *take* are used in this way. The preposition *from* in such cases cannot be omitted, i.e. only pattern A is possible.

NOTE TO THE TEACHER: In order to simplify the presentation, the following exercise requires the students to master only one pattern for production: the pattern with *to.* The other pattern can also be practiced if Exercise 1 is changed so that the stimulus sentences include the preposition *to.* For example:

     John often gives books to Mary.   JOHN OFTEN GIVES MARY BOOKS.

Exercise 1. Form sentences which include *to* and the indirect object *me.*

     John often gives Mary books.   HE NEVER GIVES ANY BOOKS
                                               TO ME.

     John often writes Mary letters.   HE NEVER WRITES ANY LETTERS
                                                 TO ME.

1. John often sells Mary pencils.
2. John sometimes lends Mary books.
3. John sometimes brings Mary flowers.
4. John sometimes gives Mary newspapers.
5. John sometimes brings Mary books.
6. John sometimes reads Mary his letters.
7. John sometimes lends Mary his books.
8. John often teaches Mary new words.

Exercise 2. For advanced students. When the direct object is a personal pronoun like *it* or *them,* the indirect object usually has *to* with it (pattern A). In the following exercise, answer the questions changing all the object noun phrases to pronouns. Use pattern A in your response, i.e., the pattern with *to.*

Is he going to give us *the history book?*   YES, HE IS GOING TO GIVE *IT* TO US TOMORROW.

Is he going to give Mr. Miller *the new books?*   YES, HE IS GOING TO GIVE *THEM* TO MR. MILLER TOMORROW.
(YES, HE IS GOING TO GIVE *THEM* TO HIM TOMORROW.)

1. Is he going to read us *the letter?*
2. Is he going to teach us *the new words?*
3. Is he going to lend Mr. Miller *his car?*
4. Is he going to tell Mr. Miller *the news?*
5. Is he going to lend Mary *his pen?*
6. Is he going to bring us *the new magazines?*
7. Is he going to pass Mr. Miller *the butter?*
8. Is he going to read us *the letter from Mr. Miller?*
9. Is he going to sell Mr. Miller *his car?*
10. Is he going to show us *his new radio?*

A.2 Notice the use of the indirect object after the verb *ask.*

B	He asked *the teacher* a question.
B	Please ask *him* his telephone number.

COMMENTS

For indirect objects after the verb *ask,* only pattern B is possible.

NOTE: There are only a very few verbs like *ask.* Among them are *cost, save, charge,* and *wish.*

The book cost me ten dollars.   The man charged me five dollars.
John saved me fifteen dollars.   He wished us a pleasant journey.

Exercise 3. Add the name *Mr. Miller* to the following statements.

He asked a question.   HE ASKED MR. MILLER A QUESTION.
He asked his name.   HE ASKED MR. MILLER HIS NAME.

1. He asked his address.
2. He asked his telephone number.
3. He asked some questions.
4. He asked a favor.

5. He asked, "What time is it?"
6. He asked the time.
7. He asked the name of the grammar book.
8. He asked the price of the grammar book.

A.3 Notice the use of *to* with the verb *explain.*

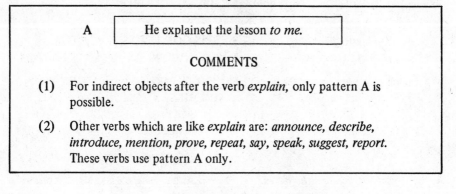

A | He explained the lesson *to me.*

COMMENTS

(1) For indirect objects after the verb *explain,* only pattern A is possible.

(2) Other verbs which are like *explain* are: *announce, describe, introduce, mention, prove, repeat, say, speak, suggest, report.* These verbs use pattern A only.

ILLUSTRATIVE EXAMPLES

1. The teacher announced the examination to the students.
2. We described our class to him.
3. He introduced his father to us.
4. He mentioned the money to Mr. Miller.
5. He didn't prove anything to us.
6. We repeated our names to him.
7. He always says "Hello" to me.
8. He is speaking English to me.
9. He didn't suggest anything to us.
10. The students reported their progress to the teacher.

Exercise 4. Practice the use of verbs like *explain* and also the verb *ask.* Repeat the statements, and add *us* or *to us* in the proper position.

He often speaks.   HE OFTEN SPEAKS TO US.
He explained the lesson.   HE EXPLAINED THE LESSON TO US.
He repeated it.   HE REPEATED IT TO US.
He usually says "yes."   HE USUALLY SAYS "YES" TO US.
He asked, "Where are you   HE ASKED US "WHERE ARE YOU
  going?"   GOING?"
They asked some questions.   THEY ASKED US SOME QUESTIONS.

1. Mary introduced it.
2. Mary usually says "Hello."
3. Mary talked.
4. She described her home.
5. She introduced John.
6. John asked the way to Detroit.
7. Mary asked our names.
8. She announced her plans.
9. The director described the English course.
10. Mr. Gomez described South America.
11. He asked our telephone numbers.
12. The people explained their customs.
13. He repeated the words.
14. The teacher asked some questions.

Exercise 5. Practice the use of verbs like *explain* and also the verb *ask*. Listen to the verbs and the statements after them. Include the words in the statements.

The student. Mary asked some questions.	MARY ASKED THE STUDENT SOME QUESTIONS.
The student. John is explaining a problem.	JOHN IS EXPLAINING A PROBLEM TO THE STUDENT.
Him. I'm going to speak English.	I'M GOING TO SPEAK ENGLISH TO HIM.
Mr. Brown. I'm going to repeat the news.	I'M GOING TO REPEAT THE NEWS TO MR. BROWN.
Them. I asked some questions.	I ASKED THEM SOME QUESTIONS.

1. Us. He described South America.
2. Us. She talked.
3. The policeman. I asked the direction to Chicago.
4. The boys. He asked their names.
5. Me. She described her new dress.
6. The teacher. We asked a question.
7. Mary and me. They explained the customs of Argentina.
8. John and Paul. He asked some questions.
9. Mary. He always says "Hello."
10. The secretary. He repeated the words.
11. Mr. and Mrs. Brown. I'm going to ask a favor.
12. My father. I'm going to introduce you.
13. Our friends. We're going to describe our house.

Exercise 6. Summary exercise for advanced students. Practice the use of three types of verbs: (1) verbs like *give*, (2) *ask*, (3) verbs like *explain*.

He's going to ask me a favor.

the question	HE'S GOING TO ASK ME THE QUESTION.
explain	HE'S GOING TO EXPLAIN THE QUESTION TO ME.
the letter	HE'S GOING TO EXPLAIN THE LETTER TO ME.
read	HE'S GOING TO READ THE LETTER TO ME.
me	HE'S GOING TO READ ME THE LETTER.

1. send	11. some books	21. the answers
2. to me	12. to me	22. explain
3. give	13. to us	23. the questions
4. me	14. they	24. ask
5. the sugar	15. send	25. repeat
6. pass	16. us	26. send
7. to me	17. some letters	27. us
8. sell	18. some news	28. the lesson
9. his car	19. tell	29. explain
10. me	20. a story	30. give

A.4   Notice the use of *for Mary.*

Previous patterns:

	A	B
(1)	Give a book *to Mary.*	Give *Mary* a book.
(2)		Ask *Mary* a question.
(3)	Explain the lesson *to Mary.*	

New patterns:

	A	B
(1)	Buy a book *for Mary.*	Buy *Mary* a book.
(3)	Open the door *for Mary.*	

COMMENTS

(1)   Some verbs pattern with *for* instead of *to.* The preposition *for* is used in front of the indirect object.

(2)   Some of the most important verbs that are used with *for* are the following:

(1)	(3)
buy	open
get	answer
make	close
find	cash
do	change
	pronounce
	prescribe

NOTES:

(1)   Two patterns are possible with verbs such as *buy;* only one pattern is possible with verbs such as *open.* However, in order to simplify the above discussions, the pattern with *for* should be emphasized. The pattern without *for,* e.g. "Buy Mary a book," can be mentioned as an alternative, important for recognition but not for production.

(2)   In the pattern of A.4, *for* usually means "for the benefit of." In addition, *for* sometimes means "in place of" or "instead of" as in "Alice is writing my letters for me because my arm is broken." This use of *for* cannot be expressed without the preposition.

Exercise 7. Answer the questions. Include *for Mary* in your answer.

Who did John open the door for?   HE OPENED IT FOR MARY.
Who did John close the windows for?   HE CLOSED THEM FOR MARY.

      1. Who did the man cash the check for?
      2. Who did the man change the money for?
      3. Who did the teacher pronounce the word for?
      4. Who did John pronounce the words for?
      5. Who did the doctor prescribe the medicine for?
      6. Who is John going to open the door for?
      7. Who is John going to buy the book for?
      8. Who is John going to get the chair for?

Exercise 8. Change the sentences, using *for* or *to*.

Please buy me a book.   PLEASE BUY A BOOK FOR ME.
Please pass John the salt.   PLEASE PASS THE SALT TO JOHN.

1. Please get Mary a chair.   6. Please get John some books.
2. Please lend Mary a pencil.   7. Please buy Mary a cup of coffee.
3. Please make John a sandwich.   8. Please do John a favor.
4. Please find Mr. Miller a chair.   9. Please give the teacher the homework.
5. Please give John a pen.   10. Please teach the class new words.

Exercise 9. Summary exercise. Include the words in the statements. Use personal pronouns for the subjects and indirect objects.

John. The teacher explained the lesson.   SHE EXPLAINED THE LESSON TO HIM.

Mary. The professor is going to ask some questions.   HE'S GOING TO ASK HER SOME QUESTIONS.

The professor. Mary's going to ask some questions.   SHE'S GOING TO ASK HIM SOME QUESTIONS.

The patients. The doctor prescribed medicine.   HE PRESCRIBED MEDICINE FOR THEM.

      1. John. The bank cashed a large check.
      2. John. Mary's going to make a cake.
      3. Me. The doctor prescribed medicine.
      4. Me. Mr. Jones is going to give a book.
      5. Mr. Jones. I'm going to sell a house.

6. John. I'm going to buy a cup of coffee.
7. The director. I asked a favor.
8. The professor. I asked a question.
9. The children. I'm going to tell a story.
10. The new students. The teacher explained the lesson.
11. Mr. Miller. I always say "How are you?"
12. The engineers. I'm going to speak.
13. The engineers. Mr. Wilson described Alaska.
14. My mother. I'm going to write a letter.
15. Me. My mother is going to write a letter.

B.1 Notice the irregular past tense forms (with vowel difference).

Previous pattern:

| SIMPLE PRESENT | We study every day. |
| PAST | We studi*ed* yesterday. |

New pattern:

| SIMPLE PRESENT | We eat every day. |
| PAST | We *ate* yesterday. |

COMMENTS

Most verbs have the regular -ED ending in the past tense. Many verbs, however, have irregular forms. These forms must be learned individually.

ADDITIONAL EXAMPLES

Class: Open your books and read all the following questions and answers in unison. Then close your books and answer the questions as the teacher reads them. (Two answers are possible.)

Did John *eat* an apple or an orange?	He *ate* an apple.
Did John *give* a book or a magazine?	He *gave* a book.
Did John *come* last night or this morning?	He *came* last night.
Did John *become* a doctor or a lawyer?	He *became* a doctor.
Did John *meet* Mary or Alice?	He *met* Mary.
Did John *read* a book or a newspaper?	He *read* a book.
Did John *sit* here or in the library?	He *sat* here.
Did John *begin* lesson eight or lesson nine?	He *began* lesson eight.
Did John *drink* tea or coffee?	He *drank* tea.

Did John *get* a chair or a table?	He *got* a chair.
Did John *forget* a book or a pencil?	He *forgot* a book.
Did John *see* a car or a train?	He *saw* a car.
Did John *tear* his shirt or a piece of paper?	He *tore* his shirt.
Did John *wear* a suit or a sportcoat?	He *wore* a suit.
Did John *speak* to George or Paul?	He *spoke* to George.
Did John *break* a cup or a plate?	He *broke* a cup.
Did John *wake* up at six o'clock or seven?	He *woke* up at six.
Did John *write* a letter or a postcard?	He *wrote* a letter.
Did John *choose* a banana or an orange?	He *chose* a banana.
Did John *take* a pencil or a pen?	He *took* a pencil.
Did John *know* the verbs or the nouns?	He *knew* the verbs.

Exercise 10. Listen to the statements with the adverb *yesterday*. Make corresponding statements about repeated action, using the adverbial *every day*.

They came yesterday.	THEY COME EVERY DAY.
He ate breakfast yesterday.	HE EATS BREAKFAST EVERY DAY.
I met him yesterday.	I MEET HIM EVERY DAY.

1. He gave me a cigarette yesterday.
2. He read it yesterday.
3. It became dark at six o'clock yesterday.
4. I sat here yesterday.
5. I began to write yesterday.
6. I drank eight glasses of water yesterday.
7. I got a letter yesterday.
8. I forgot my book yesterday.
9. I saw your car yesterday.
10. I tore my paper yesterday.
11. I wore my new shoes yesterday.
12. I spoke English yesterday.
13. Mary broke some dishes yesterday.
14. I woke up at six yesterday.
15. We wrote letters yesterday.
16. We chose a leader yesterday.
17. He took his book yesterday.
18. He knew the lesson yesterday.

Exercise 11. Repeat the teacher's statement and add either *every day* or *yesterday*.

They write it.	THEY WRITE IT EVERY DAY.
They wrote it.	THEY WROTE IT YESTERDAY.

1. They see it.
2. They saw it.
3. They drink it.
4. They get it.
5. They took it.
6. They forget it.
7. They drank it.
8. They got it.
9. They see it.
10. They tear it.
11. They tore it.
12. They wear it.
13. They break it.
14. They choose it.
15. They chose it.
16. They broke it.
17. They take it.
18. They wore it.
19. They forgot it.
20. They read it.
    (simple present or past)

Exercise 12. Repeat the negative statement with *didn't,* and add the corresponding affirmative statement, using the adverbial *this morning.* Do not change the tense.

He didn't come yesterday.   HE DIDN'T COME YESTERDAY.
                                   HE CAME THIS MORNING.

He didn't give it to me yesterday. HE DIDN'T GIVE IT TO ME
                                        YESTERDAY.
                                   HE GAVE IT TO ME THIS MORNING.

I didn't eat the pie yesterday.   I DIDN'T EAT THE PIE YESTERDAY.
                                   I ATE IT THIS MORNING.

1. I didn't choose the flowers yesterday.
2. I didn't break any dishes yesterday.
3. I didn't read it yesterday.
4. I didn't tear my shirt yesterday.
5. He didn't become president yesterday.
6. I didn't meet him yesterday.
7. I didn't give him any money yesterday.
8. I didn't sit here yesterday.
9. They didn't speak French yesterday.
10. I didn't begin my work yesterday.
11. We didn't forget our books yesterday.
12. We didn't see his wife yesterday.
13. We didn't drink the coffee yesterday.
14. I didn't get the letter yesterday.
15. I didn't wear my new shoes yesterday.
16. I didn't wake up at six yesterday.
17. I didn't write any letters yesterday.
18. I didn't know any answers yesterday.
19. I didn't choose the correct answer yesterday.

B.2 Notice the irregular past tense form (without vowel difference).

SIMPLE PRESENT	We spend some money every day.
PAST	We *spent* some money yesterday.

ADDITIONAL EXAMPLES

Did John *send* a letter or a postcard?   He *sent* a letter.
Did John *spend* $5 or $10?   He *spent* $5.
Did John *lend* a book or a newspaper?   He *lent* a book.

Did John *make* one sandwich or two?   He *made* one.
Did John *have* coffee or tea?   He *had* coffee.

84

(NO DIFFERENCES):

Did John *cut* paper or cloth?   He *cut* paper.
Did John *put* the book on the table or under it?   He *put* it on the table.
Did the book *cost* $3 or $4?   It *cost* $3.

Exercise 13. Make statements using the adverbial *every day*.

Mary sent a letter yesterday.   SHE SENDS A LETTER EVERY DAY.
Mary spent $5 yesterday.   SHE SPENDS $5 EVERY DAY.

1. Mary cut the cake yesterday.   4. Mary put the book here yesterday.
2. Mary made breakfast yesterday.   5. Mary lent John her book yesterday.
3. Mary had coffee yesterday.   6. Mary spent an hour in the library yesterday.

Exercise 14. Respond with affirmative statements which include the adverbial *on Sunday*.

They didn't send the letter on   THEY SENT THE LETTER ON
    Saturday.   SUNDAY.

She didn't spend the money on   SHE SPENT THE MONEY ON
    Saturday.   SUNDAY.

1. She didn't cut the cake on Saturday.
2. I didn't make breakfast on Saturday.
3. We didn't have coffee on Saturday.
4. We didn't put the papers here on Saturday.
5. I didn't lend him the money on Saturday.
6. The tickets didn't cost $3 on Saturday.
7. They didn't spend time in the park on Saturday.
8. She didn't make sandwiches on Saturday.

Exercise 15. Free response.

What did you send?   I SENT A BOX.
Where did you spend $5? I SPENT IT IN CHICAGO.
When did you lend it?   I LENT IT THIS MORNING.

1. What did you make?   8. How much did you lend?
2. What did you have?   9. When did you make it?
3. What did you cut?   10. When did you have it?
4. Where did you put it?   11. When did you cut it?
5. How much did it cost?   12. When did you put it there?
6. Where did you send it?   13. When did it cost $5?
7. How much did you spend?

B.3 Notice the irregular past tense form (with vowel and consonant differences).

SIMPLE PRESENT	We buy something every day.
PAST	We *bought* a book yesterday.

ILLUSTRATIVE EXAMPLES

Did John *do* his homework last night or this morning?	He *did* it last night.
Did John *feel* happy or sad?	He *felt* happy.
Did John *sleep* until seven o'clock or eight?	He *slept* until seven.
Did John *mean* "ship" or "sheep"?	He *meant* "ship".
Did John *leave* early or late?	He *left* early.
Did John *say* "Hello" or "How are you?"	He *said* "Hello."
Did John *go* to Chicago or New York?	He *went* to Chicago.
Did John *hear* a cat or dog?	He *heard* a cat.
Did John *think* fast or slowly?	He *thought* fast.
Did John *bring* a pencil or a pen?	He *brought* a pencil.
Did John *buy* a book or a magazine?	He *bought* a book.
Did John *teach* grammar or vocabulary?	He *taught* grammar.
Did John *tell* Mary or Alice?	He *told* Mary.
Did John *stand* here or at the door?	He *stood* here.
Did John *understand* everything or only something?	He *understood* everything.

Exercise 16. Make statements using the adverbial *every night*.

John did his homework last night.	HE DOES HIS HOMEWORK EVERY NIGHT.
John felt fine last night.	HE FEELS FINE EVERY NIGHT.

1. John said "Hello" last night.
2. John went to the library last night.
3. John left the library at 10 o'clock last night.
4. John heard a train last night.
5. John thought about his plans last night.
6. John brought his friend last night.
7. Mr. Miller bought some ice cream last night.

8. Mr. Miller taught the new vocabulary last night.
9. Mr. Miller told us the answers last night.
10. Mr. Miller sold John a cup of coffee last night.
11. Mr. Miller stood here last night.
12. Mr. Miller understood the explanation last night.
13. Mr. Miller slept well last night.

Exercise 17. Listen to the negative statements. Form corresponding affirmative statements using *yesterday.*

They didn't do the exercises today.	THEY DID THEM YESTERDAY.
I didn't feel well today.	I FELT WELL YESTERDAY.
He didn't mean that today.	HE MEANT THAT YESTERDAY.

1. They didn't leave school at noon today.
2. They didn't say "Thank you" today.
3. He didn't go to class today.
4. We didn't hear the speeches today.
5. I didn't think about it today.
6. We didn't bring our books today.
7. We didn't buy the books today.
8. Mr. Brown didn't teach mathematics today.
9. He didn't tell me the answers today.
10. I didn't sell him those books today.
11. I didn't stand there today.
12. The students didn't understand today.
13. I didn't sleep today.

Exercise 18. Repeat the teacher's statement and add either *every day* or *yesterday.*

They do it.	THEY DO IT EVERY DAY.
They did it.	THEY DID IT YESTERDAY.

1. They say it.	8. They bought it.	15. They sent it.
2. They said it.	9. They teach it.	16. They lend it.
3. They hear it.	10. They taught it.	17. The spent it.
4. They heard it.	11. They tell it.	18. They make it.
5. They bring it.	12. They told it.	19. They lent it.
6. They brought it.	13. They sold it.	20. They made it.
7. They thought it.	14. They send it.	

Exercise 19. Review exercise.

Did he give Alice any stamps?	YES, HE GAVE HER SOME, BUT HE DIDN'T GIVE ME ANY.
Did he send Alice any postcards?	YES, HE SENT HER SOME, BUT HE DIDN'T SEND ME ANY.

87

1. Did he lend Alice any money?   6. Did he bring Alice any food?
2. Did he tell Alice any stories?   7. Did he buy Alice any ice cream?
3. Did he teach Alice any new words?   8. Did he sell Alice any tickets?
4. Did he give Alice any books?   9. Did he cut Alice any cake?
5. Did he write Alice any letters?   10. Did he make Alice any sandwiches?

Exercise 20. Summary exercise.

I wanted breakfast yesterday.

ate	I ATE BREAKFAST YESTERDAY.
every day	I EAT BREAKFAST EVERY DAY.
make	I MAKE BREAKFAST EVERY DAY.
coffee	I MAKE COFFEE EVERY DAY.
we	WE MAKE COFFEE EVERY DAY.

1. yesterday	8. yesterday	15. he
2. had	9. bought	16. every year
3. every day	10. a car	17. chooses
4. drink	11. every year	18. several days ago
5. yesterday	12. I	19. saw
6. every morning	13. sell	20. every 5 minutes
7. bring	14. a year ago	

For more complete practice continue the exercise with these substitutions: a letter, writes, two weeks ago, got, every week, reads, a book, yesterday, the book, forgot, every morning, I, the answer, yesterday, knew, now, a week ago, heard, the speech, every month, yesterday, understood, now, all speeches, every speech, a year ago, English, spoke, every day, teach, a year ago, wrote, a letter, began, every day, send, yesterday, some paper, lent, every day, cut, yesterday, tore, this shirt, every week, wear, a week ago, took, my friend, every day, meet, a year ago, left, New York, they, every day, see, a lot of money, give, a year ago, spent, every year, lend, cost, it, a year ago, meant, every year, a lot of food, needs, he, eats, yesterday, we, some food, I, had, a pain, felt, every day, have, a problem, study, do, yesterday, had, a typewriter, broke, every month, yesterday, saw, a desk, a doctor, told, a lawyer, every year, a year ago, became, they, were, he.

(Continue the exercise with this sentence, "We come here every day.")

1. yesterday	6. slept	11. stood
2. sat	7. every night	12. every day
3. every morning	8. there	13. I
4. wake up	9. go	14. put it
5. a week ago	10. yesterday	15. a week ago

Lesson 9

A. Adverbs of manner: *correctly, well,* etc.

B. Noun phrase + modifier: *the chair near the door*

C. *Wh*-questions: Who does Mary see? Who sees Mary?

A.1 Notice the use of adverbs of manner and adjectives.

ADVERB

John answered *correctly.*

ADJECTIVE

The answer was *correct.*
It   was a *correct* answer.

ADJECTIVES	ADVERBS
correct	correctly
quiet	quietly
bad	badly
clear	clearly
quick	quickly
sad	sadly
silent	silently
wise	wisely
sincere	sincerely
careful	carefully
beautiful	beautifully
easy	easily
slow	slowly (slow)
good	well
fast	fast
hard	hard
loud	loud (loudly)

COMMENTS: In general, adverbs of manner have an *-ly* ending. Some
common exceptions are: *good, fast, hard, loud.*

Exercise 1.

> He works quietly.   HE IS A QUIET WORKER.
> He speaks clearly.   HE IS A CLEAR SPEAKER.

1. He talks slowly.
2. He works carefully.
3. He writes well.
4. He talks loud.
5. He swims fast.
6. He works hard.
7. He teaches well.
8. He runs fast.
9. He advises well.
10. He drives carefully.
11. He speaks clearly.
12. He reads fast.
13. He sings well.
14. He speaks sincerely.

Exercise 2. Listen to the statement with an adjective (*careful, quiet,* etc.). Form two corresponding statements, one with an adverb (*carefully, quietly,* etc.) and one with an adjective after a form of the verb *BE.*

> The careful student   THE STUDENT IS STUDYING CAREFULLY.
>   is studying.   HE IS CAREFUL.
>
> The quiet doctor   THE DOCTOR WORKED QUIETLY.
>   worked.   HE WAS QUIET.
>
> The sincere doctor is   THE DOCTOR IS SPEAKING
>   speaking.   SINCERELY. HE IS SINCERE.

1. The quiet student studies.
2. The careful doctor is working.
3. The prompt girl is coming.
4. The punctual student arrived.
5. The careful teacher is writing.
6. The sincere man spoke.
7. The slow teacher is talking.
8. The quiet boy is reciting.
9. The careful girl is answering questions.
10. The prompt student wrote a letter.
11. The intelligent student answered the questions.

NOTE: In addition to the adverb *well*, there is also an adjective *well* which refers to state of health. For example:

> My friend was sick, but now he is well.

A.2 Notice the position of adverbs of manner.

	VERB	DIRECT OBJECT	ADV. OF MANNER	ADV. OF PLACE	ADV. OF TIME
He	spoke	English	rapidly	in class	yesterday.
He	drives	his car	carefully	in the city	at night.
He	drives		carefully	everywhere.	

COMMENT: An adverb of manner usually follows a verb and its direct object, if any.

NOTES:

(1) The order of adverbials suggested in the frame is a very common pattern, but it is not the only one. Adverbials of place often precede adverbials of manner.

(2) Adverbials of place and time are treated in Lesson 3.

Exercise 3. Substitute the words in the proper position.

John spoke English rapidly last year.

correctly   JOHN SPOKE ENGLISH CORRECTLY LAST YEAR.

pronounced   JOHN PRONOUNCED ENGLISH CORRECTLY LAST
                YEAR.

these words   JOHN PRONOUNCED THESE WORDS CORRECTLY
                LAST YEAR.

yesterday   JOHN PRONOUNCED THESE WORDS CORRECTLY
                YESTERDAY.

he   HE PRONOUNCED THESE WORDS CORRECTLY
                YESTERDAY.

1. rapidly	11. I	21. explained (to me)
2. a week ago	12. you	22. the answer
3. this morning	13. the story	23. repeated
4. correctly	14. yesterday	24. told me
5. this word	15. the lesson	25. gave
6. the sentence	16. the lesson to me	26. the book
7. read	17. me the lesson	27. quickly
8. an hour ago	18. the words	28. this morning
9. rapidly	19. the question	29. at 8 o'clock
10. Mr. White	20. asked	30. promptly

NOTE: Adverbials of degree occupy the same position as adverbials of manner, i.e., after the verb and its object. For example:

> She doesn't like milk *very much.*
> She likes coffee *a lot.*

Compare the following two sentences, containing expressions of quantity (Lesson 6), which are *very different* in meaning from the sentences above.

> She doesn't like *very much* milk.
> She likes *a lot* of coffee.

B. Notice the use of prepositional phrases as modifiers.

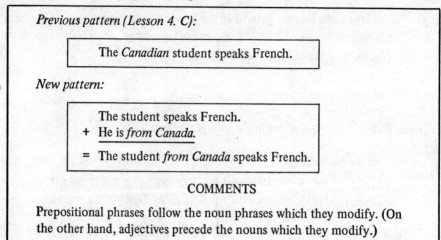

Previous pattern (Lesson 4. C):

> The *Canadian* student speaks French.

New pattern:

> The student speaks French.
> + He is *from Canada.*
> = The student *from Canada* speaks French.

COMMENTS

Prepositional phrases follow the noun phrases which they modify. (On the other hand, adjectives precede the nouns which they modify.)

NOTES: In the new pattern, the meaning of two underlying sentences is incorporated in a new sentence.

ADDITIONAL EXAMPLES

The shoestore *on State Street* is very good.
The chair *near the door* is old.
The student *at the door* is new.
The desk *in this room* is small.
The student *with Mary* is nice.

Exercise 4. Combine two statements to form one.

The girl is studying.   THE TALL GIRL IS STUDYING.
She is tall.

The girl is studying here.   THE GIRL FROM SAN FRANCISCO IS
She is from San   STUDYING HERE.
Francisco.

1. The shoestore is very good. It's large.
2. The shoestore is very good. It's on State Street.
3. The man is intelligent. He's from Brazil.
4. That man is Mr. Allen. He's beside Mr. Miller.
5. The doctor is learning English. He's with Mr. Miller.
6. The bookstore is good. It's large.
7. The large bookstore is good. It's on the corner.

8. The girl is friendly. She's tall.
9. The tall girl is friendly. She's from New York.
10. The boy speaks slowly. He's short.
11. The short boy speaks slowly. He's from Chicago.
12. The student knows the answers. He's thin.
13. The thin student knows the answers. He's in my class.
14. The store is interesting. It's big.
15. The big store is interesting. It's near the bank.
16. The story is interesting. It's short.
17. The short story is interesting. It's about baseball.
18. The doctor gave me a book. He's in my class.

NOTE: The preposition *with* can be used to express the idea of possession.

> The man is a teacher.
>
> + He has a book.
>
> = The man *with* a book is a teacher.

Exercise 5.

The man is a lawyer.   THE MAN WITH A BRIEFCASE IS
   He has a briefcase.   A LAWYER.

That boy is John. He   THAT BOY WITH A NEWSPAPER
   has a newspaper.   IS JOHN.

1. The man is nice. He has a dog.
2. The student is from Argentina. He has a tie.
3. That house is interesting. It has big windows.
4. That sentence is interesting. It has adverbs.
5. That man is a doctor. He has blond hair.
6. That tree is an apple tree. It has one funny little green apple.
7. That man is a clown. He has a banana in his ear.

NOTE FOR ADVANCED STUDENTS: Adverbs, like prepositional phrases, come after the noun they modify.

> The shoestore is very large. It is *downtown*.
> The shoestore *downtown* is very large.

Compare the position of an adjective:

> The shoestore is very large. It is *new*.
> The *new* shoestore is very large.

Examples:

> The table upstairs is long.
> People everywhere want peace.
> The teachers here are American.
> The lecture yesterday was good.

C. Compare the two *wh*-question patterns.

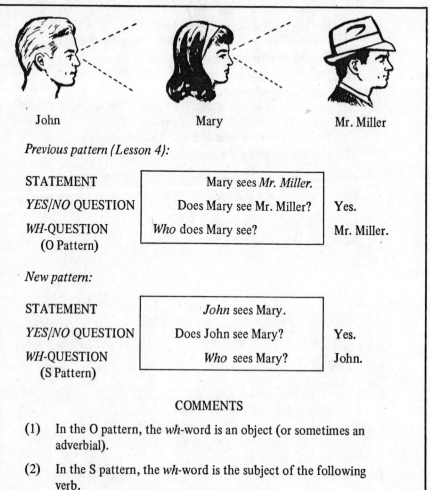

John   Mary   Mr. Miller

Previous pattern (Lesson 4):

STATEMENT	Mary sees *Mr. Miller.*	
YES/NO QUESTION	Does Mary see Mr. Miller?	Yes.
WH-QUESTION (O Pattern)	*Who* does Mary see?	Mr. Miller.

New pattern:

STATEMENT	*John* sees Mary.	
YES/NO QUESTION	Does John see Mary?	Yes.
WH-QUESTION (S Pattern)	*Who* sees Mary?	John.

COMMENTS

(1) In the O pattern, the *wh*-word is an object (or sometimes an adverbial).

(2) In the S pattern, the *wh*-word is the subject of the following verb.

NOTE: The use of *who* in the O pattern is informal standard English. *Whom* is formal English.

ILLUSTRATIVE EXAMPLES

John explained the lesson to Mary yesterday.

A. *Previous pattern*

What did John explain to Mary yesterday?
Who did John explain the lesson to yesterday?
When did John explain the lesson to Mary?
What did John do?

B.   *New pattern*

Who explained the lesson to Mary yesterday?

(Pattern S can also be used to ask for part of the subject, e.g. sentences 1 and 2 below.)

Ten students came yesterday.

1. How many students came yesterday?
2. How many came yesterday?
3. Who came yesterday?

Exercise 6. Listen to the statements. Form questions using *who, what, where,* etc. (Alternative: The teacher may give the answer as the cue. The answers are given in parentheses.)

Situation: John sells cars in Texas.

Who: WHO SELLS CARS IN TEXAS? (John)
What: WHAT DOES JOHN SELL? (Cars)
Where: WHERE DOES JOHN SELL CARS? (In Texas)

Situation: John saw Mary.

Who: WHO SAW MARY? (John)
Who(m):   WHO(M) DID JOHN SEE? (Mary)

Situation A: *John saw Mary in Detroit.*
         1.   who (John)
         2.   who(m) (Mary)
         3.   where (in Detroit)

Situation B: *This car cost $2000 a year ago.*
         4.   what (this car)
         5.   how much ($2000)
         6.   when (a year ago)

Situation C: *John visited the museum yesterday.*
         7.   who (John)
         8.   what (the museum)
         9.   when (yesterday)

Situation D: *A lot of coffee grows in Brazil.*
       10.   what (a lot of coffee)
       11.   how much coffee (a lot)
       12.   where (in Brazil)

Situation E: *Fifteen students visited the museum yesterday.*
    13. how many students (fifteen)
    14. who (fifteen students)
    15. what (the museum)
    16. when (yesterday)

Situation F: *Ten doctors learned English here a year ago.*
    17. how many doctors (ten)
    18. who (ten doctors)
    19. what (English)
    20. where (here)
    21. when (a year ago)

Situation G: *My teacher read the sentences to me this morning.*
    22. who (my teacher)
    23. who(m) (me)
    24. what (the sentences)
    25. when (this morning)

Situation H: *John is here in the morning.*
    26. who (John)
    27. where (here)
    28. when (in the morning)

Situation I: *Mr. Miller was an engineer ten years ago.*
    29. who (Mr. Miller)
    30. what (an engineer)
    31. when (ten years ago)

Situation J: *John bought the red book last week.*
    32. who (John)
    33. what (the red book)
    34. which book (the red one)
    35. when (last week)

Situation K: *Mr. Miller drove two hundred miles yesterday.*
    36. who (Mr. Miller)
    37. how far (two hundred miles)
    38. when (yesterday)

Exercise 7. Make questions based on the following sentence.

Two students gave a pound of food to the three little elephants at the zoo yesterday.

(Since it is long, the above sentence should be written on the blackboard. The exercise may be done the same way as Exercise 6.)

1. who (two students)
2. how many students (two)
3. what (a pound of food)
4. how much food (a pound)
5. which animals (elephants, little elephants, etc.)
6. which elephants (the little elephants, the three little ones, etc.)
7. how many elephants (three)
8. where (at the zoo)
9. when (yesterday)

As an alternative, the teacher may read the sentence and emphasize the part to be interrogated by saying it louder. Another possibility is for the teacher to replace the part to be interrogated with a nonsense word, such as "griffle."

ADDITIONAL SENTENCES

The new teacher read two interesting books in the library last night.
Mr. Miller does a lot of work in the office every day.

Lesson 10

REVIEW OF LESSONS 1-9*

Exercise 1. (To review questions with *be*.) Change the following statements into questions.

He is a good man.	IS HE A GOOD MAN?
It is interesting.	IS IT INTERESTING?
John was a good player.	WAS JOHN A GOOD PLAYER?

1. He was a good man.
2. These tests were hard.
3. The teacher was with the students.
4. Those books were new.
5. She is an interesting girl.
6. They are going to buy some books.
7. Mr. Smith was an important man.
8. John is late.
9. They were doing Lesson 5 today.
10. They are in Detroit now.
11. That man is a professor.
12. Bob is the winner.
13. He is going to Detroit with Paul.
14. The plane is coming this afternoon.

Exercise 2. (To review questions with *do*.) Change the following statements into questions.

John works every day.	DOES JOHN WORK EVERY DAY?
He worked in the factory.	DID HE WORK IN THE FACTORY?
They never walk home with John.	DO THEY EVER WALK HOME WITH JOHN?

1. Mary teaches in school.
2. They work every afternoon.
3. I usually work at night.
4. He often studies at night.
5. He ate here often.
6. John studies in the afternoon.
7. She never takes her book home.
8. He waited until one o'clock.
9. Bob recited this morning.
10. Paul talked to Mary yesterday.
11. They always want coffee.
12. My brother taught in high school.

*NOTE TO THE TEACHER: The exercises in this lesson attempt to review all of the patterns presented in Lessons 1-9. Patterns for which there is no specifically designated exercise are reviewed in exercises on other patterns. For example, there is no designated exercise on irregular verbs, but these forms are practiced in Exercise 11 and other exercises.

The teacher should feel free to practice all of the exercises given here, or to practice only those which review patterns that have proved especially difficult for his class. He may wish to supplement these exercises by repeating exercises from the previous lessons.

Exercise 3. (To review questions with *be* and *do*.) Change the following statements into questions.

He listens carefully.   DOES HE LISTEN CAREFULLY?
He is my uncle.   IS HE YOUR UNCLE?
They had eggs for breakfast.   DID THEY HAVE EGGS FOR
                                       BREAKFAST?

1. They are eating at the cafeteria.
2. They ate chicken for dinner.
3. Mr. Smith is going to fly to Mexico.
4. He sees a movie every week.
5. She is practicing a difficult pattern.
6. Those students are his friends.
7. Bob heard the news about John.
8. The news is good.
9. They are going to visit the museum in Toledo.
10. The students are waiting for their teacher.
11. He answered the questions.
12. Mr. Black is going to sell his car.

Exercise 4. (To review questions introduced by question words.) Change the statements into questions. Use question words which correspond to the final items in the statements.

Mary worked *yesterday*.   WHEN DID MARY WORK?
She saw him *at the movie*.   WHERE DID SHE SEE HIM?
He bought *a hat*.   WHAT DID HE BUY?
They met *John*.   WHO(M) DID THEY MEET?

1. They asked Bob yesterday.
2. They asked John.
3. They bought a car.
4. We drove to Cleveland.
5. We returned from Cleveland yesterday.
6. He saw Mary.
7. They heard the story.
8. They ate steaks.
9. We found it in New York City.
10. He visited Mary last week.
11. The student wanted Mr. Smith.
12. He met the doctor on Main Street.

Exercise 5. (To review questions with *who*.) Change the statement into two questions. Use the question word *who*. In the first question ask for the subject; in the second, ask for the object or receiver.

Mary saw John.   WHO SAW JOHN?
                           WHO(M) DID MARY SEE?

He is talking to John.   WHO IS TALKING TO JOHN?
                           WHO(M) IS HE TALKING TO?

She told John.   WHO TOLD JOHN?
                           WHO(M) DID SHE TELL?

1. Mary knows John.
2. Mr. Smith visited Mary.
3. They saw Mary.
4. John heard the teacher.
5. Paul met Mr. Smith.
6. Mary is visiting John today.
7. John waited for Mary.
8. His sister saw them.
9. The student asked the teacher.
10. We told Paul.
11. Mary understands him.
12. The teacher questioned Jane.

Exercise 6. (To review short answers to questions.) Answer the questions with short answers. Use the forms *Yes, he is; No, he doesn't; Yes, he did;* etc.

Does she like her class?	YES, SHE DOES.
What does she study?	ENGLISH.
Was she in class yesterday?	YES, SHE WAS.

1. Is he busy?
2. Do you like oranges?
3. Does she sing well?
4. Did John answer the question?
5. Does John know the answer?
6. Where do you live?
7. Are you an artist?
8. Is she an engineer?
9. What are they studying?
10. When was John sick?
11. Does Mary speak French?
12. Who sent you that letter?
13. Were the students tired?
14. Is he going to see the game?
15. What are you going to do after class?

Exercise 7. (To review answers with various question types.) Answer the questions with a full answer. Supply an appropriate answer to questions with *who, when,* etc.

Did John eat his dinner?	YES, HE ATE IT.
Was Fred at the program?	YES, HE WAS AT THE PROGRAM.
Who is with John?	MARY IS WITH HIM.
When did he arrive?	HE ARRIVED YESTERDAY.

1. Did they see the play?
2. Do the students know the way?
3. How many people are coming?
4. Does Mary like milk?
5. Who did Mary see?
6. Do you like the book?
7. Did you like the book?
8. Who saw Mary?
9. Are you a student?
10. Were they at the party?
11. Where are they living?
12. When did he come?
13. Was John with you?
14. Were we usually late?
15. Is he her friend?
16. What did he eat?
17. How much did he pay?
18. Does the bank close at three?

100

Exercise 8. (To review the formation of past time statements.) Change the statements in present time into statements in past time.

I usually buy a sandwich.	I USUALLY BOUGHT A SANDWICH.
She is making a dress.	SHE MADE A DRESS.
She is homesick.	SHE WAS HOMESICK.

1. They want a book.
2. John and Paul are friends.
3. She needs a pencil.
4. The watch is on the table.
5. His book costs $5.
6. He sits in the first row.
7. He writes a letter every day.
8. We like the weather.
9. They never eat steak.
10. Those ties are expensive.
11. He has a cold.
12. She always knows the answer.
13. It is on the desk.
14. She studies English at home.
15. He wears a hat in winter.

Exercise 9. (To review the formation of future time statements.) Change the statements in present or past time to statements in future time. Use *be* + *going to* + a verb.

He works every day.	HE IS GOING TO WORK EVERY DAY.
He ate toast for breakfast.	HE IS GOING TO EAT TOAST FOR BREAKFAST TOMORROW MORNING.
He is taking philosophy now.	HE IS GOING TO TAKE PHILOSOPHY NEXT YEAR.

1. Paul has a headache.
2. Mr. Miller is telling a joke.
3. She made a cake for dinner.
4. They are good students.
5. The pencil broke.
6. I am writing a letter.
7. Mary told us an interesting story.
8. We went downtown in a taxi.
9. They asked him a lot of questions.
10. Fred and Bill were in the same class.
11. We eat lunch at twelve.
12. The class had a good time.
13. John woke up at 6 o'clock.
14. I drank a glass of milk for breakfast.
15. The concert began at 8.
16. They walk to school with me.

Exercise 10. (To review the formation of statements with action in progress.) Change the statements from past or future time action to statements with action in progress. Use *be* + the *-ing* form of the verb. Make any other necessary changes.

She walked to school with John.	SHE IS WALKING TO SCHOOL WITH JOHN.
She is going to buy a hat.	SHE IS BUYING A HAT.
I watched a good play.	I AM WATCHING A GOOD PLAY.

1. They have dinner at home.
2. He looked for the books.
3. They went to a concert in the auditorium.

4. We are going to wait for her.
5. The director talked to the students.
6. The store on State Street had a sale.
7. I practiced my pronunciation this morning.
8. It stood by the window.
9. We are going to bring a friend.
10. He thought about home this morning.
11. Paul taught mathematics at the university.
12. I did the first lesson.
13. She felt fine today.
14. He is going to sell his car.

Exercise 11. (To review the formation of statements with repeated or habitual action.) Change the statements in past or future time to statements with repeated or habitual action. Use the simple or the -*s* form of the verb.

He did a lot of exercises every day.	HE DOES A LOT OF EXERCISES EVERY DAY.
He lived in the dormitory.	HE LIVES IN THE DORMITORY.
We are going to like English.	WE LIKE ENGLISH.

1. She ate with her friends.
2. He took a walk yesterday.
3. She usually came to school early.
4. He met me in the cafeteria.
5. He got tired of the class.
6. He took an interest in baseball.
7. Paul drank a glass of milk for breakfast.
8. The student worked for his tuition.
9. The birds went south in the winter.
10. The trees lost their leaves in the fall.
11. Mary read the newspaper in the evening.
12. It cost 50 cents.
13. He spent a lot of money for clothes.

Exercise 12. (To review adverbials of frequency and manner.) Substitute the words in proper position. Use adverbials of frequency (*usually, seldom,* etc.) before the verb. Use adverbials of manner (*quickly, carefully,* etc.) at the end of the statement.

He usually learns the lessons quickly.

rapidly	HE USUALLY LEARNS THE LESSONS RAPIDLY.
never	HE NEVER LEARNS THE LESSONS RAPIDLY.
reads	HE NEVER READS THE LESSONS RAPIDLY.
newspaper	HE NEVER READS THE NEWSPAPER RAPIDLY.

1. always
2. his lesson
3. carefully
4. studies
5. completely
6. seldom
7. does
8. his assignment
9. never
10. immediately
11. rarely
12. his work
13. efficiently
14. often
15. well
16. his grammar
17. sometimes
18. an exercise
19. usually
20. badly

Exercise 13. (To review adverbials of frequency, place and time.) Substitute the adverbials of frequency (*sometimes, never,* etc.) of place (*here, in the garden,* etc.), and of time (*in the evening, for one hour,* etc.) in proper positions.

He usually works at home in the evening.

always   HE ALWAYS WORKS AT HOME IN THE EVENING.
here   HE ALWAYS WORKS HERE IN THE EVENING.

1. in the morning	9. in the evening	17. seldom
2. sometimes	10. at home	18. here
3. never	11. always	19. at the restaurant
4. at night	12. for one hour	20. now
5. in the office	13. in the library	21. here
6. often	14. often	22. often
7. in the factory	15. on State Street	23. in New York City
8. in town	16. at noon	

Exercise 14. (To review the distribution of *a, an* with nouns.) Substitute the words. Omit *a, an* before noncount nouns and plural forms.

John ate an orange.

toast   JOHN ATE TOAST.
had   JOHN HAD TOAST.
piece of toast   JOHN HAD A PIECE OF TOAST.
peaches   JOHN HAD PEACHES.

1. tea	9. water	17. potatoes
2. sandwich	10. drank	18. napkin
3. coffee	11. cold water	19. cream
4. donut	12. glass of cold water	20. likes
5. milk	13. two glasses of water	21. salt
6. chocolate milk	14. used	22. books
7. glass of milk	15. sugar	23. easy assignment
8. fruit	16. teaspoon	24. red ties

Exercise 15. (To review the use and omission of *the*.) Substitute the words. Use the article *the* before nouns when possible. Do not use *a* in this exercise. Omit *the* before names of people, countries, time of day, streets, etc.

They visited the museum.

Canada   THEY VISITED CANADA.
saw   THEY SAW CANADA.
professor THEY SAW THE PROFESSOR.

1. Professor Smith	12. book	22. mathematics
2. art gallery	13. read	23. Mexico
3. Spain	14. philosophy	24. art
4. Mississippi River	15. books	25. president
5. New York City	16. philosophy of Aristotle	26. house
6. old city	17. grammar book	27. arrived at
7. football game	18. English	28. two o'clock
8. Paris	19. instructions	29. Miami
9. subway	20. Shakespeare	30. railroad station
10. Paul	21. discussed	31. noon
11. student		

Exercise 16. (To review the use of *this, that, these, those.*) Listen to the statement with *here* or *there*. Use *this, these* to indicate objects *here.* Use *that, those* to indicate objects *there.*

The water here is fresh.	THIS WATER IS FRESH.
The water there is clear.	THAT WATER IS CLEAR.
The houses there are old.	THOSE HOUSES ARE OLD.
The houses here are new.	THESE HOUSES ARE NEW.

1. The trees there are pine trees.
2. The problem here is difficult.
3. The apples here are ripe.
4. The man there is my cousin.
5. The student here is from Nicaragua.
6. The lady there is a teacher.
7. The light here is bright.
8. The men there are engineers.
9. The books here belong to Mary.
10. The house there is fifty years old.
11. The boys there are my nephews.
12. The flower here is a violet.
13. The automobile here is mine.
14. The movie there is good.
15. The story here is exciting.

Exercise 17. (To review modifiers of nouns.) Modify the noun in the first statement with an adjective or a prepositional phrase from the second statement.

The house is on Winter Street. It is old.	THE OLD HOUSE IS ON WINTER STREET.
The house was old. It was on Winter Street.	THE HOUSE ON WINTER STREET WAS OLD.
The red pencil is new. It is on the desk.	THE RED PENCIL ON THE DESK IS NEW.

1. My pencil is on the desk. It is new.
2. The house is on the hill. It is old.
3. He built a house. It is large.
4. He has a dog. The dog is small.
5. They have an apartment. It is luxurious.

6. We own a home. It is on Main Street.
7. My friend has a car. He is from Panama.
8. I study literature. It is American.
9. We know the students. They are Brazilian.
10. The cafeteria serves good meals. It's on Burns Avenue.
11. She bought a hat. It was expensive.
12. I read a book. It was about politics.
13. He took a test. It was important.
14. He wrote a check. It was bad.
15. She sang a song. It was about love.

Exercise 18. (To review the use of nouns as modifiers.) Combine the statements. Modify the noun in the first statement with a noun from the second statement.

He works in a factory.
   It makes cars.
                       HE WORKS IN A CAR FACTORY.

He is eating grapes. They
   come from Michigan.
                       HE IS EATING MICHIGAN
                       GRAPES.

They are students. They
   take engineering.
                       THEY ARE ENGINEERING
                       STUDENTS.

1. She is a student. She studies biology.
2. He went to a store. It sells shoes.
3. They went to a restaurant. It is on Main Street.
4. I know the book. It deals with physics.
5. We read the book. It discusses birds.
6. John is a student. He goes to the university.
7. They are workers. They work on the railroad.
8. We ate a dinner. We had steak.
9. The students had a test. It was on grammar.
10. We played a game. It was baseball.
11. They like fishing. They fish in the river.
12. The building is on Williams Street. It is a bank.
13. He is a driver. He drives a bus.
14. I bought some food. It was for my dog.
15. It's a boat. It has sails.

Exercise 19. (To review nouns as modifiers.) Change the nouns in the statements to modifiers.

He works on automobiles.   HE IS AN AUTOMOBILE WORKER.
He fights fires.   HE IS A FIRE FIGHTER.
It dries dishes.   IT IS A DISH DRYER.
It cuts glass.   IT IS A GLASS CUTTER.

1. He plays baseball.
2. He plays football.
3. It dries clothes.
4. He washes windows.
5. It washes clothes.
6. It heats water.
7. It makes noise.
8. He publishes textbooks.
9. He advises students.
10. She teaches French.
11. They speak Spanish.
12. He teaches English.
13. It cools water.
14. They cut wood.
15. He paints houses.

Exercise 20. (To review nouns in object position.) Substitute the words in proper position.

John gave me a present.

her	JOHN GAVE HER A PRESENT.
watch	JOHN GAVE HER A WATCH.
bought	JOHN BOUGHT HER A WATCH.
his father	JOHN BOUGHT HIS FATHER A WATCH.

1. a tie
2. me
3. Paul and me
4. them
5. brought
6. book
7. his picture
8. her
9. her picture
10. me
11. him
12. the picture
13. them
14. their picture
15. you
16. me
17. your picture
18. you
19. us
20. our book
21. the book
22. a book
23. him
24. you
25. me
26. her
27. our book
28. their book
29. Mary
30. him
31. Fred

Exercise 21. (To review *any, some, other, another, others, all, much, many, none, a few, a little, a lot*.) Substitute the following words in the request statements. Correlate *any, much, many* with the negative form *don't.*

Buy some apples.

peaches	BUY SOME PEACHES.
a few	BUY A FEW PEACHES.
get	GET A FEW PEACHES.
any	DON'T GET ANY PEACHES.
many	DON'T GET MANY PEACHES.
coffee	DON'T GET MUCH COFFEE.
some	GET SOME COFFEE.

1. a lot of	13. cars	25. bread
2. any	14. the others	26. coffee
3. drink	15. some	27. pencils
4. all of the	16. a few	28. the other ones
5. much	17. a little	29. books
6. use	18. sugar	30. read
7. dishes	19. any	31. all of the
8. buy	20. a lot of	32. the other
9. any	21. much	33. another
10. cars	22. apples	34. others
11. another	23. some	35. study
12. the other	24. a few	36. any others

Exercise 22. (To review the use of *me, to me, for me,* etc.) Listen to the words and the statements. Include the words in the statements.

Me
    She described the music.   SHE DESCRIBED THE MUSIC TO ME.

Them
    He asked some questions.   HE ASKED THEM SOME QUESTIONS.

John
    The teacher pronounced   THE TEACHER PRONOUNCED THE
    the word.   WORD FOR JOHN.

    1. Us.   He described the United Nations.
    2. Her.   He always says a kind thing.
    3. Them.   They waited.
    4. Me.   He told a story.
    5. John.   She made a cake.
    6. Her.   He explained the program.
    7. Him.   I asked for a cigarette.
    8. Mary.   John pronounced the sentence.
    9. Him.   We bought a present.
   10. Me.   John did the work.
   11. Bill.   Mary introduced us.
   12. Them.   He got some pencils.
   13. His mother. He wrote a letter.
   14. The class. He is going to speak about language.

107

Exercise 23. (To practice *how much, what, which,* etc., with question patterns.) Listen to the statements. Notice the words with stress in the statements. Form questions and ask for similar information about *the other car, the other word, the other man,* etc. Another person answers the question.

> This car cost *$2000.*   HOW MUCH DID THE OTHER CAR
>   COST?
>   IT COST $3000.
>
> This word means *rich.*   WHAT DOES THE OTHER WORD MEAN?
>   IT MEANS POOR.
>
> The student was   WHERE WAS THE OTHER STUDENT?
>   *in Detroit.*   HE WAS IN NEW YORK.
>
> This teacher writes   WHICH HAND DOES THE OTHER
>   *with his left hand.*   TEACHER WRITE WITH?
>   HE WRITES WITH HIS RIGHT HAND.

1. These students read *500 pages.*
2. These people left *2 years ago.*
3. That student studies *at night.*
4. One student said *"poor."*
5. This book cost *$5.*
6. These boys went *to Detroit.*
7. These girls went *to the museum.*
8. Some of this coffee comes *from Brazil.*
9. Twenty of the students studied *last night.*
10. That teacher lives *in Boston.*
11. These doctors arrived *yesterday.*
12. This student is studying *English.*
13. These students came *from Mexico.*

Lesson 11

A. Modal auxiliaries: *will, can,* etc.

B. Statement connected with *and . . . too, and . . . either,* and *but.*

A.1 Notice the forms and meanings of the modal auxiliaries.

will ——— future time . . . . . . (be going to)

can —— ability . . . . (be able to)

may —— permission . . . . . . (be permitted to, have permission to)

might —— possibility . . . . . . (It is possible that. . .)

should —— obligation . . . . . . (ought to)
desirability

must —— inference . . . . . . (I conclude that . . . ,
conclusion
probability   It is very probable that . . .)

necessity . . . . . . (have to)

I	*will*	study.	We	*will*	study.
You	*will*	study.	You	*will*	study.
He	*will*	study.	They	*will*	study.

1. We'*ll* read the book tomorrow. (We will.)
2. John *can* play the piano very well.
3. The students *can* smoke in the hall.
4. The students *may* smoke in the hall.
5. John *may* receive a letter today.
6. John *might* receive a letter today.
7. John *should* study every day.
8. Mr. Smith *must* be about forty years old.
9. Mary *must* study tonight. (She *has to.*)

COMMENTS

(1) The modal auxiliaries do not change their form for person or number. That is, there is no -*s* form for the third person singular.

(2) The normal position for the modal in a sentence is after the subject and before the rest of the sentence. (Change of position for questions will be shown later in this lesson.)

109

NOTES:

(1)   In expressing future time, *will* means about the same as *be going to:*

> I'll study the book tomorrow.
> I'm going to study the book tomorrow.

In addition, *will* is sometimes used to indicate consent or (with a negative) refusal:

> Will you help me? — Yes, I will.
> None of my friends will lend me money.

The auxiliary *shall* is used with the subject *I* or *we,* in formal style, to indicate future time. Notice, however, that in questions, the meanings of *shall* and *will* are different. For example:

> Will we go to Boston?
> > (Simple future time, asking for a prediction.)

> Shall we go to Boston?
> > (A request for your opinion or advice about going to Boston.)

(2)   Only one modal is permitted in a single verb phrase. "I presume you are able to run fast" can be expressed as:

> You *must* be able to run fast.
> Or: I presume you *can* run fast.

But it is not English to say "You *must can* run fast."

(3)   The past of *can* is *could:*

> Now she *can* speak three languages.
> Last year she *could* speak only one.

But do not use *could* for a single event in the past. To say "We *succeeded* in visiting the British Museum" you should use "we were able" rather than "we could."

> When we were in London we *were able* to visit the
> British Museum.

Exercise 1. Form sentences using the modals.

Paul is going to write a letter tomorrow.	PAUL WILL WRITE A LETTER TOMORROW.
George is able to speak French very well.	GEORGE CAN SPEAK FRENCH VERY WELL.
The students have permission to smoke in the hall.	THE STUDENTS MAY SMOKE IN THE HALL.

It is possible that George will go to Chicago.

GEORGE MIGHT GO TO CHICAGO.

Mary ought to write to her parents.

MARY SHOULD WRITE TO HER PARENTS.

It is very probable that the girls are studying. (I conclude that the girls are studying.)

THE GIRLS MUST BE STUDYING.

Paul has to take an exam next week.

PAUL MUST TAKE AN EXAM NEXT WEEK.

1. Paul and George are going to play tennis tomorrow.
2. It is possible that George is a very good tennis player.
3. John is able to swim very well.
4. We have to get up at six tomorrow morning.
5. It is possible that George will watch television tonight.
6. It is possible that Mary is home now.
7. Paul is able to read Japanese.
8. You have permission to come in and see the doctor.
9. George is going to study in the library tonight.
10. It is possible that Helen will make an apple pie.
11. My brother is in your class. I conclude that you know him.
12. Mary is able to play the violin.
13. Mr. Moro has to get a new passport soon.
14. It is possible that George is going to study business administration.
15. Mr. Moro has to take another English course.
16. Paul ought to write a letter to his parents every week.
17. It is very probable that you spend a lot of time in the laboratory. (I conclude that you spend a lot of time in the laboratory.)
18. Every student ought to read one good book every week.
19. Last year all of the students were able to read and write.

EXAMPLES OF *MUST* MEANING INFERENCE, CONCLUSION, OR REASONABLE SUPPOSITION.

1. Juan is from Mexico. He *must* speak Spanish.
2. George plays the piano very well. He *must* practice a lot.
3. George knows every one in the class. Therefore, he *must* know Paul.
4. Paul recently finished high school. Therefore, he *must* be about eighteen years old.
5. Helen lived in Japan for ten years. She *must* speak Japanese.

A.2 Notice the negative forms of the modals.

CONTRACTIONS		SHORT ANSWERS
will not	won't	No, he won't.
cannot	can't	No, he can't.
could not	couldn't	No, he couldn't.
may not		No, he may not.
might not		No, he might not.
should not	shouldn't	No, he shouldn't.
must not	mustn't	No, he mustn't.

STATEMENTS

> Mr. Miller *won't* go to Chicago tomorrow.
> Paul *can't* speak French.
> You *may not* drive without a license.
> Paul *might not* go to George's house tonight.
> Children *shouldn't* play with matches.
> Children *mustn't* play with matches.

COMMENTS

May not and *might not* are not usually contracted.

NOTE: *Cannot* is usually written as one word.

Exercise 2. Make negative statements about Mary.

George can go.	MARY CAN'T GO.
George should go.	MARY SHOULDN'T GO.
George may go out today.	MARY MAY NOT GO OUT TODAY.

1. George will go tomorrow.
2. George can play the piano.
3. George might visit us.
4. George will go to Chicago Saturday.
5. George might attend the concert.
6. George will write a letter tomorrow.
7. George can speak French.
8. George should eat fast.
9. George can swim very well.
10. George will watch television tonight.
11. George could read the sign.

A NOTE ON NEGATIVE STATEMENTS CONTAINING *HAVE TO* AND *MUST:*

The following sentences have the same meaning:

   (1) He *has to* go. =   (2) He *must* go.

However, the corresponding negative sentences do *not* have the same meaning:

   (3) He doesn*'t have to go.* ≠   (4) He must*n't go.*

In sentence 3, the entire phrase *have to go* is negated. It means "no necessity to go." But in sentence 4, *must* is affirmative and only *go* has been negated; it means "necessity *not to go.*"

Must not is usually not contracted when *must* has the meaning of inference or reasonable supposition. For example:

She must not be a student here.

Here again the scope of the *not* includes only the verb that follows it: "It *is* reasonable to suppose that she *is not a student.*"

A NOTE ON THE PAST TENSE OF *MUST:*

The past of *have to* is *had to,* which serves also as the past of *must* meaning "necessity". Sentences 5 and 6 have the same meaning. Sentence 7 is the corresponding past.

    (5) He has to wait.   =   (6) He must wait.
    (7) He had to wait.

The past of *must* in the meaning of inference will be presented in Lesson 22.

A.3 Notice the formation of questions with modals.

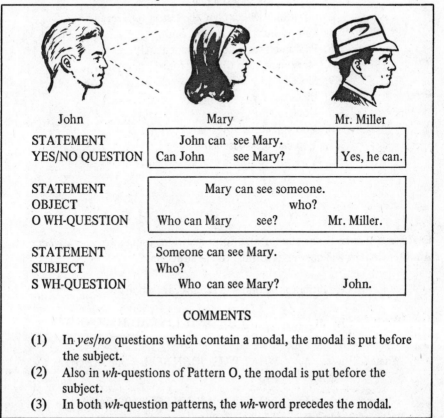

	John	Mary	Mr. Miller
STATEMENT		John can see Mary.	
YES/NO QUESTION	Can John	see Mary?	Yes, he can.
STATEMENT		Mary can see someone.	
OBJECT		who?	
O WH-QUESTION	Who can Mary	see?	Mr. Miller.
STATEMENT		Someone can see Mary.	
SUBJECT		Who?	
S WH-QUESTION		Who can see Mary?	John.

COMMENTS

(1) In *yes/no* questions which contain a modal, the modal is put before the subject.

(2) Also in *wh*-questions of Pattern O, the modal is put before the subject.

(3) In both *wh*-question patterns, the *wh*-word precedes the modal.

NOTE: Pattern O was introduced in Lesson 4.A, and Pattern S in Lesson 9.C. The use of *who* in Pattern O is informal standard English. *Whom* is formal English.

Exercise 3. Change the statements into *yes/no* questions. Another student will give a short answer.

Mary can play the piano.	Student A: CAN MARY PLAY THE PIANO? Student B: YES, SHE CAN. (NO, SHE CAN'T.)
John will study tomorrow.	Student C: WILL JOHN STUDY TOMORROW? Student D: YES, HE WILL. (NO, HE WON'T.)

1. Mary should answer the letter.
2. George can play the piano.
3. Mr. Miller will explain the lesson to George.
4. John should wait for Mr. Smith.
5. Paul must see a doctor immediately.
6. Mary may keep the book for seven days.
7. She should return it next week.
8. Birds can fly.
9. Horses can fly.
10. You will study English tomorrow.
11. You can play baseball.
12. You will go to the movies tonight.

Exercise 4. Listen to the statements. Form questions using *who, what, where,* etc. Another student will answer according to the situation.

Situation: John will sell his car tomorrow.

Who:	Student A:	WHO WILL SELL HIS CAR TOMORROW?
	Student B:	JOHN.
What:	Student A:	WHAT WILL JOHN SELL TOMORROW?
	Student B:	HIS CAR.
When:	Student A:	WHEN WILL JOHN SELL HIS CAR?
	Student B:	TOMORROW.

Situation A.   John will buy some new shoes tomorrow.
        1. who
        2. what
        3. when

Situation B.   That new student might see Mary in the library tonight.
        4. which student
        5. who
        6. whom
        7. where
        8. when

Situation C.   Fifteen students can sit in the classroom.
        9. how many students
       10. who
       11. where

Situation D.   Some of those sentences might be difficult for the new students.
       12. how many of those sentences
       13. what
       14. which students
       15. whom

Situation E.   Those students should do a lot of homework tonight.
       16. which students
       17. who
       18. how much homework
       19. what
       20. when

Situation F.   A lot of beautiful flowers will grow in that new garden.
       21. how many beautiful flowers
       22. what
       23. which garden
       24. where

Situation G.   People shouldn't throw paper on the sidewalk.
       25. who
       26. what
       27. where

B.1 Notice the affirmative statements connected with *and* and *too*.

A.	B.	John can play the piano. Alice can play the piano.
	C.	John can play the piano, and Alice can too.
D.	E.	George studies hard. Helen studies hard.
	F.	George studies hard, and Helen does too.
G.	H.	Paul is a student. Mary is a student.
	I.	Paul is a student, and Mary is too.

COMMENTS

Two simple sentences with identical predicates, such as A and B, can be joined by the word *and* to form one compound sentence, such as C. The predicate is not repeated completely in the second part of the compound sentence. An auxiliary such as *can* or *does* must be included in the second part of the sentence. Simple forms of *be* (*is, are*, etc.) are treated like auxiliaries.

ADDITIONAL EXAMPLES

Helen is going to play tennis, *and* Alice is *too*.
George wrote a letter, *and* Paul did *too*.
We have to take an exam, *and* they do *too*.

Exercise 5. Listen to the two statements. Connect them with *and* and *too*.

John can speak English.
  Mary can speak English.
	JOHN CAN SPEAK ENGLISH, AND
	  MARY CAN TOO.

He has to learn Spanish.
  She has to learn Spanish.
	HE HAS TO LEARN SPANISH, AND
	  SHE DOES TOO.

He is studying it now.
  She is studying it now.
	HE IS STUDYING IT NOW, AND
	  SHE IS TOO.

He studied French last year.
  She studied French last year.
	HE STUDIED FRENCH LAST
	  YEAR, AND SHE DID TOO.

1. He is taking a course in French now. She is taking a course in French now.
2. He is going to study French tonight. She is going to study French tonight.
3. He studies every night. She studies every night.
4. He will have an exam tomorrow. She will have an exam tomorrow.
5. He has to take the exam. She has to take the exam.
6. He should study for it tonight. She should study for it tonight.
7. He might pass the exam. She might pass the exam.

8. He passed the last exam. She passed the last exam.
9. He is a good student. She is a good student.
10. Examinations are necessary. Homework is necessary.
11. John and Mary have to do a lot of homework. We have to do a lot of homework.
12. They had to study last night. We had to study last night.

B.2 Notice the negative statements connected with *and* and *either*.

<table>
<tr><td>A.</td><td>B.
C.</td><td>John *isn't a teacher.*   Mary *isn't a teacher.*
John isn't a teacher, *and* Mary isn't *either.*</td></tr>
<tr><td>D.</td><td>E.
F.</td><td>Paul *can't play the violin.*   Alice *can't play the violin.*
Paul can't play the violin, *and* Alice can't *either.*</td></tr>
<tr><td>G.</td><td>H.
I.</td><td>Helen *doesn't play baseball.*   Alice *doesn't play baseball.*
Helen doesn't play baseball, *and* Alice doesn't *either.*</td></tr>
</table>

COMMENT

And and *either* are used to connect two negative statements when the meanings of their predicates are the same.

ADDITIONAL EXAMPLES

Alice isn't going to eat in the restaurant, *and* Helen isn't *either.*
Paul wasn't hungry, *and* George wasn't *either.*
Mr. Smith didn't forget the address, *and* Miss Ford didn't *either.*
Homework isn't always easy, *and* examinations aren't *either.*

Exercise 6.

George doesn't sing well.
   Paul doesn't sing well.
	GEORGE DOESN'T SING WELL,
	   AND PAUL DOESN'T EITHER.

George didn't play tennis
   yesterday. Paul didn't play
   tennis yesterday.
	GEORGE DIDN'T PLAY TENNIS
	   YESTERDAY, AND PAUL
	   DIDN'T EITHER.

1. George might not be here tomorrow. Paul might not be here tomorrow.
2. George isn't always early. Paul isn't always early.
3. George doesn't drink beer. Paul doesn't drink beer.
4. George wasn't at the movies yesterday. Paul wasn't at the movies yesterday.
5. Alice might not go to the movies tonight. Mary might not go to the movies tonight.
6. Alice isn't going to be late. Mary isn't going to be late.
7. Alice doesn't like cigarette smoke. Mary doesn't like cigarette smoke.
8. Alice wasn't very busy yesterday. Mary wasn't very busy yesterday.

Exercise 7. Practice *and . . . too* and *and . . . either.*

<table>
<tr>
<td>George read a good book
last night. Alice read a
good book last night.</td>
<td>GEORGE READ A GOOD BOOK
LAST NIGHT, AND ALICE DID
TOO.</td>
</tr>
<tr>
<td>George isn't hungry.
Alice isn't hungry.</td>
<td>GEORGE ISN'T HUNGRY AND
ALICE ISN'T EITHER.</td>
</tr>
</table>

1. George can't go to the party tonight. Alice can't go to the party tonight.
2. George isn't studying. Alice isn't studying.
3. He can play the piano. She can play the piano.
4. George isn't tired now. John isn't tired now.
5. Bob and Alice will be here tomorrow. We will be here tomorrow.
6. They don't have to come. We don't have to come.
7. John should write home. Mary should write home.
8. John studies every day. Mary studies every day.
9. We shouldn't arrive late. The teacher shouldn't arrive late.
10. We have to arrive on time. He has to arrive on time.
11. We don't have to arrive early. He doesn't have to arrive early.
12. John arrived late yesterday. His friend arrived late yesterday.
13. John is going to visit Canada. George is going to visit Canada.
14. My shoes were expensive. My suit was expensive.
15. They won't go to the store. I won't go to the store.
16. Mr. Hill plays volleyball very well. Mr. Smith plays volleyball very well.

NOTE: *And so* can be used in place of *and . . . too* as in the following sentences:

    (1) I can go, *and* John can *too.*
    (2) I can go, *and so* can John.

The meanings of sentences 1 and 2 are the same. Similarly, *and neither* can be used in place of *and . . . either.*

    (3) Mary can't go, *and* Helen can't *either.*
    (4) Mary can't go, *and neither* can Helen.

The meanings of sentences 3 and 4 are the same.

Note that after the expressions *and so* and *and neither* the auxiliary must be placed before the subject:

      AUX SUBJECT
  (5) . . . . and so *does Mary.*

B.3 Notice the statements which are connected with *but*.

AFFIRMATIVE   NEGATIVE

> John *is a student.*   Mr. Hill *isn't a student.*
> John is a student, *but* Mr. Hill isn't.

NEGATIVE   AFFIRMATIVE

> Mr. Hill *isn't a student.*   John *is a student.*
> Mr. Hill isn't a student, *but* John is.

COMMENTS

In the above pattern, *but* is used to connect two statements which have the same predicate except that one predicate is affirmative and the other one is negative. In the second predicate of such sentences, only the auxiliary is expressed. Simple forms of *be* are treated like auxiliaries.

NOTE: *But* is also used to connect other contrasting statements.

> John will go to Detroit, but Mary will go to Chicago.
> Helen likes chocolate ice cream, but Alice prefers vanilla.

ADDITIONAL EXAMPLES

1. John is going to go, but Mary isn't.
2. John can play the piano, but Mary can't.
3. John went, but Mary didn't.

4. Mary wasn't here, but John was.
5. Mary can't play the piano, but John can.
6. Mary didn't go, but John did.

Exercise 8. Join the two sentences with *but*. Omit part of the second predicate as shown in the examples.

John is tired. George isn't tired.	JOHN IS TIRED, BUT GEORGE ISN'T.
John won't go. George will go.	JOHN WON'T GO, BUT GEORGE WILL.

1. John lives in the city. George doesn't live in the city.
2. John wasn't happy yesterday. George was happy yesterday.
3. John isn't going to have a cup of coffee. George is going to have a cup of coffee.

4. John bought a new radio. George didn't buy a new radio.
5. John didn't know the answer. George knew the answer.
6. John watched television last night. George didn't watch television last night.
7. John should eat more for breakfast. George shouldn't eat more for breakfast.
8. John doesn't like hot dogs. George likes hot dogs.

(In each of the examples below, both parts have the same subject, but the auxiliary is changed.)

9. Paul doesn't study very much. He should study a lot.
10. Paul watches television every evening. He shouldn't watch television every evening.
11. Paul shouldn't go to the movies tonight. He might go to the movies.

Exercise 9. Summary exercise: *and . . . too, and . . . either, but.*

He can go to the party. His friends can go to the party.	HE CAN GO TO THE PARTY, AND HIS FRIENDS CAN TOO.
He doesn't wear a hat. His friends don't wear a hat.	HE DOESN'T WEAR A HAT, AND HIS FRIENDS DON'T EITHER.
John can't play the piano. Mary can play the piano.	JOHN CAN'T PLAY THE PIANO, BUT MARY CAN.

1 Mary arrived early. Her friends didn't arrive early.
2 John was here yesterday. Paul was here yesterday.
3. They weren't in Chicago. Mary was in Chicago.
4. They should come to class every day. She should come to class every day.
5 They shouldn't miss class. She shouldn't miss class.
6. They have to take an exam. She has to take an exam.
7. Mary can't go to the dance tomorrow night. John can go to the dance tomorrow night.
8. John didn't go to Mexico last summer. Bob went to Mexico last summer.
9 Mr. and Mrs. Thompson will come to the party. Their children will come to the party.
10. Mr. and Mrs. Smith might not come. Their friends might not come.
11. Uruguay isn't a very big country. Brazil is a very big country.
12 Paul and George never go to the movies. John goes to the movies.
13. Mary frequently goes to the movies. John frequently goes to the movies.
14 Bob often sees John. We rarely see John.

Lesson 12

A. Verb + preposition + object: He called *on* them.
   Verb + particle + object: He called them *up*.

B. Adverbials of purpose: He went *to buy some books.*

C. Adverbials of means: He came *by plane.*
   Adverbials of instrument: He wrote *with a pen.*

A. Notice the position of the pronoun *them* in relation to the preposition *on* and the particle *up.*

The teacher called *on* the students. He called *on them.*

The teacher called *up* the students. He called   *them up.*

COMMENTS

(1) With *prepositional* expressions, like *call on,* the pronoun object must follow the preposition.

(2) With *particle* expressions, like *call up,* the pronoun object must be placed *before* the particle.

NOTES:

(1) Common prepositions are: *on, at, to, from, for, of, into.*

(2) Common particles are: *up, down, on, off, in, out, away, back, over.*

(3) Short noun phrases may also precede particles. For example:

The teacher called John up.

ILLUSTRATIVE EXAMPLES

Prepositions

Look at the book.	Look at it.
Talk to Mary.	Talk to her.
Listen to John.	Listen to him.
Look for the pencils.	Look for them.
Ask for the package.	Ask for it.
Wait for Mr. Miller.	Wait for him.
Think of his name.	Think of it.

Particles

Fill out the form.	Fill it out.
Give back the papers.	Give them back.
Hand in the homework.	Hand it in.
Hand out the papers.	Hand them out.
Leave out the number.	Leave it out.
Look over the lesson.	Look it over.
Look up the new words.	Look them up.
Put away the books.	Put them away.
Put on your shoes.	Put them on.
Put out the cigarette.	Put it out.
Put up your hand.	Put it up.
Pick up the paper.	Pick it up.
Take off your glasses.	Take them off.
Talk over the lesson.	Talk it over.
Throw away the paper.	Throw it away.
Turn on the lights.	Turn them on.
Turn off the radio.	Turn it off.
Wake up Mr. Smith.	Wake him up.
Write down the answer.	Write it down.

(Suggestions for four exercises using the above examples:)

a. Fill out the form.	FILL IT OUT.
b. Don't fill out the form.	DON'T FILL IT OUT.
c. Let's fill out the form.	LET'S FILL IT OUT.
d. Let's not fill out the form.	LET'S NOT FILL IT OUT.

NOTE: Some of the verb + particle expressions have common synonyms. For example:

fill out, complete	*look over,* examine
give back, return	*put out,* extinguish
hand in, submit	*talk over,* discuss
hand out, distribute	*throw away,* discard
give out, distribute	*write down,* make a note of
leave out, omit	

Exercise 1. Practice the use of particles.

Did you wake up Mr. Miller?	NO, I'LL WAKE HIM UP IN FIVE MINUTES.
Did you hand in your homework?	NO, I'LL HAND IT IN IN FIVE MINUTES.

1. Did you write down the address?
2. Did you look over the lesson?
3. Did you fill out the form?
4. Did you put away the cream and sugar?
5. Did you turn on the lights?
6. Did you turn off the radio?
7. Did you put on your shoes?
8. Did you look up the new words?
9. Did you throw away the paper?
10. Did you put out the fire?

Exercise 2. Particles.

| Did John turn on the radio? | NO, HE'LL TURN IT ON IN FIVE MINUTES. |

| Did the teacher hand out the papers? | NO, HE'LL HAND THEM OUT IN FIVE MINUTES. |

1. Did Mary turn on the lights?
2. Did Mr. Miller pick up the chalk?
3. Did John look up the new words?
4. Did Mr. Miller put out the fire?
5. Did Mary turn off the television?
6. Did John hand in his homework?
7. Did John wake up Mr. Smith?
8. Did Mr. Miller take off his glasses?
9. Did the teacher look over the words?
10. Did Mr. Allen put away the book?
11. Did Mary write down the answer?
12. Did the students fill out the form?
13. Did John put on his hat?
14. Did the teacher take off his coat?
15. Did Mary put up her hand?
16. Did the teacher hand out the tests?
17. Did the students talk over the lesson?
18. Did he throw away the newspaper?

Exercise 3. Particles.

| Did John turn on the radio? | YES, HE TURNED IT ON FIVE MINUTES AGO. |

| Did the teacher hand out the papers? | YES, HE HANDED THEM OUT FIVE MINUTES AGO. |

(Continue with the items of Exercise 2.)

Exercise 4. Practice the use of both prepositions and particles. Include an adverbial of time in the response.

Did George call up Mr. Miller?	YES, HE CALLED HIM UP YESTERDAY.
Did George look at the new book?	YES, HE LOOKED AT IT LAST NIGHT.
Did George think of the answer?	YES, HE THOUGHT OF IT A MINUTE AGO.

1. Did George look for the umbrella?
2. Did George pick up the pencil?
3. Did George hand in his homework?
4. Did George ask for his picture?
5. Did George turn on the lights?
6. Did George look up the new words?
7. Did George look at the new lesson?
8. Did George write down the answer?
9. Did George put away the paper and pencils?
10. Did George talk to the new students?
11. Did George talk about the grammar lesson?
12. Did George fill out the form?
13. Did George hand in his homework?
14. Did George put on his new tie?
15. Did George put up his hand?
16. Did George wake up John?
17. Did George talk to Mary?
18. Did George take off his shoes?
19. Did George turn off the television?
20. Did George put out his cigarette?
21. Did George throw away his old hat?
22. Did George talk to Mr. Miller?

EXAMPLES OF TWO OTHER CONSTRUCTIONS

VERB + PARTICLE

Hurry up.	*Stand up.*
Sit down.	*Get up* at six o'clock.

VERB + PARTICLE followed by PREPOSITION + NOUN PHRASE

Look out for cars.
John won't *run out of paper.*
John *gets along with Paul.*

B. Notice the adverbials of purpose.

Why did John go to the store?

(in order) to + VERB EXPRESSION

John went to the store *(in order) to buy some books.*

for + NOUN PHRASE

John went to the store *for some books.*

COMMENTS

(1)   Adverbials of purpose answer the question "Why."

(2)   *In order to* is usually shortened to *to.*

(3)   Use *(in order) to* with verb expressions; use *for* with noun phrases.

NOTES:

(1)   *What ... for* means "why."

What did John go to the store for?

(2)   Questions with *why* can also be answered with *because* and *so (that).*

Why did John come here?
Because he wanted to learn English. (Lesson 23)
So that he could learn English.

Exercise 5. Practice the use of *to* with verbs and *for* with nouns.

He came to get the books.

for	HE CAME FOR THE BOOKS.
the concert	HE CAME FOR THE CONCERT.
hear the concert	HE CAME TO HEAR THE CONCERT.
study English	HE CAME TO STUDY ENGLISH.

1. cash the check
2. meet me
3. get some coffee
4. for
5. his coat
6. all of his books
7. get all of his books
8. tell me the news
9. buy some matches
10. buy matches
11. matches
12. lunch
13. eat lunch
14. find a chair
15. for
16. watch a television program
17. pick up his radio
18. for
19. an exam
20. take a test

125

Exercise 6. Listen to the statement. The first student will change it to a question with *why*. The second student will give a short answer.

John went to the store for some milk.

Student A: WHY DID JOHN GO TO THE STORE?
Student B: FOR SOME MILK.

1. John came here in order to learn English.
2. Mary went to the store in order to buy some pencils.
3. John went to the bank in order to cash a check.
4. John went to the art museum in order to see the new paintings.
5. John went to the store for a new pair of shoes.
6. John studied in order to pass the test.
7. John wrote to his friend in order to tell him about the English course.
8. Mrs. Miller went to the store for a comb.
9. Mary got up at six o'clock in order to study.
10. Mary went to the restaurant for a cup of coffee.

C.1 Notice the adverbial expressions.

Previous pattern (Lesson 9.A):

> *How* does John speak?
> He speaks *clearly.*
>
> *How* does he write?
> He writes *well.*

New patterns:

A.
> How did John come?
> He came *by plane.*
>
> How did he send the letter?
> He sent it *by airmail.*

B.
> John wrote   *with a new pen.*
> Mary answered   *with a gesture.*

COMMENTS

(1) Pattern A: Adverbials answering the question *how?* can be formed with the preposition *by* and a noun: *by airmail, by plane.* These *by* + NOUN constructions are especially common with nouns referring to communication and transportation.

(2) Pattern B: *With* + NOUN PHRASE constructions refer to an instrument or means: *with a new pen, with a gesture.*

NOTE: In expressions of Pattern A (*by plane*, etc.), the noun has no article with it, which for count nouns is contrary to the usual rules.

ILLUSTRATIVE EXAMPLES

Similar to Pattern A:

They sent the news *by radio.*   She came to class *by taxi.*
We communicated *by telephone.*   He's going to Europe *by ship.*
They travel *by land* or *by sea.*

Similar to Pattern B:

He opened the door *with a key.*
Mary took some pictures *with her new camera.*
Mrs. Miller answered *with a smile.*
Mr. Miller answered *with a nod.*

Exercise 7. Answer the questions using the suggested words. Use *by* + NOUN or *with* + NOUN PHRASE in your answer.

How did John come?   train   HE CAME BY TRAIN.

How did he close the door?   his foot HE CLOSED IT WITH HIS FOOT.

1. How did he send the package?   airmail
2. How did he go downtown?   bus
3. How did he open the box?   his hands
4. How did he go to New York?   plane
5. How did Mrs. Miller answer?   nod
6. How did John go to Chicago?   car
7. How did Mrs. Miller open the can?   can opener
8. How did Mary eat the cake?   fork

(Review the adverbs of manner from Lesson 9.A: *clearly, carefully, well,* etc.)

9. How did John speak?   clear
10. How did John work?   careful
11. How does John swim?   fast
12. How does John sing?   well
13. How does John talk?   slow
14. How does John work?   hard
15. How does John speak?   soft
16. How does John read?   rapid

127

C.2 Notice the adverbial expressions.

by + -ing VERB EXPRESSION

John passed the test	*by studying hard.*
John learned English	*by practicing a lot.*

COMMENT

The verb which follows the preposition *by* must have the *-ing* ending.

NOTE: The above comment applies to the other prepositions also: *in, of, from,* etc. In general, any verb which follows a preposition must have the *-ing* ending. (This comment does not apply to infinitive expressions, such as *to find a chair.*)

Exercise 8. Give full answers to the questions. Use the suggested verb phrase.

How did John learn English?
    practice constantly
	HE LEARNED ENGLISH
	    BY PRACTICING
	    CONSTANTLY.

How did John find Mr. Miller's address?
    look in the telephone book
	HE FOUND MR. MILLER'S
	    ADDRESS BY LOOKING
	    IN THE TELEPHONE
	    BOOK.

1. How did John earn money?   sell radios
2. How did Mr. Miller learn English?   watch movies
3. How did John learn pronunciation?   imitate the teacher
4. How did John improve his English?   practice every day
5. How did John answer the question?   shake his head
6. How did John find the post office?   ask a policeman
7. How did John entertain the class?   play a guitar
8. How did John entertain the class?   play a guitar and sing folk songs

Exercise 9. Summary exercise. Change the statement to a question with *how* or *why*. A second student will give a short answer.

John went to Chicago by train.
    Student A: HOW DID JOHN GO TO CHICAGO?
    Student B: BY TRAIN.

John found the museum by asking a policeman.
    Student B: HOW DID JOHN FIND THE MUSEUM?
    Student C: BY ASKING A POLICEMAN.

John went downtown for some books.
    Student C: WHY DID JOHN GO DOWNTOWN?
    Student D: FOR SOME BOOKS.

John called up Mary in order to ask her a question.
> Student D: WHY DID JOHN CALL UP MARY?
> Student E: IN ORDER TO ASK HER A QUESTION.

1. John went to the post office for some stamps.
2. John answered the question by shaking his head.
3. John went to Detroit in order to see a movie.
4. John got here early by running fast.
5. John put his glasses on in order to see the blackboard.
6. John talked to his mother by phone.
7. Mr. Miller has to go to the bank in order to cash a check.
8. We can improve our pronunciation by imitating native speakers.
9. We learn the meaning of new words by looking them up in a dictionary.
10. We have to study hard in order to pass our exams.

NOTE: The negative of *in order to* + VERB EXPRESSION has *not* before the word *to.*

> He came in order *not* to miss the concert.

The negative of *by* + *-ing* VERB EXPRESSION has *not* before VERB + *-ing.*

> He pleased them by *not* coming late.

Lesson 13

A. Verb + *to* + verb:
      George *wants* to *go.*

   Verb + noun phrase + *to* + verb:
      George *wants* John to *go.*
      George *told* John to *go.*

B. *Be* + adjective + *to* + verb:
      This is *easy* to *learn.*

C. *Very, too, enough.*

A.1 Notice the use of *to* before the verb *to go.*

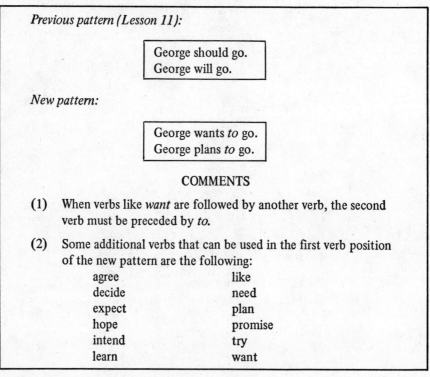

Previous pattern (Lesson 11):

> George should go.
> George will go.

New pattern:

> George wants *to* go.
> George plans *to* go.

COMMENTS

(1) When verbs like *want* are followed by another verb, the second verb must be preceded by *to.*

(2) Some additional verbs that can be used in the first verb position of the new pattern are the following:

agree	like
decide	need
expect	plan
hope	promise
intend	try
learn	want

Exercise 1. Practice the *want to* pattern.

He learned to speak English.

tried	HE TRIED TO SPEAK ENGLISH.
read the lesson	HE TRIED TO READ THE LESSON.
needs	HE NEEDS TO READ THE LESSON.

1. they	11. wants
2. all of the students	12. speak clearly
3. study grammar	13. is learning
4. John	14. must try
5. hopes	15. can learn
6. write the words	16. is going to learn
7. promises	17. needs
8. likes	18. needed
9. write letters	19. is going to try
10. plans	20. will try

Exercise 2. Practice the *want to* pattern and the modal pattern (Lesson 11). Listen to the question and the following verb or modal auxiliary. Form an answer using the suggested word and the adverb *tomorrow*.

Did John *decide to see* his lawyer today? plans	NO, BUT HE *PLANS TO SEE* HIS LAWYER TOMORROW.
Does John *need to study* the lesson today? must	NO, BUT HE *MUST STUDY* THE LESSON TOMORROW.
Will John *write* a letter today? hopes	NO, BUT HE *HOPES TO WRITE* A LETTER TOMORROW.

1. Does John hope to go to Chicago today? might
2. Does John want to watch television today? plans
3. Does John plan to visit the museum today? hopes
4. Does John have to study grammar today? must
5. Will John go to San Francisco today? plans
6. Did John decide to go to the bank today? might
7. Does Mr. Miller need to go to the bank today? should
8. Does Mr. Miller plan to read an English newspaper today? wants
9. Did Mr. Miller promise to wash his car today? might
10. Does John plan to read some interesting books today? wants
11. Did John decide to fix his bicycle today? will
12. Can Mr. Miller attend the concert today? will
13. Will John play the piano today? plans
14. Did John agree to help Mr. Miller today? might
15. Does John plan to hand in his homework today? must

Exercise 3. Practice the use of questions and short answers.

You want to study business administration.   Student A: DO YOU WANT TO
STUDY BUSINESS
ADMINISTRATION?
Student B: YES, I DO. (NO, I
DON'T.)

You can play the piano.   Student A: CAN YOU PLAY THE
PIANO?
Student B: YES, I CAN. (NO, I
CAN'T.)

1. You plan to learn Russian.
2. You like to get up at 6 o'clock.
3. You will buy a new pencil.
4. You want to go to the bank now.
5. You can speak three languages.
6. You plan to eat dinner soon.
7. You can play the guitar.
8. You like to learn languages.
9. You want to learn a lot of English.
10. You plan to study engineering.
11. You like to travel by plane.
12. You will study tonight.
13. You need to study every night.

A.2   Notice the omission of the verb expression after *to*.

Previous pattern (Lesson 11):

> John doesn't study medicine.   He should study medicine.
> *John doesn't study medicine, but he should.* _____

New pattern:

> John doesn't study medicine.   He wants to study medicine.
> *John doesn't study medicine, but he wants to.* _____

COMMENTS

(1)   In each of the above patterns, two statements are conjoined with
but.

(2)   In the example of the new pattern, the verb expression *study
medicine* is omitted, but the *to* is retained.

ADDITIONAL EXAMPLES

John didn't go, but he plans to.
Mary plans to go, but she doesn't want to.
John should study tomorrow, but he isn't planning to.

Exercise 4. Practice the two patterns.

He didn't go, but he plans to.

wants	HE DIDN'T GO, BUT HE WANTS TO.
wanted	HE DIDN'T GO, BUT HE WANTED TO.
can	HE DIDN'T GO, BUT HE CAN.
is planning	HE DIDN'T GO, BUT HE'S PLANNING TO.

1. plans
2. intends
3. hopes
4. might
5. expects
6. expected
7. is expecting

8. should
9. will
10. is intending
11. hoped
12. would like
13. will try
14. needs
15. has

16. is hoping
17. must
18. might decide
19. is going to try
20. wanted
21. can
22. wants

Exercise 5. Practice short answers beginning with *no*.
(Individually.)

Did you go to Niagara Falls?   NO, BUT I MIGHT.
                                          (NO, BUT I WILL.)
                                          (NO, BUT I WANT TO.)
                                          (NO, BUT I HOPE TO.)
                                          (NO, BUT I PLAN TO.)

1. Did you go to Chicago?
2. Do you study every day?
3. Did you meet the president?
4. Do you get up at seven o'clock?

5. Did you get a letter?
6. Do you want to study tonight?
7. Did you go to San Francisco?
8. Do you study a lot every day?

A.3   Compare the negated portions of the negative sentences.

Affirmative sentence:

George	promised	to go.

Negative sentences:

A	John	*didn't promise*	*to go.*
B	Mary	promised *not*	*to go.*

COMMENTS

(1)   In sentence A, the entire predicate is negative.

(2)   In sentence B, only that part of the predicate after the word *not* is negative. Notice that *not* precedes *to*.

Exercise 6. Pattern A.

John wants to write.	*MARY* DOESN'T WANT TO WRITE.
John tried to write.	*MARY* DIDN'T TRY TO WRITE.
John should try to write.	*MARY* SHOULDN'T TRY TO WRITE.

1. John needs to write.
2. John plans to write.
3. John planned to write.
4. John is trying to write.
5. John should write.
6. John wanted to write.
7. John can write.
8. John decided to go.
9. John should go.
10. John is going to promise to go.

Exercise 7. Pattern B.

John promised to go.	*MARY* PROMISED NOT TO GO.
John prefers to go.	*MARY* PREFERS NOT TO GO.

1. John promised to talk.
2. John tried to speak loudly.
3. John is planning to go.
4. John tried to laugh.
5. John must promise to do it again.
6. John prefers to answer.
7. John is planning to go.
8. John expected to go.
9. John hopes to take a vacation.
10. John should try to take a nap every afternoon.
11. John tried to be early.
12. John hopes to work hard.
13. John is trying to sleep.
14. John decided to study.
15. John promised to sing.

A.4   Notice the noun phrase before the word *to*.

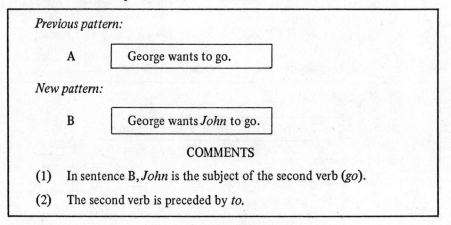

Previous pattern:

A   George wants to go.

New pattern:

B   George wants *John* to go.

COMMENTS

(1)   In sentence B, *John* is the subject of the second verb (*go*).

(2)   The second verb is preceded by *to*.

ADDITIONAL EXAMPLES

George *would like* John to go.
George *expects* John to go.
The teacher *wants* the students to learn English.
He *would like* them to practice every day.
He *expects* them to learn quickly.

Exercise 8. Practice "want somebody to do something."

| John, please open the windows. | WE WANT JOHN TO OPEN THE WINDOWS. |
| Mary, please go to the blackboard. | WE WANT MARY TO GO TO THE BLACKBOARD. |

1. John, please tell a story.
2. Mary, please sing a song.
3. Mr. Miller, please lend us a dictionary.
4. Mary, please call the airport.
5. John, please look for the pencils.
6. George, please wait for Mr. Miller.
7. John, please put the books away.
8. Mr. Smith, please turn on the lights.
9. Mary, please look over the lesson.
10. John, please wake up Mr. Miller.
11. John, please put on your gloves.
12. George, please hurry up.
13. Tom, please sit down.
14. John, please get up at seven o'clock.
15. John, please put on a coat.

NOTE: There are some additional verbs which can be followed by a noun phrase + *to* + verb.

tell	permit
advise	help
order	force
urge	get
invite	persuade

Examples:

Mr. Miller	told	John	to bring sandwiches.
The weather man	advised	us	to wear gloves.
The nurse	persuaded	the child	to eat.
Mrs. Johnson	permits	the students	to use her kitchen.
The bad weather	forced	them	to return early.
My new glasses	help	me	to read the signs.

The subject of the second verb is simultaneously the object of the preceding verb.

Exercise 9. Listen to the question and to the phrase. Use the phrase to answer the question.

| What did Mr. Miller tell John to do? —study the lesson— | MR. MILLER TOLD JOHN TO STUDY THE LESSON. |
| What did John advise Mary to do? —read the whole book— | JOHN ADVISED MARY TO READ THE WHOLE BOOK. |

1. What did Mr. Miller tell Mrs. Miller to do? —drive carefully—
2. What did the doctor persuade John to do? —drink some water—
3. What did John advise Mary to do? —send the letter by airmail—
4. What did Mrs. Miller invite the children to do? —watch television—
5. What did the doctor order Mr. Miller to do? —walk a mile every day—

6. What did Paul persuade his father to do? —listen to the music—
7. What did the teacher tell the students to do? —close their books—
8. What did Mr. Miller persuade his wife to do? —look at the map—
9. What did Mrs. Miller invite Mary to do? —have some coffee—
10. What did John advise us to do? —study hard—

B. Notice the use of *to* and a verb.

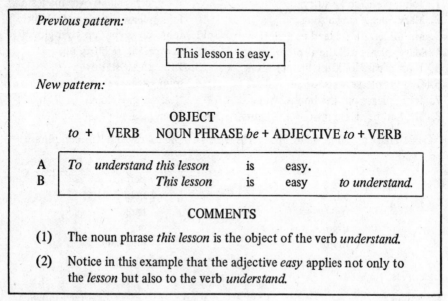

Previous pattern:

> This lesson is easy.

New pattern:

OBJECT

to + VERB   NOUN PHRASE *be* + ADJECTIVE *to* + VERB

A   To   *understand this lesson*   is   easy.
B   *This lesson*   is   easy   *to understand.*

COMMENTS

(1) The noun phrase *this lesson* is the object of the verb *understand.*

(2) Notice in this example that the adjective *easy* applies not only to the *lesson* but also to the verb *understand.*

NOTES:

(1) Pattern A above was introduced only to make the meaning of B clear. Pattern A is not as common or useful as B or as the following pattern, which is treated in Lesson 14.A:

> It is easy to understand this lesson.

(2) When a nominalization (e.g. a phrase beginning with *to*) is used as a grammatical subject, the verb is singular. See sentence 2 below.

1. *Long words* are often difficult.
2. *To pronounce long words* is often difficult.
3. *Long words* are often difficult *to pronounce.*

Exercise 10. Change the statement with the *to* nominalization in the beginning to a statement with the *to* nominalization at the end.

1. Big cars are expensive.
   To drive big cars is expensive.
   Big cars are expensive to drive.

2. These shoes are very practical.
   To wear these shoes is very practical.
   These shoes . . . . .

3. Mary's new book is interesting.
   To read Mary's new book is interesting.
   Mary's new book . . . . .

4. Our water is safe.
   To drink our water is safe.
   Our water . . . . .

5. Motorcycles can be dangerous.
   To drive motorcycles can be dangerous.
   Motorcycles . . . . .

6. John's car isn't safe.
   To drive John's car isn't safe.
   John's car . . . . .

7. Large houses are expensive.
   To live in large houses is expensive.
   Large houses . . . . .

8. Cats are interesting.
   To watch cats is interesting.
   Cats . . . . .

9. John's dog can be dangerous.
   To feed John's dog can be dangerous.
   John's dog . . . . .

10. Parks are pleasant.
    To walk in parks is pleasant.
    Parks . . . . .

NOTE: In the sentence

This lesson is easy to understand.

the noun phrase *this lesson* is the object of the verb *understand*. The subject of this verb, if expressed at all, is preceded by *for*.

This lesson is easy *for John* to understand.

Another pattern which is similar is the following:

This lesson is easy *for John.*

These patterns are practiced in the following exercise.

137

Exercise 11. Substitute the words. (Including *for* and *to* in the cue makes the exercise easier, but they may be omitted if the teacher prefers.)

This lesson is difficult for him.

(for) him to understand	THIS LESSON IS DIFFICULT FOR HIM TO UNDERSTAND.
(to) understand	THIS LESSON IS DIFFICULT TO UNDERSTAND.
easy	THIS LESSON IS EASY TO UNDERSTAND.
this exercise	THIS EXERCISE IS EASY TO UNDERSTAND.
(for) us	THIS EXERCISE IS EASY FOR US.
(for) us to write	THIS EXERCISE IS EASY FOR US TO WRITE.

1. (to) do
2. this lesson
3. (for) us to understand
4. (for) us
5. these words
6. difficult
7. (for) us to remember
8. (to) remember
9. (to) write
10. (to) spell
11. (for) the students to spell
12. (for) the students
13. easy
14. (for) them to remember
15. (to) remember
16. (to) forget
17. (to) write
18. (for) me to write
19. (for) you
20. (for) you to learn
21. these lessons
22. (to) learn
23. this exercise
24. (to) do
25. (to) practice

NOTE TO ADVANCED STUDENTS: In Frame A.1, the following pattern was introduced.

	VERB	*to* + VERB
George	wants	to go.

The following pattern is similar.

	be + ADJECTIVE	*to* + VERB
George	is ready	to go.

Notice that in both examples, *George* is the subject of the verb *go*.

Some other adjectives which can be used in the new pattern are the following: *able, unable, anxious, eager, willing, unwilling.*

This pattern is different from the one introduced in Frame B, where the subject of the sentence *(George)* is actually the object of the second verb *(understand)*:

	be + ADJECTIVE	*to* + VERB
George	is easy	to + understand

C. Notice the use of *very, too,* and *enough.*

SITUATION	NEW PATTERN
John is *very* tired. Therefore, he can't study.	John is *too* tired to study.

SITUATION	NEW PATTERN
John is 21 years old. Therefore, he can vote.	John is old *enough* to vote.

COMMENTS

(1) *Very* means "to a high degree."
     Too means "excessive."

(2) *Too tired to study* means that "to study" is something that won't (or didn't, doesn't or shouldn't) happen. You cannot use *very* in this situation.

(3) *Enough* means "sufficient." It follows the adjective (or adverb) that it modifies.

NOTE: *Enough* can either precede or follow nouns.

We have enough time.

We have time enough.

ADDITIONAL EXAMPLES

A. (*We* is the subject of *be* and *reach.*):
   We are too short. *We* can't reach the ceiling.
   We are too short   to reach it.

   We aren't tall enough. *We* can't reach the ceiling.
   We aren't tall enough   to reach it.

B. (*The ceiling* is the subject of *be* and the logical object of *reach.*):
   The ceiling is too high. We can't reach it.
   The ceiling is too high for us   to reach.
   The ceiling is too high   to reach.

   The ceiling is not low enough. We can't reach it.
   The ceiling is not low enough for us   to reach.
   The ceiling is not low enough   to reach.

Exercise 12. Listen to the situation described. Make a statement with *too*.

John is short.   JOHN IS TOO SHORT TO REACH THE CEILING.
    He can't reach the ceiling.
Mary is very tired.   MARY IS TOO TIRED TO WATCH TELEVISION.
    She can't watch television.

1. John is very busy. He can't go to New York.
2. Peter is very lazy. He doesn't work.
3. John is very angry. He can't think clearly.
4. The students are very tired. They can't study.
5. The boy is young. He can't drive.
6. Mary is sick. She can't go to class.

(In the following sentences the subject of the first is the logical object of the second.)

7. The ceiling is high. We can't reach it.

         THE CEILING IS TOO HIGH FOR US TO REACH.

8. The pencil is short. We can't use it.
9. The coffee is sweet. We won't drink it.
10. The shoes are small. I can't wear them.
11. The television set is very heavy. I can't carry it.
12. The bananas are soft. We won't eat them.
13. The car is old. We shouldn't drive it.
14. The beer is warm. We won't drink it.

Exercise 13. Practice the use of *too* and *enough*.

John is tall.   JOHN IS TALL ENOUGH
    He can reach the ceiling.   TO REACH THE CEILING.
John is very busy.   JOHN IS TOO BUSY TO
    He can't take a trip.   TAKE A TRIP.
The chalk is very short.   THE CHALK IS TOO SHORT
    We can't use it.   TO USE.
The chalk is very short.   THE CHALK IS SHORT ENOUGH
    We can throw it away.   TO THROW AWAY.

1. Mary is very sick. She can't come to class.
2. John is well. He can come to class.
3. The exercise is very easy. We can do it.
4. It is very cold. You can't go swimming.
5. It is very cold. We can go skating.
6. The bananas are very soft. We can't eat them.
7. The windows are clear. We can look through them.
8. John is very angry. He can fight.

9. It is very warm. We can go swimming.
10. It is very warm. We can't go skiing.
11. The lake is deep. We can swim in it.
12. Diamonds are valuable. You shouldn't throw them away.

(Continue using *for* and noun phrases in the responses, as "too small for Mary to see".)

13. The exercise is easy for us. We can do it.
14. The exercise is difficult for John. He can't do it.
15. This hat is small. George can't wear it.
16. The shoes are big. John can wear them.
17. The meeting is important. John shouldn't miss it.
18. The ceiling is high. John can't reach it.
19. The window is low. John can reach it.
20. The suit is small. Mr. Miller can't wear it.

Lesson 14

A. Some uses of *it* in subject position:
   It's early. It's easy to understand this lesson.

B. The expletive *there:*
   There is a book on the table.

C. Possessive *of* and *—'s:*
   The legs *of* the table. The dog'*s* legs.

D. Possessive pronouns: *mine, yours,* etc.

E. *Whose.*

F. *One* and *ones.*

A.1 Notice the use of *it* in sentences about time and weather.

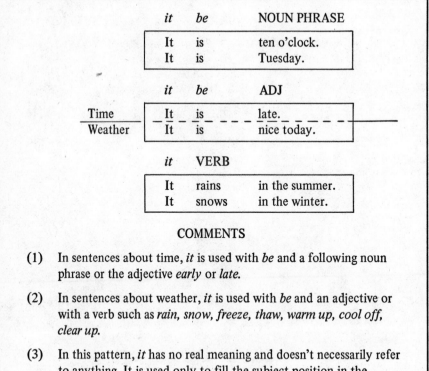

	it	*be*	NOUN PHRASE
	It	is	ten o'clock.
	It	is	Tuesday.

	it	*be*	ADJ
Time	It	is	late.
Weather	It	is	nice today.

	it	VERB	
	It	rains	in the summer.
	It	snows	in the winter.

COMMENTS

(1) In sentences about time, *it* is used with *be* and a following noun phrase or the adjective *early* or *late.*

(2) In sentences about weather, *it* is used with *be* and an adjective or with a verb such as *rain, snow, freeze, thaw, warm up, cool off, clear up.*

(3) In this pattern, *it* has no real meaning and doesn't necessarily refer to anything. It is used only to fill the subject position in the sentence.

NOTE 1: The words *it is* are usually contracted to *it's.*

NOTE 2: In the pattern which contains an adjective, certain verbs other than *be* (*seem, become, get*) may be used.

It seems late.
It gets warm in the afternoon.
It became cloudy.

ADDITIONAL EXAMPLES

What time is it?
    It's a quarter after ten.
    It's ten thirty.
    It's a quarter to eleven.
    It's 11 A.M.
    It's 12 noon.
    It's 12 midnight.

What day is it today?
    It's Wednesday.

What is the date today? (What date is it today?)
    It's October first. (second, third . . .)

What month is it?
    It's February.

Do we have much time?
    No, it's late.
    Yes, it's early.
    Yes, it seems early.
    No, it's getting late.

How is the weather?
    It's nice. (wonderful, beautiful)
    It's cold. (cool, warm, hot)
    It's cloudy. (windy, sunny)
    It seems cool and it's getting windy.

How is the weather in the winter?
    It's terrible. It snows every day and it gets very cold.

How is the weather now?
    It's raining.
    It's snowing.

Exercise 1. Listen to the question. Give a true answer beginning with *it*.

What day is it?   IT'S MONDAY.
What day was it yesterday?   IT WAS SUNDAY.

   1. What day will it be tomorrow?
   2. What time is it?
   3. What time was it an hour ago?
   4. What month is it?
   5. What month will it be next month?

6. What month was it last month?
7. What season is it?
8. What season was it three months ago?
9. What year is it?
10. What year was it last year?
11. What year will it be next year?
12. What year was it when Columbus discovered America?

Exercise 2. Ask another student how the weather is in his country, region, or city. He will answer with one or more sentences. Each sentence of the answer will begin with *it*.

> Student A: How's the weather in Thailand?
> > Student B: It's always hot. (It's very humid too.)

> Student B: How's the weather in northern India?
> > Student C: It's very hot and humid in the summer. It's pleasant in the winter.

> Student C: How's the weather in Paris?
> > Student D: It's warm in the summer. It's cool in the winter. (It often rains.)

NOTE: *It* may be used in sentences which identify persons.

Who is at the door?	It's John.
Who is on the phone?	It's Mary.
Who is at the door?	It's Helen and Alice.
Who was that?	It was my uncle.
Who was the man in the car?	It looked like Dr. Martin.

A.2. Notice the use of *it* in sentences about distance.

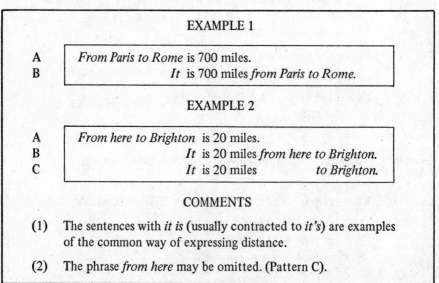

EXAMPLE 1

A   *From Paris to Rome* is 700 miles.
B   *It* is 700 miles *from Paris to Rome.*

EXAMPLE 2

A   *From here to Brighton* is 20 miles.
B   *It* is 20 miles *from here to Brighton.*
C   *It* is 20 miles   *to Brighton.*

COMMENTS

(1) The sentences with *it is* (usually contracted to *it's*) are examples of the common way of expressing distance.

(2) The phrase *from here* may be omitted. (Pattern C).

NOTE: Patterns A and B have the same meaning. Pattern A, however, is not as common or useful as B. A is introduced mainly to make the meaning of B easier to understand. In other words, when you want to express the meaning of A, use the form of B.

ADDITIONAL EXAMPLES

It is two blocks from here to the post office.
It is two blocks to the post office.
It isn't far to the post office.
It's a long way to Tipperary.
It's five hours by car from here to Chicago.
It's an hour and a half by plane from here to New York.

Exercise 3. Practice the use of *it* in expressing distance. (The following diagram may be put on the blackboard.)

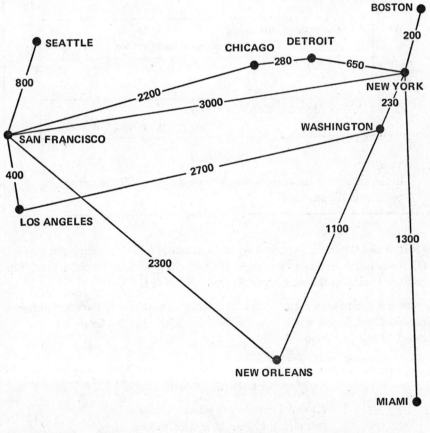

From New York to Washington   IT IS 230 MILES FROM
                                      NEW YORK TO WASHINGTON.

From New York to Miami　　　　　IT IS 1300 MILES FROM
　　　　　　　　　　　　　　　　　　　NEW YORK TO MIAMI.

1. From New York to Boston
2. From New York to Detroit
3. From Detroit to Chicago
4. From Chicago to San Francisco
5. From San Francisco to Seattle
6. From San Francisco to Los Angeles
7. From Los Angeles to Washington
8. From Washington to New Orleans
9. From New Orleans to San Francisco
10. From San Francisco to New York

A.3　Notice the use of *it*.

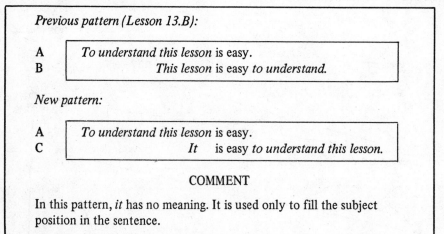

Previous pattern (Lesson 13.B):

A　　*To understand this lesson* is easy.
B　　　　　　*This lesson* is easy *to understand.*

New pattern:

A　　*To understand this lesson* is easy.
C　　　　　　*It*　is easy *to understand this lesson.*

COMMENT

In this pattern, *it* has no meaning. It is used only to fill the subject position in the sentence.

NOTE: A and C mean the same thing, but sentence A is not as common or useful as C; it was introduced mainly to make the meaning of C easier to understand. When you want to express the meaning of A, use the form of C.

Sentence B is similar to A and C, but B is special because we say the noun phrase *this lesson* first. In this way we can emphasize the fact that *this lesson* is the "topic" of our discussion.

ADDITIONAL EXAMPLES

To watch musical programs is pleasant.
It is pleasant *to watch musical programs.*

To ski can be dangerous.
It can be dangerous *to ski.*

Exercise 4. Continue as in the illustrative examples given above.

To drive big cars is expensive.   IT IS EXPENSIVE TO DRIVE BIG CARS.
To play baseball must be fun.   IT MUST BE FUN TO PLAY BASEBALL.

1. To read Mary's new book is interesting.
2. To drive motorcycles can be dangerous.
3. To drive John's car isn't safe.
4. To live in a large house is expensive.
5. To watch cats is interesting.
6. To feed John's dog can be dangerous.
7. To walk in the park is pleasant.
8. To write this exercise isn't difficult.
9. To arrive in class on time is important.
10. To come early is good.
11. To learn a new language can be very interesting.
12. To ski is exciting.
13. To pronounce long words is often difficult.
14. To get up early is sometimes difficult.
15. To have a good alarm clock is usually necessary.
16. To have two alarm clocks shouldn't be necessary.
17. To hear an alarm clock at six in the morning isn't pleasant.
18. To swim is easy.
19. To understand this lesson is easy.

Exercise 5. Give short replies using *it is.* (Individually)

Tell me something that is   IT IS INTERESTING TO
     interesting to do.   VISIT FOREIGN COUNTRIES. Or,
                           IT IS INTERESTING TO
                           MEET NEW PEOPLE.
                   (or some other original answer)

Tell me something that is   IT IS FUN TO GO
     fun to do.   SWIMMING ON A HOT DAY. Or,
                   IT IS FUN TO GO TO PARTIES .

Tell me something that is . . . . .

1. . . . difficult to do.   8. . . . hard to do.
2. . . . easy to do.   9. . . . nice to do.
3. . . . dangerous to do.   10. . . . simple to do.
4. . . . exciting to do.   11. . . . necessary to do.
5. . . . important to do.   12. . . . polite to do.
6. . . . good to do.   13. . . . unusual to do.
7. . . . impossible to do.

B.1   Notice the use of the expletive *there.*

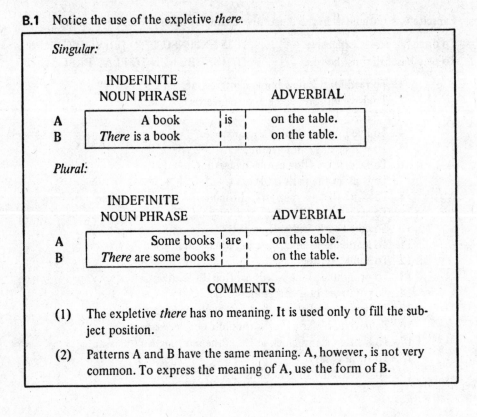

Singular:

	INDEFINITE NOUN PHRASE		ADVERBIAL
A	A book	is	on the table.
B	*There* is a book		on the table.

Plural:

	INDEFINITE NOUN PHRASE		ADVERBIAL
A	Some books	are	on the table.
B	*There* are some books		on the table.

COMMENTS

(1)   The expletive *there* has no meaning. It is used only to fill the subject position.

(2)   Patterns A and B have the same meaning. A, however, is not very common. To express the meaning of A, use the form of B.

NOTE:

(1)   The expletive *there* is different from the adverb *there,* which is used to indicate place.

> *There's*   a book   *there.*
> EXPLETIVE   ADVERB

The expletive is always unstressed. The adverb *there,* however, when it occurs in initial position, is stressed.

> Where's the pen?

> *There*   it is — on the table.
> ADVERB

(2)   In informal situations, the singular form *there is* is sometimes used before a plural noun phrase: *There's some books on the table.* The plural form is preferred, however, when the noun phrase is plural: *There are some books on the table.*

ADDITIONAL EXAMPLES

With an adverbial of place (on the table, etc.):

> There are a few books on the table.
> There are a lot of students in the classroom.
> There weren't many students here yesterday.
> There's a little milk in that glass.
> There isn't much milk in that glass.
> There were several chairs in the room.
> There are three elephants in the city zoo.

With an adverbial of time (tomorrow, etc.):

> There's going to be a party tomorrow.
> There were several parties last week.

Exercise 6. Listen to the negative statement. Make an affirmative statement. In your response, use the adverbial of place if one is given, but change the time to *today.*

There wasn't a pen here yesterday.	BUT THERE IS ONE HERE TODAY.
There wasn't a party yesterday.	BUT THERE IS ONE TODAY.
There weren't any apples on the table yesterday.	BUT THERE ARE SOME ON THE TABLE TODAY.
There wasn't any snow on the ground yesterday.	BUT THERE IS SOME ON THE GROUND TODAY.

1. There wasn't any ice here yesterday.
2. There weren't any chairs here yesterday.
3. There wasn't any coffee here yesterday.
4. There weren't any books on the table yesterday.
5. There wasn't a piece of chalk on the table yesterday.
6. There weren't any doctors in the office yesterday.
7. There wasn't a meeting yesterday.
8. There weren't any baseball games yesterday.
9. There wasn't any bread on the table yesterday.
10. There weren't any pieces of bread on the table yesterday.

NOTE: In order to make a question, put the form of *be* (or modal auxiliary) before the expletive *there*.

STATEMENT: There *is* a book here.
YES/NO QUESTION: *Is* there a book here?
SHORT ANSWERS: Yes, there is.
                      No, there isn't.

STATEMENT: There *will* be music at the party.
YES/NO QUESTION: *Will* there   be music at the party?
SHORT ANSWERS: Yes, there will.
                      No, there won't.

Exercise 7. Listen to the statement. Change it to a *yes/no* question. Another student will give a true short answer.

                      There's a blackboard in this room.
STUDENT A: IS THERE A BLACKBOARD IN THIS ROOM?
STUDENT B: YES, THERE IS.

                      There's a tiger in this room.
STUDENT A: IS THERE A TIGER IN THIS ROOM?
STUDENT B: NO, THERE ISN'T.

                      There are a lot of easy patterns in our book.
STUDENT A: ARE THERE MANY EASY PATTERNS IN OUR BOOK?
              (ARE THERE A LOT OF EASY PATTERNS IN OUR BOOK?)
STUDENT B: YES, THERE ARE.
              (NO, THERE AREN'T.)

1. There's a desk in this room.
2. There's a car in this room.
3. There are some students in this room.
4. There are a lot of trees in this city.
5. There are a few books on the teacher's desk.
6. There's a little beer in your refrigerator.
7. There's a lot of money in your bank account.
8. There's going to be some homework for us to do tomorrow.
9. There will be an examination at the end of this course.
10. There will be a party after the examination.

C. Notice the use of the preposition *of* and the suffix *-'s*.

The table has legs. THING	The legs *of the table* of the THING
The dog has legs. ANIMAL	*The dog's* legs ANIMAL'S
John has legs. PERSON	*John's* legs PERSON'S

COMMENTS

(1) The possessive form of a noun phrase referring to a THING is made by putting *of* before the noun phrase.

(2) The possessive form of a noun phrase referring to an ANIMAL or a PERSON is made by adding the suffix *'s* (apostrophe *s*) at the end of the noun phrase.

(3) In addition to their use in showing possession, the possessive forms are also used to indicate certain other relations.

> the work *of the machine*
>   of the THING

> *the boy's* work
> PERSON'S

(4) The possessive form of a noun phrase referring to TIME is made by adding *'s*.

> *today's* homework
> TIME's

> *a week's* vacation
> TIME's

NOTE: The forms recommended above are the usual ones. Occasionally, however, speakers of English will not follow these rules exactly. For example: "The father of the boy talked about the world's problems."

Exercise 8. Listen to the two statements. Make a new statement using the possessive forms.

It's a book. The boy has it.	IT'S THE BOY'S BOOK.
They're books. The boy has them.	THEY'RE THE BOY'S BOOKS.
It's a car. It belongs to Mary.	IT'S MARY'S CAR.

They're legs. They're on the   THEY'RE THE LEGS OF THE
  table.   TABLE.

1. They're legs. They're on a dog.
2. They're problems. Bob has them.
3. It's a cover. It's on this book.
4. It's homework. It's for today.
5. They're letters. They belong to John.
6. It was a speech. Mr. Miller gave it.
7. It's a top. It's on this table.
8. She's a wife. She married Mr. Miller.
9. They are walls. They are in this room.
10. It's a desk. The teacher uses it.
11. They're glasses. They belong to Mary.
12. It's an old coat. John owns it.
13. It's a house. Mr. Allen bought it.
14. They are wheels. They are on my bicycle.
15. It was a vacation. It was for a week.
16. It's a paper. It came today.
17. They're toys. The children play with them.

NOTE:

(1)   Compare -*'s* and -*s'*

        The boy has the books.   the boy's books.
        The boys have the books.   the boys' books.

After a plural noun phrase with the regular plural ending -*s*, the possessive ending does not add any further *s* sound. The singular possessive *boy's*, the regular plural *boys*, and the plural possessive *boys'* are all pronounced alike.

(2)   The noun which follows a possessive noun phrase is omitted when the meaning is clear.

        Do you have John's book?   (Singular)
           No, I have *Mary's.*

        Do you have John's books?   (Plural)
           No, I have *Mary's.*

D. Compare the possessive determiners with the possessive pronouns.

Previous pattern (Lesson 6.E):	*New pattern:*
POSSESSIVE DETERMINERS	POSSESSIVE PRONOUNS
This is *my* book. These are *my* books.	This is *mine.* These are *mine.*
your book. *your* books.	*yours.* *yours.*

his book.	*his.*
his books.	*his.*
her book.	*hers.*
her books.	*hers.*
our book.	*ours.*
our books.	*ours.*
your book.	*yours.*
your books.	*yours.*
their book.	*theirs.*
their books.	*theirs.*

COMMENTS

(1) The possessive pronouns are used after forms of *to be* with no noun phrase following. They are also used as substitutes for a noun phrase: "My books are here; YOURS are on the table."

(2) The singular and plural forms of the possessive pronouns are the same: "Mine is here. Mine are here."

Exercise 9. Listen to the two statements. Combine them with the *and . . . too* pattern. Use a possessive pronoun or the possessive form of a noun as a noun phrase substitute in the second statement.

My book is on the table.
  Your book is on the table.
	MY BOOK IS ON THE TABLE,
	  AND YOURS IS TOO.

His car can go very fast.
  Her car can go very fast.
	HIS CAR CAN GO VERY FAST,
	  AND HERS CAN TOO.

John's cat likes fish.
  Mary's cat likes fish.
	JOHN'S CAT LIKES FISH, AND
	  MARY'S DOES TOO.

1 Your grammar book is green. My grammar book is green.
2. His dictionary is very large. Her dictionary is very large.
3. My friends can speak English. Your friends can speak English.
4. Her friends always speak Spanish. His friends always speak Spanish.
5. Our examination will be difficult. Your examination will be difficult.
6. Your homework was difficult. Their homework was difficult.
7. Their teachers give difficult assignments. Our teachers give difficult assignments.
8. Mary's new car goes very fast. John's new car goes very fast.
9. The girl's hair is long. The boy's hair is long.
10. Mr. and Mrs. King's daughter works hard. Mr. and Mrs. Thompson's daughter works hard.

Exercise 10. Listen to the statement and the name or pronoun after it. Make a parallel statement with the name or pronoun as subject and the corresponding possessive pronoun as direct object.

I have my books. John.   JOHN HAS HIS.

I put my books on the table.   JOHN AND MARY PUT THEIRS
   John and Mary.   ON THE TABLE.

He is reading his book. I.   I AM READING MINE.

1. I brought my books to class. John.
2. I brought my paper to class. Mary.
3. I mailed my letters. Mary.
4. I am doing my homework. Fred.
5. We don't like our car. Mr. and
    Mrs. Smith.
6. They visited their brothers.
    Mr. Smith.
7. They bought their tickets. We.
8. I read my letter before class. You.
9. You did your work before class. I.
10. I read my assignments last night. You
    and John.
11. They wrote their compositions this
    morning. We.
12. Mr. Peterson is going to sell his car. I.

E. Notice the formation of questions with *whose*.

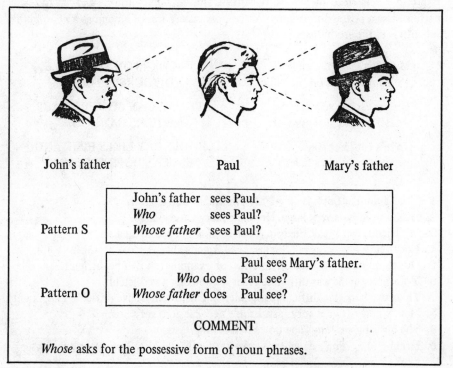

John's father   Paul   Mary's father

Pattern S	John's father	sees Paul.
	Who	sees Paul?
	Whose father	sees Paul?

Pattern O		Paul sees Mary's father.
	Who does	Paul see?
	Whose father does	Paul see?

COMMENT

Whose asks for the possessive form of noun phrases.

NOTE: *Wh*-questions have been practiced in the following lessons: 4, 9.C, and 11.A.3.

The pronunciation of *whose* and *who's* (=who is) is the same. The meanings are, of course, very different.

"Whose father is in the living room?"   "Mary's."

"Who's in the living room?"   "Mary's father."

Exercise 11. Listen to the statement. Make a corresponding question with *whose*. Another student will give a short answer.

John's father sees Paul.

STUDENT A: WHOSE FATHER SEES PAUL?

STUDENT B: JOHN'S.

Paul sees Mary's father.

STUDENT B: WHOSE FATHER DOES PAUL SEE?

STUDENT C: MARY'S.

1. We can see John's book.
2. John's pencil is on the table.
3. Mary's pencils are on the table.
4. Mary is reading her book.
5. John's apartment is near the university.
6. John's brother lives in New York.
7. Mary likes Helen's green dress.
8. John's pencil fell on the floor.
9. Alice likes the Millers' new house.
10. Bill likes to ride our bicycle.
11. Betty likes my new apartment.
12. Mr. Smith's house is on fire.
13. Mrs. Miller is feeding her cat.
14. John's pen is on the floor.
15. John wants to borrow our car.
16. We can see Bill's house from ours.
17. We might see Betty's mother tomorrow.

NOTE: The noun which follows *whose* is omitted when the meaning is clear.

"*Whose book* do you have?"

"John's_____. *Whose* _____ do you have?

"Mary's."

F. Notice the use of *one* and *ones.*

Previous pattern (Lesson 7.C):

One, used as a substitute for a singular indefinite noun phrase.

> "Did you buy *a pencil?*"
> "No, I'm going to buy *one* tomorrow."

New patterns:

One, used as a substitute for a singular noun.

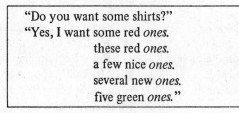

> "Do you want a shirt?"
> "Yes, I want   this *one.*
>   that *one.*
>   a large *one.*
>   a good *one.*
>   the red *one.*
>   this red *one.* "

Ones, used as a substitute for a plural noun.

> "Do you want some shirts?"
> "Yes, I want some red *ones.*
>   these red *ones.*
>   a few nice *ones.*
>   several new *ones.*
>   five green *ones.* "

COMMENTS

(1)   *One* is used as a substitute for a singular noun after *this, that,* or a descriptive adjective such as *large, good, red.*

(2)   *Ones* is used as a substitute for a plural noun after a descriptive adjective only, but not after words like *these* or *several.* Compare the following examples:

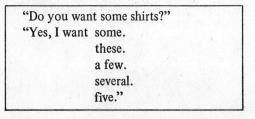

> "Do you want some shirts?"
> "Yes, I want some.
>   these.
>   a few.
>   several.
>   five."

Words such as *some, these, a few, several, five* are not descriptive adjectives. Therefore, they cannot be followed by *ones.*

Exercise 12. Listen to the statements. Make a new sentence(s) without the noun *book*. Use *one* and *ones* when necessary.

I want this book.	I WANT THIS ONE.
I want that book.	I WANT THAT ONE.
I want five books.	I WANT FIVE.
I want a new book.	I WANT A NEW ONE.
I want some new books.	I WANT SOME NEW ONES.
I want your new book.	I WANT YOUR NEW ONE.
I want your book.	I WANT YOURS.
I want these books.	I WANT THESE.

1. I want these new books.
2. I want those books.
3. I want those black books.
4. I want several black books.
5. I want that red book.
6. I want this old book.
7. I want ten books.
8. I want ten red books.
9. I want several books.
10. I want a few books.
11. I want a very good book.
12. I want three books.
13. I want three good books.
14. I want this green book.
15. I want five new books.
16. I want a new book.
17. I want some good books.
18. I want a few books.
19. I want some other books.
20. I want a big book.
21. I want this big book.
22. I want this book.
23. I want these books.
24. I want my book.
25. I want my books.
26. I want her book.
27. I want his book.
28. I want Mary's book.
29. I want your books.
30. I want their book.
31. I want our book.

Lesson 15

Expressions of Comparison

    A.   *the same as, different from, like*
           the same . . . as, as . . . as

    B.   *more . . . than*
           -er than

    C.   *the most*
           the . . .-est

A.1 Notice the use of *the same as* and *different from.*

> My pencil and your pencil are the same.
> There is no difference.
>
>   My pencil is *the same as* yours.

> John's coat is large and brown.
> Paul's coat is small and gray.
>
>   John's coat is *different from* Paul's.

COMMENT

The same as and *different from* are used to compare two persons, things, places, animals, etc.

NOTE: *Different than* is sometimes used in place of *different from.* However, *different from* is preferred in writing.

Exercise 1.

My shoes are brown and size ten and yours
   are too There is no difference.

MY SHOES ARE THE SAME
AS YOURS.

This book is red. It's very small. That one
   is black. It's big.

THIS BOOK IS DIFFERENT
FROM THAT ONE.

1. This is a grammar book. That book is too. There is no difference.
2. This radio is small, but that one is large.
3. Four times three is twelve and three times four is, too.
4. John's pen is blue. Mary's pen is green.

5. John is short. He's always happy. Paul is tall and he's seldom happy.
6. Two times three is six and three times two is, too.
7. Mary's address is 804 Washington Street. Nancy lives there, too.
8. John's address is 909 Fifth Street. Bob's address is 910 Main Street.
9. John's coat is brown. Paul's is black.

NOTE: In a sentence such as "My coat is like yours", the word *like* means "almost the same" or "similar."

Exercise 2. Make sentences with *like*.

John's coat is similar to Paul's.   JOHN'S COAT IS LIKE PAUL'S.

John's new car looks almost the   JOHN'S NEW CAR LOOKS LIKE
    same as Paul's.   PAUL'S.

1. John is very similar to his father.
2. Paul's eyes are almost the same as his mother's.
3. John looks similar to his father.
4. John works very hard and a horse does too.
5. Paul eats a lot and a horse does too.
6. Mary eats very little and a bird does too.

A.2 Notice the use of *the same . . . as* and *as . . . as*.

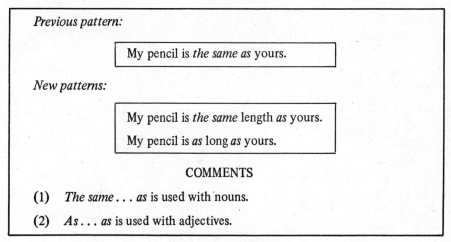

Previous pattern:

My pencil is *the same as* yours.

New patterns:

My pencil is *the same* length *as* yours.

My pencil is *as* long *as* yours.

COMMENTS

(1)   *The same . . . as* is used with nouns.

(2)   *As . . . as* is used with adjectives.

ILLUSTRATIVE EXAMPLES
(These examples can be used to form two or more exercises.)

This pencil is the same *length* as the other one.
         This pencil is as *long* as the other one.   (short)

This street is the same *width* as the other one.
         This street is as *wide* as the other one.   (narrow)

This book is the same *thickness* as the other one.
        This book is as *thick* as the other one.   (thin)

This shelf is the same *height* as the other one.
        This shelf is as *high* as the other one.   (low)

This student is the same *height* as the other one.
        This student is as *tall* as the other one.   (short)

This lake is the same *depth* as the other one.
        This lake is as *deep* as the other one.   (shallow)

This piece of metal is the same *hardness* as the other one.
        This piece of metal is as *hard* as the other one.   (soft)

This student is the same *age* as the other one.
        This student is as *old* as the other one.   (young)

This chair is the same *weight* as the other one.
        This chair is as *heavy* as the other one.   (light)

This chair is the same *size* as the other one.
        This chair is as *big* as the other one.   (small)

This chair is the same *price* as the other one.
        This chair is as *expensive* as the other one.   (inexpensive)

This train is the same *speed* as the other one.
        This train is as *fast* as the other one.   (slow)

This store is the same *distance* as the other one.
        This store is as *far* as the other one.   (near, close)

NOTE: The expression *as . . . as* is also used with expressions of quantity *(much, many, little, few)* and expressions of quantity followed by nouns. See Exercise 3.

Exercise 3. (individually)

Bob bought five books, and George did too.	BOB BOUGHT AS MANY BOOKS AS GEORGE. (BOB BOUGHT AS MANY AS GEORGE.)
Bob had two cups of coffee, and George did too.	BOB HAD AS MUCH COFFEE AS GEORGE. (BOB HAD AS MUCH AS GEORGE.) (BOB HAD AS MANY CUPS OF COFFEE AS GEORGE.)

1. Bob has two dogs, and George does too.
2. Bob drank two glasses of milk, and George did too.
3. Bob ate three sandwiches, and George did too.
4. Bob drinks a glass of milk every day, and George does too.
5. Bob bought two shirts, and George did too.

6. Bob talked to two students, and George did too.
7. Bob uses ten pieces of paper every day, and George does too.
8. Bob reads two magazines every week, and George does too.
9. Bob wants a gallon of ice cream, and George does too.
10. Bob wrote three letters, and George did too.

NOTE: The expression *as . . . as* is also used with adverbs. See Exercise 4.

Exercise 4. Practice the use of *as . . . as* with adverbs. (The sentences in parentheses are alternate cues.)

John speaks very clearly, but Paul doesn't. (John is a very clear speaker, but Paul isn't.)	PAUL DOESN'T SPEAK AS CLEARLY AS JOHN.
John sings very well, but Paul doesn't. (John is a very good singer, but Paul isn't.)	PAUL DOESN'T SING AS WELL AS JOHN.

1. John talks very slowly, but Paul doesn't.
    (John is a very slow talker, but Paul isn't.)
2. John works very carefully, but Paul doesn't.
    (John is a very careful worker, but Paul isn't.)
3. John writes very well, but Paul doesn't.
    (John is a very good writer, but Paul isn't.)
4. John swims very fast, but Paul doesn't.
    (John is a very fast swimmer, but Paul isn't.)
5. John works very hard, but Paul doesn't.
    (John is a very hard worker, but Paul isn't.)
6. John teaches very well, but Paul doesn't.
    (John is a very good teacher, but Paul isn't.)
7. John runs very fast, but Paul doesn't.
    (John is a very fast runner, but Paul isn't.)
8. John drives very carefully, but Paul doesn't.
    (John is a very careful driver, but Paul isn't.)
9. John speaks very clearly, but Paul doesn't.
    (John is a very clear speaker, but Paul isn't.)
10. John reads very fast, but Paul doesn't.
    (John is a very fast reader, but Paul isn't.)
11. John walks very slowly, but Paul doesn't.
    (John is a very slow walker, but Paul isn't.)

Exercise 5. Idioms.

John is quick. A wink is quick.   JOHN IS AS QUICK AS A WINK.

Our bread is hard. A rock is hard.   OUR BREAD IS AS HARD AS A
                                       ROCK.

1. Mary is quiet. A mouse is quiet.
2. The joke is old. The hills are old.
3. Mary is pretty. A picture is pretty.
4. Mr. Smith is cold. Ice is cold.
5. His word is good. Gold is good.
6. His face is red. A beet is red.
7. Mary is sweet. Honey is sweet.
8. Mary's watch is light. A feather is light.

Exercise 6. Summary exercise: *the same . . . as* and *as . . . as.*

The color of your suit is blue. The   YOUR SUIT IS THE SAME
  color of mine is blue too.   COLOR AS MINE.

The size of your suit is thirty-six,   YOUR SUIT ISN'T THE SAME
  but the size of mine is forty.   SIZE AS MINE.
                                          (or) YOUR SUIT ISN'T AS
                                                  BIG AS MINE.

Your books are interesting, and   YOUR BOOKS ARE AS
  mine are too.   INTERESTING AS MINE.

John writes carefully, and Mary   JOHN WRITES AS CAREFULLY
  does too.   AS MARY.

1. Mary speaks clearly, and John does too.
2. John's height is five feet. Paul's height is five feet.
3. John's weight is 150 pounds. Paul's weight is 150 pounds too.
4. John's age is twenty-four. Paul's age is twenty-two.
5. John speaks rapidly. The professor speaks rapidly.
6. The color of John's hat is gray. The color of the professor's is gray too.
7. My family has two cars. Your family has two cars.
8. Mary is nineteen years old. James is nineteen years old too.
9. The price of the new book is three dollars. The price of the old one is three
     dollars too.
10. John is big. Paul is big too.
11. Mary is beautiful. Helen is beautiful too.
12. Peter ate three hamburgers. Paul ate three hamburgers too.
13. John works slowly. Paul works slowly too.
14. The quality of this shirt is excellent. The quality of that one is excellent too.

Exercise 7. Summary exercise: Compare one tree with several other trees. (They may be drawn on the blackboard.) Use the expressions *the same . . . as* and *as . . . as.*

size	THIS TREE IS THE SAME SIZE AS THOSE.
type	THIS TREE IS THE SAME TYPE AS THOSE.
big	THIS TREE IS AS BIG AS THOSE.
tall	THIS TREE IS AS TALL AS THOSE.

1. beautiful	4. old	7. age	10. tall
2. color	5. height	8. big	11. good
3. short	6. shape	9. size	12. price

NOTE FOR ADVANCED STUDENTS: The expression *as . . . as* can be followed by a group of words which corresponds to a sentence. For example:

1. John speaks English as fast as *he reads it.*

Often only part of the sentence appears:

2. Mary reads English as fast as Paul (reads English).
3. Mary reads English as fast as (she reads) French.

In example 2, the verb phrases (*reads English*) of the first and second parts of the sentence are the same. We don't repeat the verb phrase; it is, however, understood. Example 3 is similar. The subject and verb of the two parts of the sentence are the same, and it is, therefore, not necessary to say *she reads.* It is, of course, understood.

In example 2, where the verb phrases of the two parts are the same, the auxiliary *does* can be used in place of the second verb phrase, giving us example 4:

4. Mary reads English as fast as Paul *does.*

Similarly, forms of *be* or a modal auxiliary can be used in place of the complete verb phrase:

5. She is as tall as Paul *is.*
6. She can swim as fast as Paul *can.*

The words *does, is, can* are optional in sentences 4, 5, and 6; they can be included or omitted. If, however, *Paul* is replaced with the corresponding personal pronoun *he,* the words *does, is, can* are usually included:

7. Mary reads English as fast as *he* does.
8. She is as tall as *he* is.
9. She can swim as fast as *he* can.

The comments in this note apply to the following expressions (all of which include *as* or *than*):

A. the same as (But not *like.*)
    the same . . . as
    as . . . as

B. more . . . than (See Exercise 9.)
    -er than

B. Notice the comparative forms with -*er* and *more*.

Paul is tall.	Paul is careful.
John is very tall.	John is very careful.
John is tall*er* than Paul.	John is *more* careful than Paul.

COMMENTS

The suffix -*er* is used

(a)   with adjectives and
adverbs of one syllable:

tall	taller
clear	clearer
fast	faster
hard	harder
nice	nicer
quick	quicker
soon	sooner

(b)   with adjectives that end
in -*y* (2 syllables):

busy	busier
easy	easier
happy	happier
heavy	heavier
lazy	lazier
pretty	prettier
early	earlier

The word *more* is used

(a)   with most adjectives and
adverbs of two or more
syllables:

careful	more careful
beautiful	more beautiful
expensive	more expensive
interesting	more interesting
important	more important
necessary	more necessary
often	more often

(b)   with adverbs that have the
adverb suffix -*ly*:

carefully	more carefully
clearly	more clearly
easily	more easily
quickly	more quickly
rapidly	more rapidly

Note the following irregular forms:

good	better
well	better
bad	worse
badly	worse
far	farther (further)

NOTE: In general *farther* and *further* can be used interchangeably. However, only *further* can be used to mean "additional." For example: "a further example."

Exercise 8.

Is George tall?	YES, HE IS *TALLER* THAN I AM.
Did George come early?	YES, HE CAME *EARLIER* THAN I DID.
Did George write carefully?	YES, HE WROTE *MORE CAREFULLY* THAN I DID.

1. Is George careful?
2. Did George work hard?
3. Did George answer quickly?
4. Is George busy?
5. Is George fast?
6. Did George run fast?
7. Did George speak clearly?
8. Is George young?
9. Did George jump high?
10. Did George read fast?

Exercise 9.

| This pencil isn't long enough. | LET ME GET YOU *A LONGER ONE.* |
| This picture isn't beautiful enough. | LET ME GET YOU *A MORE BEAUTIFUL ONE.* |

1. This car isn't fast enough.
2. This glass isn't big enough.
3. This book isn't interesting enough.
4. This table isn't strong enough.
5. This watch isn't old enough.
6. This chair isn't big enough.
7. This suit isn't nice enough.
8. This raincoat isn't cheap enough.
9. This shirt isn't good enough.
10. This story isn't interesting enough.
11. This magazine isn't new enough.
12. This spoon isn't clean enough.
13. This knife isn't sharp enough.
14. This fish isn't fresh enough.

Exercise 10. This is a summary exercise to practice the use of adjectives and adverbs in expressions of comparison. Use *as . . . as, more . . . than* and *-er than.*

John is six feet tall, but Mary is only five feet tall.	JOHN IS TALLER THAN MARY.
Alice is very interesting, but her sister isn't.	ALICE IS MORE INTERESTING THAN HER SISTER.
John is the same height as Paul.	JOHN IS AS TALL AS PAUL.

1. Mary is very happy, but Alice isn't.
2. This lesson is very easy, but the other one isn't.
3. The post office is very near, but the bookstore isn't.
4. John talks very fast, but Mary doesn't.

5. Mary is the same height as Alice.
6. This book is very expensive, but the other one isn't.
7. We entered very quietly, but they didn't.
8. Mary talks very slowly, but Mr. Smith doesn't.
9. John speaks very rapidly, but Paul doesn't.
10. Mary is the same age as Alice.
11. Alice is very happy, but John isn't.
12. The first lesson was very easy, but the second one wasn't.
13. This lesson is very difficult, but the other one wasn't.
14. This table is the same size as that one.
15. This chair is very comfortable, but that one isn't.
16. This diamond is the same price as that one.

C. Notice the superlative forms, which are made with *-est* and *most*.

John is taller than Paul, but George is *the* tall*est*.	John is more careful than Paul, but George is *the most* careful.

COMMENTS

(1)   The suffix *-est* is used with the same words that *-er* is used with.

    (a)   Adjectives and adverbs of one syllable:

tall	taller	the tallest
clear	clearer	the clearest
fast	faster	the fastest
hard	harder	the hardest
nice	nicer	the nicest
quick	quicker	the quickest

    (b)   Adjectives that end in *-y* (2 syllables):

busy	busier	the busiest
easy	easier	the easiest
happy	happier	the happiest
heavy	heavier	the heaviest
lazy	lazier	the laziest
pretty	prettier	the prettiest
early	earlier	the earliest

Note the following irregular forms:

good	better	the best
well	better	the best
bad	worse	the worst
badly	worse	the worst
far	farther	the farthest

(2)   The word *most* is used with the same words that *more* is used with.

     (a)   Adjectives of two or more syllables:

careful	more careful	the most careful
beautiful	more beautiful	the most beautiful
expensive	more expensive	the most expensive
interesting	more interesting	the most interesting
important	more important	the most important
necessary	more necessary	the most necessary

     (b)   Adverbs that have the adverb suffix -*ly:*

carefully	more carefully	the most carefully
clearly	more clearly	the most clearly
easily	more easily	the most easily
quickly	more quickly	the most quickly
rapidly	more rapidly	the most rapidly

Exercise 11. Practice -*est* and *most.*

John is taller than Peter.	BUT GEORGE IS THE TALLEST.
John is more careful than Peter.	BUT GEORGE IS THE MOST CAREFUL.

1. John is younger than Peter.
2. John is busier than Peter.
3. John is quicker than Peter.
4. John is nicer than Peter.
5. John is happier than Peter.
6. John is faster than Peter.
7. John swims faster than Peter.
8. John works harder than Peter.
9. John reads faster than Peter.
10. John is more intelligent than Peter.
11. John is smarter than Peter.
12. John is friendlier than Peter.

NOTE: The expressions *more . . . than* and *the most* are used also with nouns (See Exercise 12.)

Exercise 12.

books	MARY HAS *MORE BOOKS THAN ALICE.* HELEN HAS *THE MOST BOOKS.*
money	MARY HAS *MORE MONEY THAN ALICE.* HELEN HAS *THE MOST MONEY.*

1. pencils	7. pieces of furniture	12. bread
2. chalk	8. hats	13. diamonds
3. pieces of chalk	9. apples	14. homework
4. flowers	10. fruit	15. assignments
5. chairs	11. sandwiches	16. time
6. furniture		

NOTES:

(1) We can also use *more* and *most* without a following noun:

> Alice has a lot of intelligence.
> Mary has more than Alice.
> Helen has the most.

(2) *Less* is the opposite of *more.*
Least is the opposite of *most.*

In general, *less* and *least* are used with the same words that *more* and *most* are used with.

ADJECTIVE

> John and Paul are *more careful* than George.
> George is *less careful* than John and Paul.
> George is *the least careful.*

ADVERB

> John and Paul write *more carefully* than George.
> George writes *less carefully* than John and Paul.
> George writes *the least carefully.*

NON-COUNT NOUN

> John and Paul have *more time* than George.
> George has *less time* than John and Paul.
> George has *the least time.*

COUNT NOUN (Use *fewer* and *the fewest*)

> John and Paul have *more books* than George.
> George has *fewer books* than John and Paul.
> George has the *fewest books.*

Lesson 16

(This lesson corresponds to Lesson XVII [seventeen] in the third editions of *English Sentence Patterns* and *English Pattern Practices*.)

A.   Embedded statements: I know *that he lives here.*

B.   Embedded *wh*-clauses: I know *who lives here.*

A.   Notice the use of *that* + statement in place of a noun phrase.

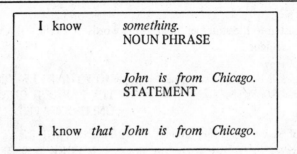

I know	*something.* NOUN PHRASE
	John is from Chicago. STATEMENT
I know *that John is from Chicago.*	

COMMENTS

1. A noun phrase (*something, someone, the new student, John,* etc.) can follow *I know*. In addition, an embedded statement (*John is from Chicago*) can function as a noun phrase.

2. The word *that* may be included or omitted in this pattern.

ADDITIONAL EXAMPLES

I believe that John is from Chicago.
I think it rained yesterday.
I imagine that John is going to be late.

Exercise 1.   Practice the use of *I think (that)* . . .   (The word *that* is optional.)

Which do you think is bigger — New York or Chicago?	I THINK (THAT) NEW YORK IS BIGGER.
Which do you think is older — London or New York?	I THINK (THAT) LONDON IS OLDER.

1. Which do you think is more expensive — a Cadillac or a Volkswagen?
2. Which do you think is more dangerous — a mouse or a tiger?
3. Which do you think is deeper — a lake or an ocean?
4. Which do you think is higher — Mt. Blanc or Mt. Everest?
5. Which do you think is lighter in weight — a horse or a cat?
6. Which do you think is longer — a mile or a kilometer?
7. Which do you think is faster — a mouse or a turtle?
8. Which do you think is sharper — a butter knife or a steak knife?
9. Which do you think is sweeter — an orange or a lemon?
10. Which do you think is taller — the Empire State Building or the White House?
11. Which do you think is warmer — Miami or Boston?
12. Which do you think is older — Montreal or Paris?
13. Which do you think is heavier — a car or a plane?
14. Which do you think is stronger — an elephant or a car?

Exercise 2. Listen to the statement and to the words that follow it. Combine them to form a new sentence.

New York is the largest city in the United States.
I know —

I KNOW THAT NEW YORK IS THE LARGEST CITY IN THE UNITED STATES.

Much of New York is surrounded by water.
I understand —

I UNDERSTAND THAT MUCH OF NEW YORK IS SURROUNDED BY WATER.

1. Most of the city is on islands. I guess —
2. New York is the busiest port in the United States. I suppose —
3. A ship arrives or departs every twenty minutes. I heard —
4. Approximately eight million people live in New York. I understand —
5. The United Nations is on the island of Manhattan. I assume —
6. The Empire State Building is more than 1,200 feet tall. I think —
7. The average temperature in New York in February is 28 degrees. I believe —
8. The average temperature in July is 74 degrees. I understand —
9. The first European arrived in New York in 1524. I learned —
10. His name was Verrazano. I believe —
11. The Dutch purchased Manhattan for $24. I heard —
12. The city became British in 1664. I understand —

NOTE: *That* clauses cannot be used after the verb *want*. The verb after *want* must be in the infinitive form with *to*:

I want *John to go.*
I want *to study.*

Want is discussed in Lesson 13.

NOTE TO ADVANCED STUDENTS: The verbs of Exercise 2, that is, verbs like *know*, plus some additional verbs of the same type, are listed below:

agree	doubt	hope	regret
answer	dream	imagine	remember
assume	feel	know	say
believe	forget	learn	suppose
conclude	guess	notice	think
decide	hear	realize	understand
discover			

A similar pattern includes verbs like *tell:*

> I told him (that) Louise came early.

In this sentence, an object (*him*) follows the verb. In fact, the verb must be followed by a personal object. Notice that there is no personal object following verbs like *know:*

> I know (that) Louise came early.
> I said (that) Louise came early.

Some additional verbs like *tell* are the following:

assure	notify
convince	remind
inform	

In a third pattern, an optional personal object follows the verb:

> He wrote (me) that John is in Paris.

Some additional verbs like *write* are the following:

promise	teach
show	warn

In a fourth pattern, an optional *to* + object follows the verb:

> He explained (to us) that a quick answer was important.

Some additional verbs like *explain* are the following:

admit	prove	report
announce	read	say
mention	repeat	suggest
point out	reply	write

B. Notice how a *wh*-clause is used after verbs like *know*.

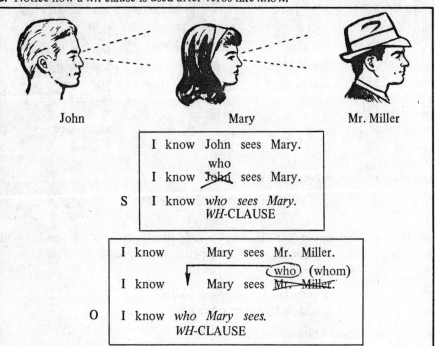

John   Mary   Mr. Miller

	I know John sees Mary.
	who
	I know ~~John~~ sees Mary.
S	I know *who sees Mary.*
	WH-CLAUSE

	I know Mary sees Mr. Miller.
	who (whom)
	I know Mary sees ~~Mr. Miller.~~
O	I know *who Mary sees.*
	WH-CLAUSE

COMMENTS

1. In Pattern S, the *wh*-word replaces the subject. For example, *who* replaces *John*.

   In Pattern O, the *wh*-word replaces the object (or some other part of the verb phrase). For example, *who* replaces *Mr. Miller*.

2. In either case, the *wh*-word comes at the beginning of the *wh*-clause.

   S. ... *who* sees Mary.

   O. ... *who* Mary sees.

3. The verb (or auxiliary) of the *wh*-clause immediately follows the subject of the *wh*-clause.

   S. I know *who*   sees Mary.
             SUBJECT   VERB

   I know *who*   *can* see Mary.
          SUBJECT   AUX.

   O. I know who *Mary*   sees.
              SUBJECT   VERB

   I know who *Mary*   *can* see.
           SUBJECT   AUX.

NOTE: The use of *who* in Pattern O is informal standard English. *Whom* is formal English.

Exercise 3. The word order of *wh*-clauses in questions is the same as in the corresponding statements. In this exercise, change the statements to questions. Remember the word order of the *wh*-clause does not change.

Pattern S

John knows who was here.   DOES JOHN KNOW WHO WAS HERE?

Mary knows who answered the   DOES MARY KNOW WHO ANSWERED
   telephone.   THE TELEPHONE?

1. She knows what happened here.
2. John told Mary which answer was correct.
3. He told her which was correct.
4. John remembers whose book was on the desk.
5. John asked Mary how many students went on the picnic.
6. Mary can tell us how many went.
7. She will explain how much money is necessary.
8. She remembers how much is necessary.

Pattern O

John remembers who he talked to.   DOES JOHN REMEMBER
                                             WHO HE TALKED TO?

John asked where Mary was from.   DID JOHN ASK WHERE
                                             MARY WAS FROM?

9. John knows which book we want.
10. He remembers which one we want.
11. He can tell us how many books we need.
12. He told us how much they will cost.
13. Mary knows what time it is.
14. She knows when the plane will leave.
15. John explained where Boston is.
16. He can understand why Mary wants to go there.
17. Mary would like to know how far it is.
18. Mary learned how often John practices English.
19. She found out how long he practices every day.
20. Everyone knows how well he can speak English now.
21. Mary knows how difficult it is.
22. George knows how late the store is open.

Exercise 4. Answer the questions with *No, I don't know,* etc. + a *wh*-clause. Then ask another student the same question. He should give an original answer.

Tchr: Do you know who he is?   St. A: NO, I DON'T KNOW WHO HE IS.
DO YOU KNOW WHO HE IS?
St. B: YES, HE IS MR. SMITH. (or some other original answer)

Tchr: Do you know where he comes from?   St. A: NO, I DON'T KNOW WHERE HE COMES FROM.
DO YOU KNOW WHERE HE COMES FROM?
St. B: YES, HE COMES FROM MEXICO. (JAPAN, ARGENTINA, etc.)

1. Do you know who came last night?
2. Do you know who John saw last night?
3. Do you know how old he is?
4. Do you know where he is from?
5. Do you know what he said?
6. Do you know how he came?.
7. Did you ask him where he went?
8. Did you ask him where his friends are?
9. Did you ask him how his family is?
10. Do you know where he lives?
11. Do you know where he is now?
12. Do you know what time it is?

NOTE TO THE TEACHER: Each box contains a statement with an underlined noun phrase. Put the statement on the board and cross out the underlined words. Ask the students (1) to form a sentence beginning with *I know* and (2) to form a *wh*-question. Replace the crossed-out words with *wh*-words.

Pattern S   Pattern O

VERBS	
John sees Mary.	Mary sees <u>Mr. Miller</u>.
1. I know *who* sees Mary.	1. I know *who* Mary sees.
2. *Who* sees Mary?	2. *Who* does Mary see?
BE	
<u>John</u> is a student.	John is <u>a student</u>.
1. I know *who* is a student.	1. I know *what* John is.
2. *Who* is a student?	2. *What* is John?
MODAL AUXILIARIES	
<u>John</u> can play tennis.	John can play <u>tennis</u>.
1. I know *who* can play tennis.	1. I know *what* John can play.
2. *Who* can play tennis?	2. *What* can John play?

Exercise 5. Practice pattern O. Listen to the question and the partial response. Complete the response as shown in the examples. (To the teacher: An alternative way of presenting this exercise is to list the suggested cue words "I don't know," "They didn't say," etc., on the blackboard so that the student may choose any appropriate one in his answer.)

Who is that man? I don't know—   I DON'T KNOW WHO THAT MAN IS.
What is the date of the party?   I DON'T KNOW WHAT
  I don't know—   THE DATE OF THE PARTY IS.
Where were they? They didn't say—   THEY DIDN'T SAY WHERE THEY
                                      WERE.
Whose book did he find?   DO YOU REMEMBER WHOSE BOOK
  Do you remember—   HE FOUND?

1. When is the party? I don't know —
2. How far is Detroit from here? I don't know —
3. Which did he want? Do you remember —
4. What is his name? Do you know —
5. Who is that man? Do you know —
6. What are you going to do when you leave the United States? Do you know —
7. Where was the concert? Who knows —
8. How many boys were there? Who knows —
9. What section was he in? Who knows —
10. Why wasn't he there? He didn't say —
11. Why weren't they in class? They didn't say —

12. Where are they going? Do you remember —
13. When did Mary arrive? Do you remember —
14. Why did they want to go? Do you remember —
15. Where is he from? Do you know —
16. Who is the girl in the blue dress? Do you know —
17. Where is the new student from? Do you know —
18. Where was the fire? Who knows —
19. Why wasn't the bank open? Who knows —
20. Where is he from? I don't remember —
21. How old is he? Do you know —
22. What is his profession? He didn't say —
23. Why was he late? I can't imagine —
24. When is he leaving? I'm not sure —
25. Where is he going? Ask him —
26. What time is it? I don't have any idea —
27. How tall is the Empire State Building? Ask Alice —
28. What is that? Do you know —
29. Whose book is that? Do you know —
30. How much time is there? Do you know —
31. What is the population of New York? Can you tell me —
32. What is he laughing at? Tell me —
33. What does he want? Ask him —
34. How much does it cost? Guess —
35. What does this word mean? Will you tell me —
36. How far is it? Do you know —
37. Where is the bus station? Do you know —
38. What time is it? Do you know —
39. Where is the post office? Can you tell me —
40. Where is the hospital? I don't know —
41. Where can I buy some towels? Can you tell me —
42. Where can I buy a good pen? Can you tell me —
43. Where can I buy some flowers? Do you know —
44. What did he want? I don't know —
45. Where was the lecture? Who knows —
46. How many students are there in the English course? Who can tell me —
47. What did he say? I don't know —
48. Who did you meet there? Do you remember —
49. How many did you buy? Do you remember —
50. What did he mean? I don't know —
51. What did he find? I don't know —
52. What did he do? I don't know —
53. What did he say? Do you remember —
54. What did he lose? I don't know —
55. What did he buy? I don't know —
56. What did he choose? I don't know —
57. What did John say? Can you remember —
58. How much did it cost? Do you know —

59. What did he say? I can't remember —
60. What did he sing? I don't know —
61. What did he leave? I don't know —
62. What did he tell them? I don't know —
63. What did he eat? I don't know —
64. Where did he go? Do you remember —
65. How old is he? I wonder —
66. What time is it? I wonder —
67. Where did he go? I wonder —
68. Who drank my coffee? I wonder —
69. Why did he come? I'll ask —

Exercise 6. Answer the questions with *I don't know* + *wh*-clause.

Is he from Chicago or New York?	I DON'T KNOW WHERE HE IS FROM.
Is he twenty-four or twenty-five years old?	I DON'T KNOW HOW OLD HE IS.
Did John come or did Paul come?	I DON'T KNOW WHO CAME.

1. Is this answer correct or is that answer correct?
2. Was John here or was Paul here?
3. Is he a doctor or is he a lawyer?
4. Did ten people come or did fifteen people come?
5. Is your friend in Detroit or is he in New York?
6. Was he here yesterday or last week?
7. Was it 3 o'clock or was it 4 o'clock?
8. Is it forty miles or is it fifty miles to Detroit?
9. Is that Paul or is that John?
10. Were ten people or were fifteen people at the party?
11. Does he want a course in English or a course in geography?
12. Can I buy my books here or in a drugstore?
13. Was the doctor here or was the lawyer here?
14. Did he come by plane or by ship?

NOTE: The embedded statements and *wh*-clauses in this lesson can also be used in subject position.

I heard *that John was happy.*
That John was happy made me happy.

I know *how he traveled.*
How he traveled was easy to discover.

I know *why he left early.*
Why he left early is a difficult question.

177

NOTE: The previous exercise deals with embedded *wh*-questions. It is also possible to embed *yes-no* questions. Such embedded *yes-no* questions must be preceded by *if* (or *whether*). Notice that the embedded clause has the word order of a statement, not a question.

Exercise 7. Listen to the statement and the words that follow it. Combine them to form a new sentence.

Is he home? I wonder —   I WONDER IF HE IS HOME.

Did he go? I'll ask —   I'LL ASK IF HE WENT.

1. Is he feeling better? I'll ask —
2. Is Professor Brown in his office? I'll ask —
3. Does John speak Japanese? I wonder —
4. Is he going to arrive soon? I wonder —
5. Are these answers correct? Can you tell me —
6. Is my tie straight? Can you tell me —
7. Does my hair look all right? Can you tell me —
8. Did I turn off the shower? I don't remember —
9. Did you take out the dog? Do you remember —
10. Can Mary go to the party? He wants to find out —
11. Does he like steak? I'd like to know —
12. Am I going with you tonight? I'm not sure —
13. Did we do Lesson 12 yesterday? Do you recall —
14. Did Paul tell her the joke? I wonder —
15. Are we going to have class on Friday? Do you know —
16. Did he answer the question? I'm not sure —
17. Did Mary bring her raincoat? I'm not sure —
18. Did George find his bicycle? Do you know —
19. Did the mail come? Do you know —
20. Will the governor be re-elected? I'd like to know —
21. Will the police catch the criminal? I'd like to know —
22. Will I return to my country after the course? I'm not sure —
23. Will the Democrats win the next election? I'm not sure —
24. Should we go to the baseball game or the movies? I don't know —
25. Should I watch television or study for my exam? I don't know —
26. Does she have her appointment at 3 or 4? Mary doesn't remember —

Lesson 17

(This lesson corresponds to Lesson XVI in the third editions of *English Sentence Patterns* and *English Pattern Practices.*)

A. Relative clauses

B. *for, during*
when, while
before, after, until

A.1 Notice the relative clauses.

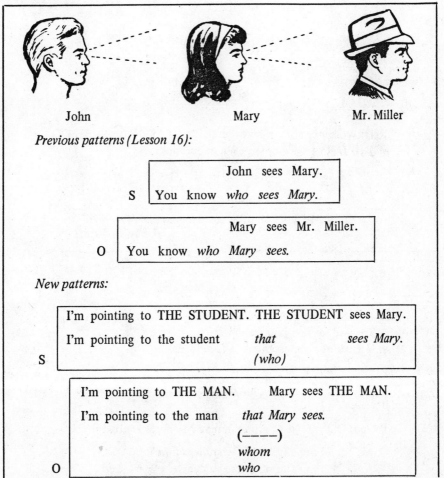

John   Mary   Mr. Miller

Previous patterns (Lesson 16):

John sees Mary.

S You know *who sees Mary.*

Mary sees Mr. Miller.

O You know *who Mary sees.*

New patterns:

I'm pointing to THE STUDENT. THE STUDENT sees Mary.

I'm pointing to the student   *that*   *sees Mary.*
                               (who)

S

I'm pointing to THE MAN.   Mary sees THE MAN.

I'm pointing to the man   *that Mary sees.*
                           (————)
                           whom
                           who

O

179

COMMENTS

1. In the S pattern, the *wh*-word is the subject of the following verb. In the O pattern, the *wh*-word is an object (or sometimes an adverbial).

$$\text{S.} \quad \underset{\text{SUBJECT}}{\textit{that}} \quad \text{sees Mary}$$

$$\text{O.} \quad \underset{\text{OBJECT}}{\textit{that}} \quad \text{Mary sees.}$$

2. In both patterns the verb (or auxiliary) comes immediately after the subject.

S.	*that*	*sees* Mary
	SUBJECT	VERB

O.	that	*Mary sees*
		SUBJECT VERB

S.	*that*	*can* see Mary
	SUBJECT	AUX.

O.	that	*Mary can* see.
		SUBJECT AUX.

3. Relative clauses always have the SUBJECT-VERB (or SUBJECT-AUXILIARY) word order, even in questions:

    S.   Are you pointing to the student *that sees* Mary?
                                    SUBJECT VERB

    O.   Are you pointing to the man that *Mary sees?*
                                      SUBJECT VERB

NOTES:

(1)   *Who* and *whom* are used for persons.
      Which is used for things and animals.
      That is used for persons, things, and animals.

(2)   In Pattern S, *that* is more common for things and animals than *which* is. Both *who* and *that* are very common for persons. However, sometimes *who* is preferred.

(3)   In Pattern O, the relative pronoun may be omitted entirely.

        I'm pointing to the student that Mary sees.
        I'm pointing to the student   Mary sees.

In clauses of this type, the *that* form or the omission is generally preferable to *who, whom* or *which.*

(4)   *Whom* can be used in Pattern O only. *Whom* is used in formal writing and speeches.

         Mr. Miller is the teacher *whom* Mary sees.

Exercise 1. Listen to the statements. Form a new statement which contains a relative clause. Use *that* as the relative pronoun in each sentence. (Suggested variations:

     1. Use *who, whom* or *that* for persons and *that* or *which* for things.

     2. Use *that* for pattern S and omission of the relative for pattern O.)

Be sure to put the relative clause immediately after the noun phrase it modifies.

S. I saw the man.
   The man helped us.   I SAW THE MAN THAT HELPED US.
O. I saw the man.
   We helped the man.   I SAW THE MAN THAT WE HELPED.
S. We ate the cake.
   It was on the table.   WE ATE THE CAKE THAT WAS ON THE TABLE.
O. We ate the cake.
   Mary baked it.   WE ATE THE CAKE THAT MARY BAKED.

     1.S. I will read the book. The book describes New York.
     1.O. I will read the book. John described the book.

     2.S. This is the homework. It is from Lesson 16.
     2.O. This is the homework. We did it yesterday.

     3.S. I saw the man. The man wrote the book.
     3.O. I saw the man. John described the man.

     4.S. This is the building. The building belongs to the city.
     4.O. This is the building. We like the building.

     5.S. Those men are the teachers. They talked to us.
     5.O. Those men are the teachers. We talked to them.

     6.S. She read the book. The book tells about Lincoln.
     6.O. She read the book. John told her about the book.

     7.S. That is the pen. It was on the president's desk.
     7.O. That is the pen. The president writes with it.

     8.S. That is the man. He waited for us yesterday.
     8.O. That is the man. We waited for him yesterday.

     9.S. That is the painting. It was on the wall yesterday.
     9.O. That is the painting. We looked at it yesterday.

     10.S. Mr. Miller is the man. The man spoke to John.
     10.O. Mr. Miller is the man. Mary spoke to the man.

Exercise 2. Listen to the statement and the question. Answer the question. Include information from the statement in your answer. (Individually)

S. The book describes California.   YES, I READ THE BOOK THAT
    Did you read the book?   DESCRIBES CALIFORNIA.

O. Mr. Miller described the book.   YES, I READ THE BOOK THAT
    Did you read the book?   MR. MILLER DESCRIBED.
                                    (NO, I DIDN'T READ THE BOOK
                                    THAT MR. MILLER
                                    DESCRIBED.)

1.S. The man wrote the book. Did you see the man?
1.O. John described the man. Did you see the man?

2.S. A car stopped at your house. Did you see the car?
2.O. John bought a car. Did you see the car?

3.S. A boy spoke to John. Do you know the boy?
3.O. Mr. Miller spoke to the boy. Do you know the boy?

4.S. The book tells about New York. Did you read the book?
4.O. John told you about the book. Did you read the book?

5.S. An architect owns this building. Did you find him?
5.O. Mrs. Miller recommended an architect. Did you find him?

6.S. The girl speaks French. Did you meet her?
6.O. John talked to the girl. Did you meet her?

NOTE: In the preceding exercise, the relative clauses modified the object in every case. However, relative clauses may be used to modify noun phrases in other positions also. In the following examples, the relative clauses modify subject noun phrases.

Pattern S:

      THE MAN   gave me a map.
  +   THE MAN drove the bus.

  = The man   who drove the bus gave me a map.

Pattern O:

      THE MAN   gave me a map.
  +   I was talking to THE MAN.

  = The man I was talking to   gave me a map.

Exercise 3. Listen to the two statements. Form a new statement that contains a relative clause. Put the information of the first statement inside the second one.

PATTERN S.

The man was here yesterday.	THE MAN THAT WAS HERE
He is in New York now.	YESTERDAY IS IN NEW YORK NOW.
The doctor came yesterday.	THE DOCTOR THAT CAME
He saw Mr. Miller.	YESTERDAY SAW MR. MILLER.

1. The man wrote the letter. He will talk to you tomorrow.
2. The student wrote the poem. He is from Panama.
3. The book fell down. It is a grammar book.
4. The person called on the telephone. He asked for Mr. Olsen.
5. The man sold the car. He is Mr. Smith.
6. The doctor gave the prescription. He is my brother.

PATTERN O.

(Listen to the subject noun phrase and the two statements. As before, put the information of the first statement inside the second one.)

The man. Mary talked to the man.	THE MAN THAT MARY TALKED
He is in New York now.	TO IS IN NEW YORK NOW.
The book. John bought the book.	THE BOOK THAT JOHN BOUGHT
It is not very expensive.	IS NOT VERY EXPENSIVE.

7. The doctor. Mary called the doctor. He came yesterday.
8. The car. John wants the car. It can go a hundred and twenty miles an hour.
9. The cake. Mary made the cake. It smells good.
10. The men. John spoke to the men. They are teachers.
11. The book. You ordered the book. It came yesterday.
12. The man. I talked to the man. He is from Spain.
13. The book. John was looking at the book. It is at home.

Exercise 4. Practice the use of pattern O relative clauses. Answer the question and include the information of the statement in the answer.

Mary sang a song.	YES, THE SONG THAT
Was the song beautiful?	MARY SANG WAS BEAUTIFUL.
John described a house.	YES, I SAW THE HOUSE
Did you see the house?	THAT JOHN DESCRIBED.

1. You read a book. Was the book interesting?
2. Mr. Smith wrote a book. Should I buy the book?
3. John spoke to a man. Is Mr. Miller the man?
4. John described a book. Was the book interesting?

5. The teacher pronounced some words. Did you repeat the words?
6. John saw a letter. Was it from Mr. Miller?
7. John lives in a new house. Is the house on Fifth Street?
8. Mary spoke about a man. Do you know him?
9. John drank some coffee. Did Mary make the coffee?

A.2   Notice the use of *whose* in relative clauses.

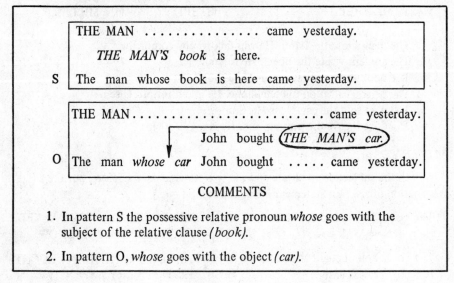

THE MAN . . . . came yesterday.

    THE MAN'S book is here.

S | The man whose book is here came yesterday.

THE MAN. . . . . came yesterday.

    John bought *THE MAN'S car.*

O | The man *whose car* John bought . . . . . came yesterday.

COMMENTS

1. In pattern S the possessive relative pronoun *whose* goes with the subject of the relative clause *(book)*.

2. In pattern O, *whose* goes with the object *(car)*.

Exercise 5. Practice pattern S. Listen to the statements. Form a new statement which contains the clause *whose father visited our class.*

John met the girl.   JOHN MET THE GIRL WHOSE
  The girl's father visited our class.   FATHER VISITED OUR CLASS.

1. John called the girl. The girl's father visited our class.
2. John wrote to the girl. The girl's father visited our class.
3. The girl went downtown. The girl's father . . . . .
4. John waited for the girl. The girl's father . . . . .
5. The girl took off her hat. The girl's father . . . . .
6. The girl left early. The girl's father . . . . .
7. John knows the girl. The girl's father . . . . .
8. The girl is looking for her brother. The girl's father . . . . .
9. The girl is going to buy a new book. The girl's father . . . . .
10. The girl is talking with John. The girl's father . . . . .
11. The girl answered all the questions. The girl's father . . . . .

Exercise 6. Practice pattern O. Listen to the statements. Form a new statement which contains the clause *whose home we visited* (modifying *teacher*).

The teacher bought a new car. THE TEACHER WHOSE HOME
We visited the teacher's home.   WE VISITED BOUGHT A NEW CAR.

John helped the teacher. JOHN HELPED THE TEACHER
We visited the teacher's home.   WHOSE HOME WE VISITED.

1. Mr. Smith introduced the teacher. We visited the teacher's home.
2. The teacher laughed at the joke. We visited the teacher's home.
3. The teacher lent John a book. We visited . . . . .
4. John lent his pen to the teacher. We visited . . . . .
5. The teacher likes to listen to jazz. We visited . . . . .
6. Mr. Smith called up the teacher. We visited . . . . .
7. The teacher sings well. We visited . . . . .
8. John wrote to the teacher. We visited . . . . .

NOTE TO ADVANCED STUDENTS: The relative clauses which have been presented in this lesson are called limiting, restrictive, or defining relative clauses. There is also a second type, called additive, nonrestrictive, or appositive relative clauses. For example:

RESTRICTIVE:
The girl who lives in New York brought the book.

ADDITIVE:
Mary, who lives in New York, brought the book.

Restrictive clauses help identify or define the noun phrases which they modify. Additive clauses, on the other hand, give further information which is not essential to the meaning or identification of the noun phrase; they are equivalent to separate statements.

Notice that additive relative clauses are set off by commas in writing and by pauses in speaking. *That* cannot be used in additive clauses.

NOTE: In the following relative clauses the word *ever* means "at any time."

Mr. Miller is the tallest man that I *ever* saw.
Mr. Miller is the tallest man that *ever* entered this room.
The best book that I *ever* read was an old one.

Each sentence contains a noun preceded by a superlative form of an adjective (*tallest, best*) and followed by a relative clause containing *ever.*

185

A.3 Notice the relative clauses with *that is* and the equivalent expression without *that is*.

A	The man *that is talking to Mary* is Mr. Smith.
B	The man *talking to Mary* is Mr. Smith.

C	The book *that is on the table* is expensive.
D	The book *on the table* is expensive.

COMMENTS

1. There is no change in meaning when *that + be* is omitted from a relative clause.

2. It is especially common to delete *that + be* from a relative clause when *be* is followed by (1) an *-ing* form of verb, e.g. *talking* (see example B) or (2) a prepositional phrase, e.g. *on the table* (see example D).

3. Sentences like example D were introduced and practiced in Lesson 9.

ADDITIONAL EXAMPLES

The man (that is) sitting in the car is my brother.
My brother is the man (that is) sitting in the car.
The student (that is) from Canada speaks French.
The store (that is) near the bank sells briefcases.

Exercise 7. Repeat the following sentences and delete *that + be*.

I gave the book to the man that is writing the letter.	I GAVE THE BOOK TO THE MAN WRITING THE LETTER.
The book that is on the table is not very expensive.	THE BOOK ON THE TABLE IS NOT VERY EXPENSIVE.

1. The student that is watching television is from Peru.
2. A girl that is from your country is studying here.
3. The girl that is writing the letter is going to study economics.
4. Mr. Miller is the man that is speaking to the students.
5. The boy that was wearing a red hat kicked the ball.
6. The bookstore that is on State Street is very good.
7. We talked to the old man that was sitting beside the road.
8. The doctor that is in your class is from Mexico.
9. Who is the man that is talking to John?
10. The restaurant that is on the corner serves good meals.

186

(*That* + *be* can be deleted when it is followed by a phrase containing *as . . . as* or *like*.)

11. I never read a book that was as good as that one.
12. I'm going to get a bicycle that is like yours.
13. I want a shirt that is as colorful as John's.
14. There aren't many cities that are as beautiful as this one.

NOTE FOR ADVANCED STUDENTS: *That* may be omitted from the relative clause in the following sentence.

I saw a fish that weighed thirty pounds.

If *that* is omitted, the verb must be replaced with its *-ing* form:

I saw a fish *weighing* thirty pounds.

Only a small number of relative clauses can be changed in this way. It depends on the verb. The clauses which can be changed correspond to sentences containing verbs that cannot occur in the *-ing* form.

The fish was ~~weighing~~ 30 pounds.

Some additional examples:

Peter bought a bicycle *that cost* $1.00.
Peter bought a bicycle *costing* $1.00.

He used a relative clause *that began* with *that is*.
He used a relative clause *beginning* with *that is*.

He wrote a sentence *that contained* a relative clause.
He wrote a sentence *containing* a relative clause.

I read a book *that describes* the early history of California.
I read a book *describing* the early history of California.

The book *that belongs* to Mr. Smith is on the table.
The book *belonging to* Mr. Smith is on the table.

B.1 Notice the use of *for* and *during*.

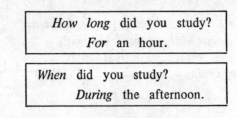

> How *long* did you study?
> *For* an hour.

> *When* did you study?
> *During* the afternoon.

COMMENTS

1. *For* is used with noun phrases which denote a quantity of time, such as *an hour, two hours, eight weeks, a long time. For* answers the question "how long?"

2. *During* is used with noun phrases which refer to a period of time, such as *the afternoon, the course, the summer. During* answers the question "when?"

ILLUSTRATIVE EXAMPLES WITH *FOR* AND *DURING*

How long did you study?

We studied *for*	one	hour.
We studied *for*	twenty	minutes.
We studied *for*	several	days.
We studied *for*	a few	minutes.
We studied *for*	an	hour.
We studied *for*	a little	while.
We studied *for*	a long	time.

When did you study?

We studied *during* our vacation.
We studied *during* the summer.
We studied *during* the afternoon.
We studied *during* the day.
We studied *during* the noon hour.

NOTE: *For* may be omitted. It doesn't change the meaning. However, *during* may not be omitted.

Exercise 8. Practice the use of *for* and *during*.

two hours	I WORKED HARD FOR TWO HOURS.
the summer	I WORKED HARD DURING THE SUMMER.
several days	I WORKED HARD FOR SEVERAL DAYS.
the course	I WORKED HARD DURING THE COURSE.
a little while	I WORKED HARD FOR A LITTLE WHILE.

1. the night	4. the afternoon	7. six years	10. two days
2. three weeks	5. a few minutes	8. the day	11. several hours
3. many years	6. the evening	9. my vacation	12. the school year

B.2   Notice the use of *while* and *when*.

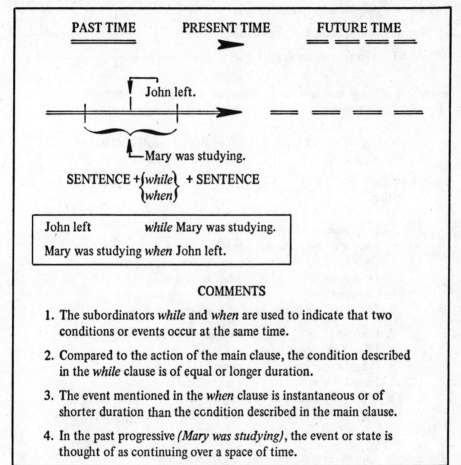

SENTENCE + {*while* / *when*} + SENTENCE

John left *while* Mary was studying.

Mary was studying *when* John left.

COMMENTS

1. The subordinators *while* and *when* are used to indicate that two conditions or events occur at the same time.

2. Compared to the action of the main clause, the condition described in the *while* clause is of equal or longer duration.

3. The event mentioned in the *when* clause is instantaneous or of shorter duration than the condition described in the main clause.

4. In the past progressive *(Mary was studying)*, the event or state is thought of as continuing over a space of time.

NOTE: *When* is sometimes used in place of *while*. However, *while* can never be used in place of *when*.

ADDITIONAL EXAMPLES

The time in the first part of the sentence below is represented by the line or lines above the shaft of the arrow, the time in the second part by the line or lines below the shaft.

The phone rang while I was studying.

I was studying when the phone rang.

Mary was reading while John was writing.

John left when the bus arrived.

Exercise 9. Change the statements with *when* to similar statements with *while*. Change the statements with *while* to similar statements with *when*.

I was studying *when* my friends arrived.	MY FRIENDS ARRIVED WHILE I WAS STUDYING.
John came *while* I was eating.	I WAS EATING WHEN JOHN CAME.

1. I was reading when the storm began.
2. I was working when he opened the door.
3. I was having a cup of coffee when he took my picture.
4. I was practicing my lesson when he arrived.
5. I was watching the baseball game when it began to rain.
6. I was listening to some music when the phone rang.

7. I dropped the book while I was drinking some tomato juice.
8. I found the pencil while I was moving the furniture.
9. It began to snow while I was working in the garden.
10. I saw John while I was walking to class.
11. John came while I was writing a letter.
12. The taxi broke down while I was going to the airport.

Exercise 10. Join the two statements using *when* or *while*.

I was studying. My friends arrived.	I WAS STUDYING WHEN MY FRIENDS ARRIVED.
I arrived. John was working.	I ARRIVED WHILE JOHN WAS WORKING.

1. John was watching television. I began to write.
2. I dropped the book. I was walking to class.
3. I was cleaning my room. I found the pencil.
4. John was listening to the radio. The phone rang.
5. It began to rain. John was fixing his bicycle.

6. Mary was playing the piano. John answered the telephone.
7. The child woke up. Mary was sleeping.
8. The train was moving. Mary got off.
9. John called. Mary was playing the piano.

B.3 Notice the use of *before, until,* and *after* in expressions of time.

$$\left\{ \begin{array}{l} before \\ until \\ after \end{array} \right\} + \begin{array}{l} \text{EMBEDDED} \\ \text{SENTENCE} \end{array}$$

The phone rang				*before*	John	arrived.
Mary studied				*until*	John	arrived.
Mary turned on the radio				*after*	John	arrived.

$$\left\{ \begin{array}{l} before \\ until \\ after \end{array} \right\} + \text{NOUN PHRASE}$$

The phone rang				*before*	five o'clock.
Mary studied				*until*	five o'clock.
Mary turned on the radio				*after*	five o'clock.

COMMENT

The subordinators *before, until,* and *after* can be followed by an embedded sentence *(John arrived)* or by a noun phrase *(five o'clock).*

NOTES:

(1) With the subordinators *before* and *after* you may also use an *-ing* verb expression:

> Mary studied before *eating.*
> Paul left after *getting his money.*

In such sentences the subject of the *-ing* expression is assumed to be identical with the main subject *(Mary* and *Paul* in the examples). Note that "to eat" or "to get" cannot be used here. Never say "before to eat" or "after to get the money."

(2) Do not use *until* with expressions of place or distance: "until today" is correct, but not "until the drugstore." Use *as far as* with expressions of place: "as far as the drugstore."

Exercise 11. Listen to the statements, which begin with a subordinator. Put the subordinated phrase or clause after the main clause.

Before he went to the movies, John ate supper.	JOHN ATE SUPPER BEFORE HE WENT TO THE MOVIES.
Until he ate a sandwich, John was very hungry.	JOHN WAS VERY HUNGRY UNTIL HE ATE A SANDWICH.

1. Before he went to New York, Mr. Miller bought an umbrella.
2. After breakfast, Mr. Smith went to work.
3. Before lunch, John wrote a letter to his parents.
4. After she ate lunch, Mary went to the museum.
5. Before dinner, John watched television.
6. Until it got dark, John and Paul played tennis.
7. After they heard the weather report, Mr. and Mrs. Smith left for California.
8. Until he was ten years old, John lived in a small town.
9. After it saw the cat, the dog made a lot of noise.

NOTE: The words *after* and *afterwards* are different. *Afterwards* means "later," "after that," "then," or "at a later time."

Compare the following sentences:

1. He went to class *after* he ate breakfast.
2. John ate breakfast. *Afterwards* he went to class.

The meanings of 1 and 2 are the same. However, the order in which the information is presented is different.

Lesson 18

A. The present perfect: *have studied*
B. The present perfect progressive: *have been studying*
C. The past perfect: *had studied*
D. Short answers: *Yes, I have; No, I haven't.*
E. Irregular verbs: *go, went, gone,* etc.

A.1 Notice the use of *have* and the past participle.

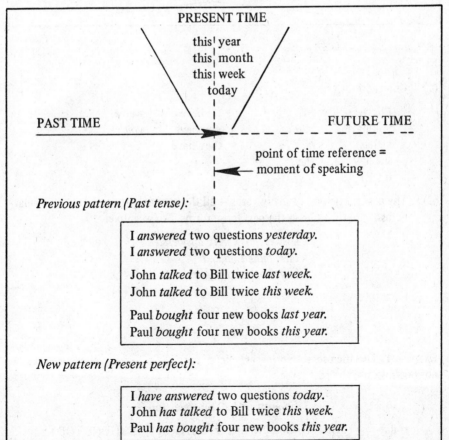

PRESENT TIME

this year
this month
this week
today

PAST TIME   FUTURE TIME

point of time reference =
← moment of speaking

Previous pattern (Past tense):

> I *answered* two questions *yesterday.*
> I *answered* two questions *today.*
>
> John *talked* to Bill twice *last week.*
> John *talked* to Bill twice *this week.*
>
> Paul *bought* four new books *last year.*
> Paul *bought* four new books *this year.*

New pattern (Present perfect):

> I *have answered* two questions *today.*
> John *has talked* to Bill twice *this week.*
> Paul *has bought* four new books *this year.*

COMMENTS

(1)   In the example sentences of the previous pattern, the events occurred before the moment of speaking. Therefore, it is possible to use the past tense in these sentences.

(2)   In the example sentences of the new pattern, the events occurred before the moment of speaking also. However, since the events occurred in the present time (today, this week, this year), the present perfect can be used. It is used when the speaker wishes to indicate that the event is relevant (important) in the present or future time. (For further explanation, see the note following Exercise 3.)

(3)   Notice that the adverbials *today, this week, this year* all refer to the present time. Past time adverbials *yesterday, last night, a minute ago, before John came,* cannot be used with the present perfect. Therefore, the following sentence is incorrect:

~~I have opened the window *a minute ago.*~~
~~PAST TIME~~

NOTES:

(1)   Contractions.

I have	*I've*	we have	*we've*
you have	*you've*	you have	*you've*
he has	*he's*	they have	*they've*
she has	*she's*		
it has	*it's*		

(2)   The past participles of many verbs — all the regular verbs and many irregular verbs — are the same as the past tense forms. For example:

answer, *answered, answered*
talk, *talked, talked*
buy, *bought, bought*

Exercise 1. Use the present perfect *whenever possible* in this exercise. When it is not possible, use the past tense.

John answered all our questions.

today   JOHN HAS ANSWERED ALL OUR QUESTIONS TODAY.

last night   JOHN ANSWERED ALL OUR QUESTIONS LAST NIGHT.

give a talk

1. yesterday	7. today
2. ten minutes ago	8. before he ate breakfast
3. this morning	9. this week
4. this week	10. before he came to class
5. before George came	11. from seven o'clock to eight o'clock
6. last week	this morning

NOTE: The present perfect is also used with *just* and *recently* in order to indicate that something that happened a short time ago is still relevant (important) in the present time:

> John has *just* opened the window.
> Mary has *recently* written home.
> John has given a talk *recently*.

The expression *so far* means "to the moment of speaking."

> We've completed 17 lessons *so far.*
> I've lived in this city one month and have liked it *so far.*

A.2 Notice the use of *since* and *for.*

> We have studied *since seven o'clock.*
> John has waited *for twenty minutes.*

COMMENT

In the sentences above, the present perfect forms (*have studied, has waited*) describe actions (or situations) which began in the past and which *continue in the present time.*

NOTES:

(1) A form of *have* and the past participle is required with any verb which is modified by a time expression beginning with *since.* For example:

> She has waited *since* early this morning.

(2) Time adverbials beginning with *for* may be used in present perfect sentences and also in past tense sentences. In the latter case (that is, past tense) the sentences do not express the idea that the action (or situation) has continued to the present time. Examples:

> I have studied for two years. (= the last two years)
> I studied for two years. (any two years, for
> example, five to seven years ago)

(3) A time expression which follows *since* represents *a point in time:*

> since seven o'clock
> since yesterday
> since last week

195

A time expression which follows *for* represents *a quantity of time:*

>for two hours
>for three days
>for a week

(4)   Negative present perfect sentences are formed by adding *n't* (or *not*) to the auxiliary *have.*

>John *hasn't* eaten breakfast.
>We *haven't* studied since yesterday.

Compare sentences where *have* is not used as an auxiliary.

>John *doesn't have* our bicycle.
>We *don't have* any red pencils.
>We *don't have* to study tonight.

Exercise 2. Practice *since* and *for* with the present perfect of verbs expressing states or situations.

Bill *owns this house.* He bought it in January.	BILL *HAS OWNED THIS HOUSE* SINCE JANUARY.
Jane *belongs to the club.* She joined it three weeks ago.	JANE *HAS BELONGED TO THE CLUB* FOR THREE WEEKS.

1. We *know this song.* We learned it three weeks ago.
2. We *know Mr. Smith.* We met him three weeks ago.
3. The Johnsons *live in Canada.* They moved there in January.
4. Mrs. Brown *holds the position of treasurer.* She obtained the position in January.
5. George *has a cold.* He caught it three weeks ago.
6. Betty *owes me a dollar.* She borrowed it in January.
7. Alice *is in the hospital.* She went there three weeks ago.
8. Charles *belongs to the Socialist Party.* He joined it in January.
9. Dr. Hill *owns this machine.* He bought it three weeks ago.

Exercise 3. Listen to the statements. They tell about situations that began in the past and continue to the present. Give the same information using the present perfect.

I liked American movies in 1965, and I like them now.	I'VE LIKED AMERICAN MOVIES SINCE 1965.
I wanted to see this movie a year ago, and I want to see it now.	I'VE WANTED TO SEE THIS MOVIE FOR A YEAR.
I had blond hair when I was a child, and I still have blond hair now.	I'VE HAD BLOND HAIR EVER SINCE I WAS A CHILD.

1. I needed a new coat two years ago, and I need one now.
2. I wanted to visit Washington when I came to the United States, and I still want to visit it.
3. I stopped smoking last Monday, and I haven't smoked again. *(on monday) for the last time*
4. Monday was the last time I played baseball. *(on monday)*
5. I liked fish when I was a child, and I like it now.
6. I preferred history at the beginning of the course, and I still prefer it.
7. I began to like languages ten years ago, and I like them now.
8. I started to collect stamps in 1968, and I still collect stamps now.
9. I began to attend the university three years ago, and I still attend the university now.
10. I began to work here in March, and I still work here now.

NOTE: In general, the present perfect (that is, *have* + past participle) is used when the action or state described is one which is relevant at the time of speaking. Thus the present perfect is used only when one of the following two conditions is met:

1) The state described by the verb or the results of the action continue into the present.

> John has been here for ten minutes. (He is here now.)
> John has opened the window. (It is still open.)

Compare:

> John was here for ten minutes. (He is somewhere else now.)
> John opened the window. (Perhaps it is closed now.)

2) The action described by the verb can be repeated in the present or future.

> John has visited New York three times. (He can visit it again.)

Compare:

> George Washington visited New York many times.

In questions, the use of *have* indicates that the action or situation described is still possible at the time of speaking or in the future. For example, the question "Have you eaten breakfast?" will be used only in the morning, when it is still possible to eat breakfast. It will not be used at suppertime or in the evening.

Consider also these negative examples:

A. I haven't eaten breakfast this morning.
B. I didn't eat breakfast this morning.

Sentence A can be used in the morning, but later in the day, when you can no longer change the situation, you should use Sentence B.

Similarly, Sentence C below asks about something which is possible to do, while Sentence D asks about something which can no longer be done.

C. Have you seen the President on TV?
D. Did you ever see John F. Kennedy in person?

If you are presently in the United States, people might ask you questions similar to the following:

> Have you visited New York?
> Have you seen the Rocky Mountains?

The use of *have* in the above sentences implies that it is still possible for you to visit New York or see the Rocky Mountains. In your own country, after you have returned from a visit to the United States, the questions will most likely be formed with *did:*

> Did you visit New York?
> Did you see the Rocky Mountains?

If, on the other hand, you make repeated trips to the United States, these questions could be formed with *have* also, since opportunities to visit places in the United States will recur in the future.

B. Notice the use of the present perfect progressive.

1	John has studied.	*have* + participle
2	+ John is studying.	*be* + *studying*
3	= John has been studying.	*have* + participle *be* + *studying*

COMMENTS

(1)　Sentence 1 states that John studied and that this is relevant in the present.

(2)　Sentence 2 states that John is studying now.

(3)　Sentence 3 states that John's studying began in the past and is continuing in the present. The fact that the studying continues (is in progress) in the present time is emphasized.

Exercise 4. Listen to the sentences in the present progressive. Make sentences in the present perfect progressive. Include "for two hours" in your sentences.

John is talking to the teacher.	JOHN HAS BEEN TALKING TO THE TEACHER FOR TWO HOURS.
The teacher is explaining a difficult pattern.	THE TEACHER HAS BEEN EXPLAINING A DIFFICULT PATTERN FOR TWO HOURS.
Mary is watching television.	MARY HAS BEEN WATCHING TELEVISION FOR TWO HOURS.

1. John is working.
2. John is studying at the library.
3. Mary is singing folk songs.

4. George is painting a picture.
5. Paul is looking up words in the dictionary.
6. Bill is writing letters.
7. Bob is listening to the radio.
8. Mrs. Miller is talking to Mrs. Allen.
9. John is studying mathematics.
10. George is doing his homework.

Exercise 5. Practice *since* and *for* with the present perfect progressive of verbs expressing activities or events.

The phone is *ringing.* It started two minutes ago.	THE PHONE *HAS BEEN RINGING* FOR TWO MINUTES.
The water is *running.* I turned it on at nine o'clock.	THE WATER *HAS BEEN RUNNING* SINCE NINE O'CLOCK.

1. We're *discussing politics.* We started an hour ago.
2. The police are *helping us.* They started helping us at nine o'clock.
3. Mr. Jones is *listening to the radio.* He turned it on an hour ago.
4. The children are *watching television.* They started watching at nine o'clock.
5. The engine is *running smoothly.* It started an hour ago.
6. Billy is *wearing his mother's glasses.* He put them on ten minutes ago.
7. Barbara is *studying Greek.* She started in September.
8. Paul is *playing the piano.* He started playing an hour ago.
9. It's *raining.* It started at nine o'clock.
10. The refrigerator is *making funny noises.* It started half an hour ago.

C. Notice the use of the past perfect: *had* + participle.

A	John answered all the questions correctly.
B	He *had studied* very hard.

COMMENT

Both sentences A and B are about the past. But the use of *had* + participle indicates that the action described in sentence B happened *before* that described in sentence A.

Exercise 6. Combine two sentences to form a new one which contains the word *because.* When you change the order of the two sentences, use the past perfect.

John studied very hard. He answered all the questions correctly.	JOHN ANSWERED ALL THE QUESTIONS CORRECTLY BECAUSE HE HAD STUDIED VERY HARD.

> Mary played tennis all afternoon yesterday. She was tired last night.

> MARY WAS TIRED LAST NIGHT BECAUSE SHE HAD PLAYED TENNIS ALL AFTERNOON.

1. The boys walked for a long time. Then they decided to rest.
2. Mary waited for the bus for a long time. She decided to take a taxi.
3. John needed a new coat for a long time. He bought one yesterday.
4. Mary saved enough money for a plane ticket. She went to Europe.
5. John worked hard all year. He took a long vacation.
6. John's old car broke down. He bought a new one.
7. John slept for ten hours. He was wide awake yesterday morning.
8. John practiced for many years. He played the piano very well yesterday.

NOTES:

(1) *Had* + participle is used to indicate that something happened before something else. However, when the words *before* or *after* are included in the sentence, it is not absolutely necessary to use the past perfect. The simple past is sufficient. For example, *had* is optional in the following sentences.

> George packed his suitcase immediately after he (had) decided to go.
> Susan (had) finished her homework before she went to the meeting.

(2) To indicate that one activity was in progress before some other action in the past, we use the form *had been* VERB-*ing*.

> John had been walking in the park before it rained.
> George had been writing letters before Paul came.

This grammar point is practiced in Exercise 26 in Review Lesson 20.

D. Notice the question pattern and the use of short answers.

QUESTION	Have you visited the museum?
ANSWERS	Yes, I have.
	No, I haven't.

ANSWERS

Yes, I have.	No, I haven't.
Yes, you have.	No, you haven't.
Yes, he has.	No, he hasn't.
Yes, we have.	No, we haven't.
Yes, you have.	No, you haven't.
Yes, they have.	No, they haven't.

Exercise 7. Short answers. (Individually)

Have you visited New York?   YES, I HAVE. (NO, I HAVEN'T.)

Have you seen the Empire   YES, I HAVE. (NO, I HAVEN'T.)
State Building?

1. Have you read any interesting books recently?
2. Have you received any letters from your family this week?
3. Have you had any coffee today?
4. Have you learned any new words today?
5. Have you seen any American football games?
6. Have you played American football?
7. Have you studied mathematics?
8. Have you attended any concerts this semester?

NOTE: *Had* and *hadn't* complete the short answers to questions beginning with *had*.

Had he completed his studies when he went to France?

Yes, he had.

E.1 Notice the irregular verbs. The past tense and past participle forms (second and third forms) are the same for each of these verbs.

read	read	have read	cost	cost	have cost
feed	fed	have fed	cut	cut	have cut
bleed	bled	have bled	hit	hit	have hit
lead	led	have led	hurt	hurt	have hurt
meet	met	have met	put	put	have put
			let	let	have let
keep	kept	have kept	set	set	have set
sleep	slept	have slept	find	found	have found
sweep	swept	have swept	bind	bound	have bound
feel	felt	have felt	wind	wound	have wound
deal	dealt	have dealt			
mean	meant	have meant	bring	brought	have brought
leave	left	have left	think	thought	have thought
			catch	caught	have caught
bend	bent	have bent	teach	taught	have taught
lend	lent	have lent	buy	bought	have bought
send	sent	have sent	fight	fought	have fought
spend	spent	have spent			
build	built	have built	sell	sold	have sold
			tell	told	have told
say	said	have said			
hold	held	have held	sit	sat	have sat
			shoot	shot	have shot
have	had	have had	slide	slid	have slid
make	made	have made			
stand	stood	have stood	lose	lost	have lost
understand	understood	have understood			

Exercise 8. Listen to the statement. Expand the statement with *but . . . since.* Use *haven't* and *hasn't* in the added part. In this exercise, omit time expressions after the word *since.* The time expressions are already in the sentence and are therefore not repeated. They are understood.

I met several architects last year.	I MET SEVERAL ARCHITECTS LAST YEAR, BUT I HAVEN'T MET ANY SINCE.
I read a French book last semester.	I READ A FRENCH BOOK LAST SEMESTER, BUT I HAVEN'T READ ANY SINCE.

1. I sent Mary two letters last week.
2. I spent some money last Friday.
3. John lent me something a week ago.
4. I made some mistakes yesterday.
5. He had two operations last month.
6. My brother cut some wood last week.

7. I put some paper there an hour ago.
8. He left a package last Tuesday.
9. Last month he said some intelligent things.
10. Mary brought two notebooks to class last week.
11. I bought a shirt last summer.
12. I taught a lot of English two years ago.
13. The teacher told us a story last week.
14. He sold a lot of hats last week.
15. We kept records of our income in 1969.
16. They fed us some meat last week.
17. They held three meetings two weeks ago.
18. Mr. Miller built two houses last summer.
19. I found some money two years ago.
20. John lost some weight five years ago.
21. Mary set some fresh flowers on the table last month.

E.2 Notice the irregular verbs. In most cases, the three forms differ from each other.

drive	drove	have driven	sing	sang	have sung
write	wrote	have written	sink	sank	have sunk
ride	rode	have ridden	ring	rang	have rung
			drink	drank	have drunk
break	broke	have broken	shrink	shrank	have shrunk
wake	woke	have woken	begin	began	have begun
choose	chose	have chosen	swim	swam	have swum
freeze	froze	have frozen	run	ran	have run
speak	spoke	have spoken			
steal	stole	have stolen	swing	swung	have swung
wear	wore	have worn	wring	wrung	have wrung
tear	tore	have torn	win	won	have won
swear	swore	have sworn	hang	hung	have hung
			dig	dug	have dug
blow	blew	have blown	strike	struck	have struck
grow	grew	have grown			
know	knew	have known	get	got	have gotten
throw	threw	have thrown	forget	forgot	have forgotten
fly	flew	have flown			
			bite	bit	have bitten
draw	drew	have drawn	hide	hid	have hidden
eat	ate	have eaten	see	saw	have seen
give	gave	have given	lie	lay	have lain
come	came	have come	go	went	have gone
become	became	have become	do	did	have done
			be	was	have been
fall	fell	have fallen			
shake	shook	have shaken	show	showed	have shown
take	took	have taken			

Exercise 9. Make replies beginning with the word *but*. Use the present perfect.

He didn't write anything yesterday.	BUT HE HAS WRITTEN SOMETHING TODAY.
He didn't break anything yesterday.	BUT HE HAS BROKEN SOMETHING TODAY.

1. He didn't eat anything yesterday.
2. He didn't take anything yesterday.
3. He didn't sing anything yesterday.
4. He didn't drink anything yesterday.
5. He didn't begin anything yesterday.
6. He didn't get anything yesterday.
7. He didn't forget anything yesterday.
8. He didn't hide anything yesterday.
9. He didn't see anything yesterday.
10. He didn't do anything yesterday.
11. He didn't give anything yesterday.
12. He didn't break anything yesterday.
13. He didn't choose anything yesterday.
14. He didn't tear anything yesterday.
15. He didn't throw anything yesterday.
16. He didn't draw anything yesterday.
17. He didn't shoot anything yesterday.
18. He didn't steal anything yesterday.
19. He didn't bite anything yesterday.

Exercise 10. Make replies beginning with the word *but*. Use the present perfect.

He didn't drive a car yesterday.	BUT HE HAS DRIVEN ONE TODAY.
He didn't sing a song yesterday.	BUT HE HAS SUNG ONE TODAY.

1. He didn't write a letter yesterday.
2. He didn't eat an apple yesterday.
3. He didn't take a picture yesterday.
4. He didn't drink a cup of coffee yesterday.
5. He didn't win a game of chess yesterday.
6. He didn't hang up a picture yesterday.
7. He didn't do a homework exercise yesterday.
8. He didn't break a glass yesterday.
9. He didn't wear a tie yesterday.
10. He didn't tear a piece of paper yesterday.

Exercise 11. (for advanced students). Listen to the statement and to the words that follow it. Combine them to form a new sentence. Notice that, if the main verb is in a past tense, the verb of the *that*-clause is in a past tense. If the original statement was expressed in the past tense, the verb of the *that*-clause can be in the past perfect tense.

"You look very happy." She told me—	SHE TOLD ME THAT I LOOKED VERY HAPPY.
He is going to graduate soon. He wrote me—	HE WROTE ME THAT HE WAS GOING TO GRADUATE SOON.
Apollo 11 landed on the moon. They announced—	THEY ANNOUNCED THAT APOLLO 11 HAD LANDED ON THE MOON.
We have been working very hard. You knew—	YOU KNEW THAT WE HAD BEEN WORKING VERY HARD.

1. It is raining. I thought—
2. I am wrong. I admitted—
3. It is time to leave. He reminded his wife—
4. They often speak Spanish in class. I realized—
5. He left his billfold home. John realized—
6. She's going to Europe this summer. She told me—
7. Henry sings beautifully. They told us—
8. "I'm getting bored." She said—
9. "We're going to eat dinner in Detroit." They said—
10. He has been studying all day. His roommate noticed—
11. He'll write soon. He promised me— (use *would*)

(Use *if* or *whether* instead of *that* in the following responses:)

Do they want to buy my car? I asked them—	I ASKED THEM IF THEY WANTED TO BUY MY CAR.

12. Is he from Mexico or Venezuela? I wondered—
13. Will he be here soon? I wondered—
14. Did he turn the lights off? He couldn't remember—
15. Can Fred play tennis? I wasn't sure—
16. Has he been coming to class every day? I asked—
17. Is he still sick? I wanted to know—
18. Did he gain any weight? Did you notice—
19. Has he ever been in Hawaii? I asked him—
20. Does Martha know how to ski? Did you notice—

Lesson 19

A. Passive sentences: *The letters were written.*
B. The use of *still, any more, already,* and *yet.*
C. Past participles as modifiers: John is *interested.*
    Adjectives in *-ing:* The story is *interesting.*
D. Adjective + preposition combinations: *interested in* music, *excited about* music.

A. Notice the active and passive sentences.

PRESENT

ACTIVE	*They*	*write*	*letters*	every day.
			OBJECT	
PASSIVE	*Letters*	*are*	*written*	every day.
	SUBJECT	BE	PAST PARTICIPLE	

PAST

ACTIVE	They	*wrote*	*letters*	yesterday.
			OBJECT	
PASSIVE	*Letters*	*were*	*written*	yesterday.
	SUBJECT	BE	PAST PARTICIPLE	

COMMENTS

(1) The object of an active sentence is the subject of the corresponding passive sentence.

(2) In a passive sentence, a form of *be* appears before the main verb.

(3) In the active form, the tense is shown by the main verb (present *write,* past *wrote.*) In the passive form, the tense is shown by the form of *be:* present *am, is, are;* past *was, were.*

(4) The main verb of a passive sentence is in the past participle form.

206

NOTE:

	If the main verb of the active sentence is:	then *be* of the corresponding passive sentence is:
a)	present tense	present tense: *am, is, are*
b)	past tense	past tense: *was, were*
c)	infinitive	infinitive: *be*
d)	*-ing*	*-ing: being*
e)	past participle	past participle: *been*

		ACTIVE	PASSIVE
a)	SIMPLE PRESENT	They *write* letters every day.	Letters *are* written every day.
b)	SIMPLE PAST	They *wrote* letters yesterday.	Letters *were* written yesterday.
c)	INFINITIVE	They are going to *write* letters tomorrow.	Letters are going to *be* written tomorrow.
	(future with *will*)	They will *write* letters tomorrow.	Letters will *be* written tomorrow.
	(modal *should*)	They should *write* letters.	Letters should *be* written.
	(*have to*)	They have to *write* letters.	Letters have to *be* written.
d)	PROGRESSIVE	They are writ*ing* letters.	Letters are be*ing* written
		They were writ*ing* letters.	Letters were be*ing* written.
e)	PERFECT	They have writt*en* letters.	Letters have be*en* written.
		They had writt*en* letters.	Letters had be*en* written.

Exercise 1. Change the following active sentences into their corresponding passive sentences.

a)	They write letters every day.	LETTERS ARE WRITTEN EVERY DAY.
	Someone locks the door every night.	THE DOOR IS LOCKED EVERY NIGHT.

1. Someone explains the lesson every day.
2. Someone closes the window every day.
3. We need action now.
4. The government spends billions of dollars every year.
5. People lose many things every day.

b)

    6. They completed the building before I left.

    7. The teacher explained that lesson yesterday.

    8. They finished the building recently.

    9. Edison invented the electric light before I was born.

  10. Napoleon wrote that letter many years ago.

  11. Bizet composed the opera "Carmen" in the nineteenth century.

  12. The Romans built Rome a long time ago.

  13. Michelangelo painted that picture many years ago.

  14. The Egyptians constructed the pyramids many years ago.

c)

  15. We must stop inflation now.

  16. We should build more houses next year.

  17. We must build more hospitals immediately.

  18. You should answer their questions immediately.

  19. They will write letters tomorrow.

  20. They are going to write letters tomorrow.

  21. The doctor is going to perform the operation.

  22. They are going to bring the books tomorrow.

d)

  23. They are writing the letters.

  24. They are completing the building.

  25. They are reading the book now.

e)

  26. They have written letters.

  27. They have closed the windows.

  28. They have sharpened the pencils.

  29. They have done the homework.

  30. They have made the telephone call.

NOTES:

(1) Passive sentences are used in place of the corresponding active sentences when the subject of the active sentence is unimportant or unknown.

Where was that car made?

It was made in England.

The logical subject — the people who made the car — is unknown to the speaker.

In addition, passive sentences are used when the logical object of the verb is the topic of the discussion. In the following sentence, the letter — not its writer — is the main topic of discussion.

That letter was written many years ago.

Finally, passive sentences are used whenever the speaker (or writer) wants to delay or avoid mentioning the subject.

(2)   When the subject of an active sentence is expressed in the corresponding passive sentence, this logical subject is preceded by the preposition *by* and follows closely after the verb.

> Napoleon wrote that letter many years ago.
> That letter was written by Napoleon many years ago.

B.1   Notice the use of *still* and *any more.*

John	still	lives in New York.
John	still	doesn't own a car.
Mary	still	isn't here.
She is	still	in Chicago.
She can	still	skate very well.

Alice isn't here *any more.*

COMMENTS

(1)   The word *still* indicates that a situation continues the same as before, either affirmative or negative.

(2)   *Any more* is used in negative sentences to indicate that a situation existed before, but does not continue.

(3)   *Still* precedes main verbs and negative words, but usually follows *be* and auxiliaries such as *can.*

(4)   The normal position for *any more* is at the end of the sentence.

ADDITIONAL EXAMPLES

1. Carol lived in Japan when she was a child, and she can still speak Japanese.
2. Alice has been in Japan a year, but she still can't speak Japanese.
3. Ralph spoke both Japanese and English as a child, but he can't speak Japanese any more.

Exercise 2. Listen to the statements describing two situations, past and present. Summarize in one statement with *still* or *any more.*

Mary often played the piano last year. She doesn't play the piano now.	MARY DOESN'T PLAY THE PIANO ANY MORE.
John didn't play the piano before. He doesn't play the piano now.	JOHN STILL DOESN'T PLAY THE PIANO.
Paul played the piano two years ago. He plays the piano now.	PAUL STILL PLAYS THE PIANO.

1. The price was five dollars. The price is five dollars.
2. John was eating breakfast. John is eating breakfast now.
3. Mr. Black lived in New York. Mr. Black doesn't live in New York now.
4. Mr. Brown lived in New York. Mr. Brown lives in New York now.
5. Mr. Black had been living in New York. Mr. Black was living in New York when I left.
6. I wanted to study last night. I want to study now.
7. I tried to study yesterday. I am trying to study now.
8. He attended the university last semester. He doesn't attend the university now.
9. He didn't speak very well last year. He doesn't speak very well now.
10. I wanted him to study before. I want him to study now.
11. They complained about the heat last week. They are complaining now.
12. My father worked there last year. He doesn't work there now.

B.2 Notice the use of *already* and *yet.*

> Alice is in New York *already.*
> Paul hasn't read the book *yet.*

COMMENTS

(1) *Already* indicates a time earlier than expected. *Yet* indicates a time later than expected.

(2) *Already* applies to affirmative situations, and *yet* applies to negative situations.

NOTES:

(1) The meaning of *yet* includes the idea of a possible change in the situation: "Nobody in the class speaks French" simply describes the situation, but "Nobody in this class speaks French yet" may suggest that some of the students are making progress toward learning the language.

(2) *Already* can be placed either at the end of the sentence or in the middle. If it is placed in the middle, it comes before the main verb but after a form of *be* or an auxiliary.

(3) The usual position for *yet* is at the end of the sentence.

ADDITIONAL EXAMPLES

1. They know the answer already. (Or, they already know the answer.)
2. They're here already. (Or, they're already here.)
3. They've left already. (Or, they've already left.)
4. They aren't here yet.
5. We don't know the answer yet.
6. We haven't received the information yet.

Exercise 3. Repeat the following statements and include *already* or *yet*. For example:

It's only eight o'clock and Dr. Brown is here.	IT'S ONLY EIGHT O'CLOCK AND DR. BROWN IS HERE ALREADY.
The class should begin now, but Mr. Green isn't here.	THE CLASS SHOULD BEGIN NOW, BUT MR. GREEN ISN'T HERE YET.
It's only 10:55, but the eleven o'clock class has begun.	IT'S ONLY 10:55, BUT THE ELEVEN O'CLOCK CLASS HAS BEGUN ALREADY.

1. They didn't expect to come early, but they are here.
2. They expected to come yesterday, but they aren't here.
3. I expected them yesterday, but they aren't here.
4. I expected them today, but they haven't come.
5. They had a lot of work, but they have finished.
6. I expected them to go later, but they have left.
7. I expected them to go early, but they haven't left.
8. They had very little work today, but they haven't finished.
9. We have just started to work, but Mr. Appleton is tired.
10. We had just started to work when you came, but Mr. Appleton was tired.
11. I'm waiting for a friend, but he hasn't come.
12. These students began to study English a short time ago, but they speak very well.

C. Notice the use of past participles and *-ing* forms of verbs.

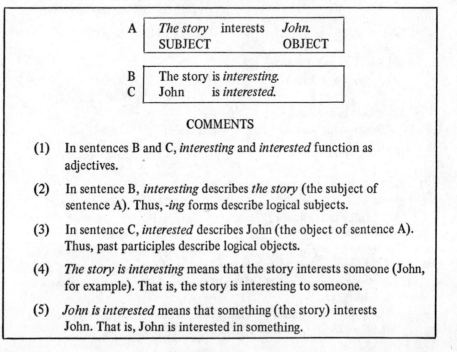

A	*The story*	interests	*John.*
	SUBJECT		OBJECT

B	The story is *interesting.*
C	John is *interested.*

COMMENTS

(1) In sentences B and C, *interesting* and *interested* function as adjectives.

(2) In sentence B, *interesting* describes *the story* (the subject of sentence A). Thus, *-ing* forms describe logical subjects.

(3) In sentence C, *interested* describes John (the object of sentence A). Thus, past participles describe logical objects.

(4) *The story is interesting* means that the story interests someone (John, for example). That is, the story is interesting to someone.

(5) *John is interested* means that something (the story) interests John. That is, John is interested in something.

NOTES:

(1) The sentences of this frame that contain a past participle are very similar to passive sentences.

Past Participle Used as an Adjective:

The dish is *broken.*

Passive Sentence:

The dish was broken by John.

(2) The sentence *The dish was broken* can be interpreted either way. In one case, *broken* is like an adjective which describes the condition of the dish. In the other interpretation the sentence is passive and it reports an event: Someone broke the dish.

(3) Many past participles and *-ing* forms can be used in front of nouns in the same way as ordinary adjectives.

John is interested. He is an *interested* person.
The story is interesting. It is an *interesting* story.
The *excited* people were listening to an *exciting* speech.

Exercise 4. Produce sentences which contain past participles and *-ing* words used as adjectives.

The story interested John.
  (Describe the story.)   THE STORY WAS INTERESTING.
                                               (THE STORY IS INTERESTING.)

(Describe John.)   JOHN WAS INTERESTED.

Mr. Smith closed the door.
  (Describe the door.)   THE DOOR IS CLOSED.
                                               (THE DOOR WAS CLOSED.)
The movie bored John.
  (Describe the movie.)   THE MOVIE WAS BORING.

(Describe John.)   JOHN WAS BORED.

1. Mrs. Smith broke the dish. (Describe the dish.)
2. Mr. Smith was watching some children. The children amused Mr. Smith.
    (Describe the children.) (Describe Mr. Smith.)
3. It was an intelligent answer. It surprised the people. (Describe the answer.)
    (Describe the people.)
4. The good news excited John. (Describe the news.) (Describe John.)
5. The long answer confused Mr. Miller. (Describe the answer.) (Describe
    Mr. Miller.)
6. The explanation convinced the class. (Describe the explanation.) (Describe
    the class.)

7. The tiger frightened the little boy. (Describe the tiger.) (Describe the little boy.)
8. The news disappointed the class. (Describe the news.) (Describe the class.)
9. The trip tired the professor. (Describe the trip.) (Describe the professor.)
10. John's story amazed the class. (Describe the story.) (Describe the class.)
11. The animals entertained the children. (Describe the animals.) (Describe the children.)
12. The magazine disgusted the artist. (Describe the magazine.) (Describe the artist.)

D. Notice the use of adjective + preposition combinations.

> John is *interested in* classical music.
> Mary is *interested in* attending a concert.
> George is *excited about* a new book.
> Susan is *excited about* going to California.

COMMENT

Adjective + preposition combinations are followed by noun phrases, such as *classical music* and *a new book,* or *-ing* verb phrases, such as *attending a concert* or *going to California.*

NOTE: Prepositions are used idiomatically after ordinary adjectives like *happy* (*about* something) as well as with those which are made from verbs (as for example, *worried about* something). These combinations must be learned as units.

ADDITIONAL EXAMPLES

tired of	worried about
bored with	happy about
accustomed to	unhappy about
disappointed with (or, in)	in favor of
pleased with	surprised at

Exercise 5. Practice the use of adjective + preposition combinations.

Mrs. Miller is going to London. She is excited.	MRS. MILLER IS EXCITED ABOUT GOING TO LONDON.
Mary said, "I don't like to read. It makes me tired."	MARY IS TIRED OF READING.
John said, "I travel all the time. It's my usual habit."	JOHN IS ACCUSTOMED TO TRAVELING.

1. John said, "I like geography. I think it's very interesting."
2. John is going into the army. He is worried.

3. Mary wants to write long compositions. She is in favor of this.
4. Mr. Gray doesn't want to work hard any more. He says, "It is tiring."
5. Some people drink water with their meals. They say, "It's our custom."
6. Mrs. Brown has a new hat. She says, "It pleases me."
7. Mary is away from home. She is unhappy.
8. Mary doesn't like her job. She is bored.
9. John often stays up very late. He is accustomed to this.
10. John thinks he might forget his suitcase. He is worried.
11. Mr. Miller is learning a new language. He is excited.
12. John doesn't like to listen to people's complaints. He is tired of this.
13. Mary wants to visit a museum. She thinks it will be interesting.
14. Mr. Miller likes to travel in foreign countries. He is accustomed to this.
15. John doesn't want to eat cereal for breakfast any more. He is tired of it.
16. John doesn't like his new car. He is disappointed.
17. Mary wants to ride the bus. She is in favor of this.

NOTE: *Be used to* means the same as *be accustomed to.*

> John *is used to* reading a lot.
> John *is accustomed to* reading a lot.

There is another construction, *used to* which is very different from *be used to.*

> John *used to* read a lot.

Used to can be inserted before a verb in order to express customary events or states in the past. It implies that the event or state stopped and does not continue in the present.

EXAMPLES

1. Mary studied late at night last year, but she doesn't any more.

MARY USED TO STUDY LATE AT NIGHT.

2. Two years ago Alice got up at six o'clock every day, but she doesn't any more.

ALICE USED TO GET UP AT SIX O'CLOCK.

3. When he was a child, John usually spent his summers in the mountains, but now he doesn't.

JOHN USED TO SPEND HIS SUMMERS IN THE MOUNTAINS.

Lesson 20

Review of Lessons 11-19*

Exercise 1. (To review expressions of comparison in questions.) Listen to the statement which contains an expression of comparison. Ask a question about Mary in a similar situation.

John is taller than Fred.	IS MARY TALLER THAN FRED?
He took a bigger one.	DID MARY TAKE A BIGGER ONE?
John has the blackest hair in class.	DOES MARY HAVE THE BLACKEST HAIR IN CLASS?

1. John is shorter than Bob.
2. Rose is more beautiful than Jane.
3. They paid more money than John did.
4. She types most efficiently in the morning.
5. He was the tallest in his class.
6. His bag is heavier than mine.
7. The boy looks just like his father.
8. He seems different from the other students.
9. You are as slow as Bob is.
10. He works more effectively at home.
11. This course is the most practical.
12. They are going to take the earliest bus.

Exercise 2. (To review expressions of comparison with *more* or *-er.*) Listen to the statement which describes John. Produce a statement which compares Paul. Use the form *more* or *-er,* and the word *than.*

John is young.	PAUL IS YOUNGER THAN JOHN.
John is patient.	PAUL IS MORE PATIENT THAN JOHN.
John has a good car.	PAUL HAS A BETTER CAR THAN JOHN.

1. John's hair is gray.
2. John has traveled often.
3. John is tall.
4. John is interesting.
5. We know that John is a good student.
6. John has walked a long distance.
7. John has had experience in teaching.
8. John is going to the concert early.
9. John has a wide knowledge of physics.
10. John has a bad temper.
11. John talks English fluently.
12. John's nose is small.

*NOTE TO THE TEACHER: Each teacher may plan a review lesson suited to the needs of his particular class by making a selection of exercises from the ones included in this lesson. Exercises from previous lessons may also be reviewed.

Exercise 3. (To review expressions of comparison with *most* or *-est*.) Listen to the statement about one or more people. Produce a statement of comparison about Mary. Use the expressions of comparison *most* or *-est*.

There are many good students in this class.	MARY IS THE BEST STUDENT IN THIS CLASS.
Jane and Betty are charming.	MARY IS THE MOST CHARMING.
Jane and Betty are pretty.	MARY IS THE PRETTIEST.

1. John and Bill work hard.
2. Those students have answered often.
3. All of the students were industrious.
4. The boys took a big piece of cake.
5. The girls acted silly.
6. John answered the questions promptly.
7. The students took a lot of time to write their compositions.
8. John has more ambition than Jane.
9. Their hair is long.
10. Bill and Betty traveled a long distance on their vacation.
11. John and Jane had many friends.
12. Both Mary and Jane are sick.

Exercise 4. (To review the expressions of comparison *like, the same as, different from, the same . . . as, as . . . as*.) Substitute the following words and make the necessary changes. Use *as . . . as* with adjectives and adverbs; use *the same . . . as* with nouns.

John talks like his father.

same	JOHN TALKS THE SAME AS HIS FATHER.
differently	JOHN TALKS DIFFERENTLY FROM HIS FATHER.
as clearly	JOHN TALKS AS CLEARLY AS HIS FATHER.
loud	JOHN TALKS AS LOUD AS HIS FATHER.
languages	JOHN TALKS THE SAME LANGUAGES AS HIS FATHER.

1. quietly	10. his brother	19. reads
2. little	11. as polite	20. books
3. much	12. the same	21. magazines
4. frequently	13. different	22. as much
5. like	14. is	23. the same
6. looks like	15. is like	24. practices
7. different	16. speaks	25. like
8. as old	17. as softly	26. acts
9. seems	18. as rapidly	

216

Exercise 5. (To review the forms *very, enough,* and *too.*) Listen to the statements which describe a situation. Produce a statement with *is* which summarizes the situation. Use *too, very,* or *enough* and *to* + a verb in the statement.

The coat is small. John can't wear the coat.	THE COAT IS TOO SMALL FOR JOHN TO WEAR.
John wants to play ball. He is eager.	JOHN IS VERY EAGER TO PLAY BALL.
John will do the work. He is ambitious.	JOHN IS AMBITIOUS ENOUGH TO DO THE WORK.

1. John can afford to take a trip. He is wealthy.
2. Bill is afraid to take a trip. He is timid.
3. Mary can't study. She is sick.
4. John isn't able to see the sign. He is nearsighted.
5. Paul can swim across the lake. He is strong.
6. John can't sit up. He is weak.
7. John wants to take a trip. He is anxious.
8. John can't take a trip. He is tired.
9. Mary hates to see the team lose. She is sorry.
10. John can reach the ceiling. He is tall.
11. Bill can't reach the ceiling. He is short.
12. Fred can't play football. He is small.

Exercise 6. (To review the forms *of* or *-'s.*) Listen to the following situations. Produce statements with the forms *of* or *-'s.* Use *-'s* with the names of people and *of* with things.

This book belongs to John.	THIS IS JOHN'S BOOK.
The book is interesting in the beginning.	THE BEGINNING OF THE BOOK IS INTERESTING.
This is Webson College. Mr. Smith is President.	MR. SMITH IS PRESIDENT OF WEBSON COLLEGE.

1. He is using the book that belongs to Mary.
2. John has a new book.
3. The flower has a red color.
4. The book has the name "Flower Arrangement."
5. The typewriter keys are broken.
6. He works in Bright Hall. He works in the basement.
7. I am correcting a composition. It was written by Miss Cross.
8. I found a glove yesterday. It belongs to Mary.
9. The president lives in this house.
10. The club elected a new secretary. Bob is the secretary.
11. I bought a car. I bought it from John.
12. John has an injured hand.

Exercise 7. (To review *his, her, mine, one, ones, these,* etc.) Listen to the statements with *my book, this book, John's book,* etc. Produce equivalent statements without using the word *book.*

John may use my book.	JOHN MAY USE MINE.
He bought another book.	HE BOUGHT ANOTHER ONE.
	(or) HE BOUGHT ANOTHER.
I have Mary's book.	I HAVE HERS.
Your book is on the desk.	YOURS IS ON THE DESK.

1. I want John's book.
2. Are these their books?
3. I lost my book.
4. I have read several books this month.
5. He lost interest in those books.
6. John borrowed a few books from the library.
7. They didn't bring their books with them.
8. John hadn't read that book.
9. They forgot their books.
10. Do you have your book with you?
11. What did you do with her books?
12. I haven't read this book yet.
13. What happened to those books?
14. Have you seen the new books for the course?
15. My friend didn't care for this book.
16. These books are too heavy to carry.

Exercise 8. (To review *yet, still, already, any more.*) Listen to the questions and the words which follow. Answer the questions and use the words in the answers. Use *any more* and *yet* in negative statements and *already* in affirmative statements. Use *still* in negative and affirmative statements.

Where is John? still	JOHN IS STILL EATING BREAKFAST.
Have they studied Lesson Five? already	THEY'VE STUDIED IT ALREADY.
Has the class studied Lesson Six? yet	IT HASN'T STUDIED IT YET.
Does John work here? any more	JOHN DOESN'T WORK HERE ANY MORE.

1. Has John left? yet
2. Have you seen the new auditorium? already
3. Has Fred come here lately? any more
4. Have you seen Mary this morning? yet
5. Is Jane going downtown this afternoon? already
6. Do you like jazz music? any more
7. Do you like symphony music? still
8. Is Betty going to take the American literature course? already

9. Have you eaten at the Union Cafeteria lately? any more
10. Have you seen the director? yet
11. Has Bob returned the book to you? still
12. Where is Tom? already

Exercise 9. (To review *to* + verb after *like, want,* etc.) Answer the questions with *to* + verb. Use the verb which is given.

What does he want? buy   HE WANTS TO BUY A BOOK.

What did John expect? get   JOHN EXPECTED TO GET A LETTER
                                   TODAY.

What do they like? swim   THEY LIKE TO SWIM IN THE LAKE.

1. What is she learning? speak
2. What does he need? study
3. What did he promise? go
4. What does Paul plan? answer
5. What did Mary decide? drive
6. What is he beginning?
    read
7. What do you hope? see
8. What did he ask us? come
9. What is he continuing? use
10. What did the teacher want from
     them? write
11. What is he trying? sell
12. What did he want from us? pay

Exercise 10. (To review the production of *can, must,* etc., in questions.) Listen to the statements. Ask parallel questions about Bob.

I can see the top of the   CAN BOB SEE THE TOP OF THE
   mountain.   MOUNTAIN?

You should report to the director   SHOULD BOB REPORT TO THE
   immediately.   DIRECTOR IMMEDIATELY?

Mary must hand in her   MUST BOB HAND IN HIS
   composition today.   COMPOSITION TODAY?

1. John may go to the movie.
2. I should take another course in English.
3. He might forget his books.
4. Our professor will answer the letter in the morning.
5. He will answer my question tomorrow.
6. The students should pay their fees now.
7. I can send the package later.
8. You could have forgotten the letter.
9. He could see the traffic light in the dark.
10. He must answer the letter today.
11. I might go to Detroit tomorrow.
12. John could go to the late show.
13. They must return the application blank next week.
14. They might find an apartment on Main Street.

15. He would like to have a conference.
16. I can understand it.
17. She may turn the television on.
18. You can come tomorrow.
19. You can do the paper tomorrow.
20. You may use the telephone.

Exercise 11. (To review the use of *can, might, will, may, must, should.*) Listen to the situation statements. Produce statements with *might, can,* etc. which are suitable to these situations.

A.   (To review *might.*) Listen to the statement about John and make a related statement which shows that John is undecided or that some action is possible. Use *might* and the verb which is given.

John wants to go to the play, but he   HE MIGHT GO TO THE
   is undecided. go   PLAY.

John is thinking of buying a car. buy   HE MIGHT BUY A CAR.

        1. John is planning a trip to San Francisco. go
        2. John is waiting for a letter. get
        3. John is working for a degree. get
        4. John wants to eat breakfast. have
        5. John has a toothache. go
        6. John drives very carelessly in his car. have
        7. John is homesick. What can he do? talk
        8. John is looking for an apartment. find

B.   (To review *can.*) Listen to the following situations about Tom. Produce a related statement. Show what he is able to do. Use *can* plus the verb which is given.

Tom is a good musician. play   HE CAN PLAY THE PIANO.

Tom has no time to see you today.   HE CAN SEE YOU TOMORROW.
   see

        1. Tom has a good memory. memorize
        2. Tom does not need the book today. wait
        3. Tom plays many sports. swim, play tennis, and ski
        4. Tom has no one to go with him. go
        5. Tom is looking for a copy of Moby Dick. get
        6. Tom wants to talk to you. talk
        7. Tom is not doing anything this afternoon. go
        8. Tom understands English very well. speak

C.   (To review *should*.) Listen to the situation about Bob. Indicate what Bob has the obligation to do in this situation. Use *should* and the verb which is given.

Bob has low grades. study   HE SHOULD STUDY HARDER.

Bob is wanted by the director.   HE SHOULD REPORT TO THE
    report   DIRECTOR.

      1. Bob is sick. see
      2. Bob is tired from playing ball. rest
      3. Bob lost all of his money. borrow
      4. Bob is sleepy in class. sleep
      5. Bob writes home only once a month. write
      6. Bob has poor pronunciation. practice
      7. Bob comes to class late every day. come
      8. Bob has owed John five dollars for the last two years. pay

D.   (To review *must*.) Listen to the situation about Fred. Make a judgment and tell what he is required to do. Use *must* and the verb which is given.

Fred is late for his class. hurry   HE MUST HURRY.

Fred wants to study   HE MUST TAKE COURSES IN
   engineering. take   MATH.

      1. Fred is using Mary's book and she needs it. return
      2. Fred refuses to take the medicine which the doctor gave him. take
      3. Fred lost his eyeglasses and he can't see. get
      4. Fred has a composition to write. hand in
      5. Fred has not studied today. work
      6. Fred has not paid his tuition yet. pay
      7. Fred found John's wallet. return
      8. Fred is going to attend summer school. Registration is tomorrow.
        register

E.   (To review *may*.) Listen to the situation. Make a statement about Paul which indicates that he has or does not have permission. Use *may* and the verb which is given.

Paul has permission to be absent.   HE MAY BE ABSENT.
   be

Paul asked to use the laboratory.   HE MAY NOT USE THE
   He was refused. use   LABORATORY.

1. Paul asked the director for a vacation. The director said no. have
2. Paul asked to use the television set. use
3. The landlady has given Paul permission to use her phone. use
4. Paul was forbidden to drink coffee by the doctor. drink
5. Paul has received permission to visit Canada. visit
6. The government refused to give Paul a driver's license. drive
7. Paul is allowed to take sixteen credit hours this semester. take
8. Paul is not allowed to take Spanish. take

F.   (To review *will*.) Listen to the situations about Mary. Indicate what Mary is or is not going to do. Use *will* and the verb which is given.

Mary is standing in the rain. get   SHE WILL GET WET.

Mary missed the grammar   SHE WON'T KNOW HER
   class today. know   LESSON TOMORROW.

1. Mary canceled her trip to England. take
2. Mary has a book to give you tomorrow. give
3. Mary has decided to take a vacation in Mexico. take
4. Mary has promised to write when she arrives in France. write
5. Mary is writing a composition. finish
6. Mary is angry at Jane. speak
7. Mary got the letter yesterday. reply
8. Mary has chosen too many courses. find

Exercise 12. (To review the contrast between *I want to find*, etc., and *I can find*, etc.) Substitute the following words. Do not use *to* after *must, can, should*, etc.

I want to see the director.

   must   I MUST SEE THE DIRECTOR.
   have   I HAVE TO SEE THE DIRECTOR.
   speak   I HAVE TO SPEAK TO THE DIRECTOR.

1. may	9. visit	17. might	25. report
2. want	10. must	18. find	26. can
3. could	11. won't	19. must	27. should
4. had	12. should	20. intend	28. am going to
5. should	13. can't	21. can	29. want
6. will	14. intend	22. should	30. will
7. need	15. may	23. won't	31. expect
8. am going to	16. wish	24. have	32. wish

Exercise 13. (To review verbs + *up, on, off,* etc.) Listen to the statements. Repeat the statements and use pronouns like *him, it, them,* etc.

I woke up John at ten this morning.	I WOKE HIM UP AT TEN THIS MORNING.
I put my hat on.	I PUT IT ON.
I got out of the boat.	I GOT OUT OF IT.

1. I picked up my books.
2. I took my hat off.
3. I paid up my debts.
4. I found out about the lesson.
5. I turned the alarm off.
6. I turned on the radio.

7. I walked over to the drugstore.
8. I called up John.
9. I jumped out of bed.
10. I jumped into bed.
11. I sat down by the man.
12. I ran into John.

Exercise 14. (To review short answers to questions.) Answer the questions with a short answer. You may make your answers affirmative or negative.

Can you read his writing?	NO, I CAN'T.
Whose book is this?	MINE.
Is there going to be a concert tonight?	NO, THERE ISN'T.

1. Will John go by train?
2. Have you forgotten about the play?
3. May John use your telephone?
4. Did he ask you about it?
5. Why is John here tonight?
6. How did you get to Ann Arbor?
7. Is he a member of the club?
8. Could you find his address?
9. Is it far to California?
10. Would you like to go on a picnic today?
11. Whose pencil is this?
12. Might they come for the meeting?
13. Why did Mary go to the bookstore?
14. Should he make an appointment with the doctor?
15. Has she been studying Lesson Six?
16. Do you want to study in the library?
17. Had you gotten the news before you left?
18. Can Mary play the piano?
19. Are there any mountains in this area?
20. How are you traveling to New York City?

Exercise 15. (To review statements with *it's.*) Answer the following questions with *it's* or *it.*

Who is it at the door?	IT'S JOHN.
What do you think of the movie?	IT'S TERRIBLE.
Why are you waiting?	IT'S TOO EARLY TO GO TO THE PLAY.
Why didn't you go to the restaurant?	IT WASN'T OPEN.

1. What time is it?
2. How far is it to Detroit?
3. What is the weather like today?
4. What was the weather like yesterday?
5. What month is it?
6. What day is it?
7. What do you think of the play?
8. Why do you practice so much?
9. What year is it?
10. Who is talking to Professor Smith?
11. How is your cold?
12. When is the game?

Exercise 16. (To review statements with *there is, are.*) Answer the questions with *there is* or *there are.* Use the words which are given after the questions.

Where is there a gasoline station? Baker Street	THERE'S ONE ON BAKER STREET.
Where can I find a telephone? room	THERE'S ONE IN THE NEXT ROOM.
Do you have any matches? table	THERE ARE SOME ON THE TABLE.

1. Where is there a drugstore? Greenwood Street
2. Where can I buy some bananas? grocery store
3. Where can I find some soap? drugstore
4. Where can I find a mechanic? garage
5. Do you see any pencils? desk
6. Where can I find a room? hotel
7. Where could I buy a candy bar? candy counter
8. Where can I get some aspirin? drugstore
9. Do you have some paper? table
10. Where can I see a good play? New York
11. Where are some apples? refrigerator
12. Where can I get some good ice cream? drugstore

Exercise 17. (To review embedded statements after *know, believe, remember,* etc.) Listen to the statement and the verb which follows it. Include the verb and the statement in another statement.

John is a good student. know	I KNOW THAT JOHN IS A GOOD STUDENT.
Mary wore a green hat to the tea. remember	I REMEMBER THAT MARY WORE A GREEN HAT TO THE TEA.
He has a cold. suspect	I SUSPECT THAT HE HAS A COLD.

1. John went to Canada by train. wrote
2. They are going to be married. heard
3. There is no course in statistics next semester. learned
4. Professor Jones will not be here today. presume
5. The New York Yankees will win the pennant. predict
6. Nobody can survive at that altitude. said
7. There will be no war. believe
8. The teacher assigned a new lesson. forgot
9. I had bought the shirt the day before. explained
10. Jane was selected for a scholarship. learned
11. The library is open on Sundays. discovered
12. Tom has taken a job in Venezuela. understand

Exercise 18. (To review relative clauses.) Listen to the statements. Combine the statements using the words *who, which,* or *that.*

The book is here. I want it.	THE BOOK WHICH I WANT IS HERE.
John is a good student. He works hard.	JOHN IS A GOOD STUDENT WHO WORKS HARD.
The math teacher is my friend. John visited him.	THE MATH TEACHER THAT JOHN VISITED IS MY FRIEND.
The math teacher is my friend. He visited John.	THE MATH TEACHER THAT VISITED JOHN IS MY FRIEND.

1. Mary saw it in the book. Jim found the book.
2. Paul met the new student. I know the student.
3. My friend teaches English. He is visiting Italy.
4. They know the man. John met him yesterday.
5. They know the man. He talked to John yesterday.
6. The professor knows my mother. He teaches Spanish.
7. Fred has the camera. Mary found it.
8. I returned the book. John wanted it.
9. The secretary wrote me a letter. John knows her.
10. The secretary wrote me a letter. She knows John.
11. She talked with a professor. He praised Jim.
12. She talked with a professor. Jim praised him.

Exercise 19. (To review embedded questions introduced by the words *what, where, why, when, how much, who.*) Listen to the statement about John. Indicate that you know the information. Use *I know* plus an embedded statement introduced by *what, where,* etc.

John studies in the morning.	I KNOW WHEN JOHN STUDIES.
John studies algebra and physics.	I KNOW WHAT JOHN STUDIES.
John is talking to Fred.	I KNOW WHOM JOHN IS TALKING TO.
Professor Smith met John.	I KNOW WHO MET JOHN.
John works for a living.	I KNOW WHY JOHN WORKS.

1. John reads novels and plays.
2. John works in the factory.
3. Mary saw John.
4. John reads for pleasure.
5. John is acquainted with Professor Smith.
6. John earns $100 a week.
7. John met Miss Jones.
8. Miss Brown introduced John.
9. John paid fifty dollars for his suit.
10. John is going to Florida.
11. John takes a walk in the evening.
12. Bill forgot about John.
13. John is going to buy a hat and a pair of shoes.
14. John might come this afternoon.
15. Fred went with John.
16. John is studying to become a librarian.
17. John has forgotten about Bill.
18. Mr. Allen spoke to John.
19. John spoke to Mr. Allen.
20. Paul is John's friend.

Exercise 20. (To review passive sentences.) Listen to the statements. Make the word which receives the action the subject of a similar statement. Use a form of *be* in each statement.

The director wants John immediately.	JOHN IS WANTED IMMEDIATELY.
I saw the book on the table.	THE BOOK WAS SEEN ON THE TABLE.
They took him to the hospital.	HE WAS TAKEN TO THE HOSPITAL.

1. I returned the books yesterday.
2. The police examined the car.
3. The doctor examined Fred thoroughly.
4. We warned Paul not to go swimming.
5. He improved his pronunciation a lot this week.
6. I found my hat under the table.
7. They are inspecting the building now.
8. We must pay the bill at once.

9. We took a picture of John and Mary.
10. John and Mary took a picture of me.
11. They promised the book to us yesterday.
12. We ate it for breakfast.

Exercise 21. (To review the *-ing* and past participle forms as modifiers.) Listen to the statements. Produce related statements with *-ing* and past participle forms after *be*. One student produces an *-ing* form and another student the past participle form.

John amuses us.	JOHN IS AMUSING. WE ARE AMUSED.
They entertained us.	THEY WERE ENTERTAINING. WE WERE ENTERTAINED.
The newspaper convinced Mary.	THE NEWSPAPER WAS CONVINCING. MARY WAS CONVINCED.

1. They deceived us.
2. The book inspired him.
3. She charmed the audience.
4. The movie pleased us.
5. John displeases his teacher.
6. The long walk discouraged me.
7. The exam is going to frighten the students.
8. The movie disgusted us.
9. The examination frustrated Paul.
10. The lecture convinced us.
11. The accident depressed everybody.
12. The play interests the critic.

Exercise 22. (To review verb constructions with *have, had* and to contrast them with other constructions.) Answer the following questions. Use the verb constructions indicated in the question.

What have you been doing lately?	I'VE BEEN TAKING A COURSE IN MATH.
What does he have in his hand?	HE HAS A COIN IN HIS HAND.
What had you been working on when I came?	I HAD BEEN WORKING ON MY GRAMMAR LESSON.

1. Where are you going?
2. What have you been doing in your free time?
3. What have you done with your car?
4. What are you going to do next summer?
5. What did you do last summer?
6. What have you done this summer?
7. When did you sell your car?
8. What have you done with your book?
9. What have you been doing with your book?
10. What color pencil does John have?

    11. What color pencil has he taken?
    12. What had you bought before you came here?
    13. What has John been forgetting?
    14. What has John forgotten?

Exercise 23. (To review *have* + the past participle form.) Listen to the statement. Add another statement with *but . . . since . . .* Use *haven't, hasn't* plus the past participle form of the verb that is given after the statement.

John is a good student. study	JOHN IS A GOOD STUDENT, BUT HE HASN'T STUDIED SINCE NOVEMBER.
They work hard. complete	THEY WORK HARD, BUT THEY HAVEN'T COMPLETED AN ASSIGNMENT SINCE TUESDAY.
They earn a lot of money. buy	THEY EARN A LOT OF MONEY, BUT THEY HAVEN'T BOUGHT A CAR SINCE 1965.

1. He knows John. seen	7. Dr. Smith is a dentist. worked
2. They see John every day. talked	8. They are fishing. caught
3. Mary wants to come. talked	9. Bob likes boiled eggs. had
4. Fred has a test. studied	10. He has a camera. taken
5. He bought a car. driven	11. He knows Mary. talked
6. They know the rules. observed	12. She has a cold. taken

Exercise 24. (To review *have been* + the *-ing* form.) Listen to the statement. Add another statement with *and . . . lately* which tells related information. Use *have been* plus the *-ing* form of the verb which is given.

John is a good student. study	JOHN IS A GOOD STUDENT AND HE HAS BEEN STUDYING HARD LATELY.
They work hard. complete	THEY WORK HARD AND THEY HAVE BEEN COMPLETING THEIR WORK LATELY.
They earn a lot of money. buy	THEY EARN A LOT OF MONEY AND THEY HAVE BEEN BUYING A LOT OF CLOTHES LATELY.

(Continue with the items of Exercise 23.)

Exercise 25. (To review *had* + the past participle form of a verb.) Listen to the statements in past time. Repeat the statements and add other statements which express an action which occurred previously. Use *after . . . had* + the past participle form of the verb which is given.

He recovered. get	HE RECOVERED AFTER HE HAD GOTTEN SICK.
He waited. miss	HE WAITED AFTER HE HAD MISSED THE BUS.
He answered. receive	HE ANSWERED AFTER HE HAD RECEIVED THE LETTER.

1. She cried. hear
2. He protested. see
3. We left. report
4. He slept. eat
5. He went to bed. study
6. They celebrated. win

7. We rested. watch
8. We talked. hear
9. I returned home. visit
10. I dressed. sleep
11. They replied. get
12. She telephoned. arrive

Exercise 26. (To review *had been* + the *-ing* form of a verb.) Listen to the two statements. Combine them in a single statement. Use *had been* + the *-ing* form to indicate the action in progress before the second event took place.

I was studying. John came.	I HAD BEEN STUDYING BEFORE JOHN CAME.
I was studying. I took a walk.	I HAD BEEN STUDYING BEFORE I TOOK A WALK.
He was reading. Mary telephoned.	HE HAD BEEN READING BEFORE MARY TELEPHONED.

1. They were talking. John arrived.
2. Mary was working. She left town.
3. They were eating. He telephoned.
4. They were talking. The concert began.
5. He was smoking. The program began.
6. Mary was walking. She went to the drugstore.

7. I was eating. I telephoned John.
8. The man was singing. The police arrived.
9. I was writing a letter. John called.
10. They were eating. Bob knocked on the door.
11. She was reading. She called up Jane.
12. I was walking. It started to rain.

Exercise 27. (To practice *one, some,* and personal pronouns.) Answer the following questions using a personal pronoun (*it, her, him,* etc.) or an indefinite pronoun (*one, some*). Use the word *yesterday* in your answer.

Have you ever seen an elephant?	YES, I SAW ONE YESTERDAY.
Have you ever seen any white horses?	YES, I SAW SOME YESTERDAY.
Have you ever seen my cat?	YES, I SAW IT YESTERDAY.

Have you ever seen . . .?

1. a tiger?
2. any squirrels?
3. a brown bear?
4. any silver dollars?
5. a car factory?
6. the new post office?
7. any green chalk?
8. a British penny?
9. the city hall?
10. an electric can opener?
11. black bread?
12. boys with long hair?
13. my bicycle?
14. a red and green table lamp?
15. any green apples?
16. the chief of police?
17. a pocket watch?
18. my sister?
19. the director's office?
20. a solar eclipse?

Lesson 21

A. Verb + Noun Phrase + Verb: *See* him *go.*

B. Wish sentences: I wish they knew.

C. *Wh*-word + *to* + verb: They decided *when to go.*

A. Compare the verbs with *to* and without *to* after the object of the main verb.

Previous pattern (Lesson 13):

> We *told* him *to go.*

New pattern:

> We *saw* him *go.*

COMMENTS

(1) In the new pattern, *saw* is followed by a direct object and the simple form of another verb. The second verb *(go)* is never preceded by *to.*

(2) The new pattern contains verbs of perception in the first verb position: *see, hear, watch, feel.*

(3) The verbs *let, make,* and *have* can also be used in the first verb position:

> We *let* him *go.*

NOTES:

(1) *See, hear, feel, watch* also occur in another pattern where the second verb is in the *-ing* form (see Lesson 27).

> We saw him *going.*

> We heard him *going.*

Let, make, and *have* (in the sense of *cause*) are not used in this pattern with *-ing* forms.

(2) *Let* in the new pattern means "to permit."
Make means "to cause" or "to force."

> We let him go.　= We permitted him to go.
> We made him go. = We forced him to go.

to have authority over some
the right and powe

(3) *Have* in the new pattern is used in the situation where one person asks a second person to do something and the second person agrees to do it. Usually the first person has authority over the second:

> The boss had the secretary call the airport.
> Mrs. Smith had her daughter clean her room.

Sometimes no real authority is involved. Instead, the second person performs a service for the first person and is paid for it:

> Mr. Miller had the architect design a new house.
> Mrs. Smith had the mechanic fix her car.

(4) *Help* can also be used in the first verb position of the new pattern. After the verb *help* and a direct object, the use of *to* before a second verb is optional.

> We helped him *to* find the answer.
> We helped him   find the answer.

Exercise 1. Repeat after your teacher.

1. We'll make them sing.
2. We'll have them sing.
3. We'll let them sing.
4. We'll help them sing.
5. We'll see the bus move.
6. We'll hear the bus move.
7. We'll feel the bus move.
8. We'll watch the bus move.

Exercise 2. Review the pattern with *to*. Repeat the first sentence below. Then substitute the words given by the teacher.

He advised me to go to Florida.

> told   HE TOLD ME TO GO TO FLORIDA.
> persuaded   HE PERSUADED ME TO GO TO FLORIDA.

1. invited
2. asked
3. expected
4. wanted
5. told
6. permitted

Continue the exercise with this question pattern:

Did they advise you to go with them?

> remind   DID THEY REMIND YOU TO GO
>   WITH THEM?
> invite   DID THEY INVITE YOU TO GO
>   WITH THEM?

7. order
8. advise
9. force
10. permit
11. persuade
12. tell
13. expect
14. ask

Exercise 3. Answer the questions using the verbs given.

    1. A: Did the children take the medicine? (made)
       B: ——Yes. We made them take the medicine.

    2. A: Did Mr. Smith call the police? (had)
       B: ——Yes. We had him call the police.

    3. A: Did the girls use the car? (let)
       B: ——Yes. We let them use the car.

    4. A: Did the children take the medicine? (saw)
       B: ——Yes. We saw the children take the medicine.

    5. A: Did Mr. Green answer the telephone? (heard)
       B: ——Yes. We heard Mr. Green answer the telephone.

    6. A: Did the bus move? (felt)
       B: ——Yes. We felt the bus move.

    7. A: Did Alfred paint his bicycle? (watched)
       B: ——Yes, we watched Alfred paint his bicycle.

Exercise 4. Substitute the words given by the teacher.

They persuaded me to sell the car.
    made   THEY MADE ME SELL THE CAR.
    paint the car   THEY MADE ME PAINT THE CAR.
    wanted   THEY WANTED ME TO PAINT THE CAR.

1. buy the car	11. helped
2. advised	12. asked
3. wash the car	13. drive the car
4. forced	14. permitted
5. saw	15. let
6. park the car	16. watched
7. push the car	17. move the car
8. persuaded	18. had
9. told	19. reminded
10. made	20. heard

Exercise 5. Use the following noun phrases and verb expressions to make sentences with the verbs in the list given below.

NOUN PHRASES	VERB EXPRESSIONS
the children	take some pictures
Mr. & Mrs. Brown	open the door
all my relatives	get off the boat
the other people	arrive on time
Professor Johnson	look up the number
the secretary	put a hat on
the bus driver	turn the radio on
	talk about politics
	play the piano
	put everything away

asked	I ASKED THE CHILDREN TO GET OFF THE BOAT.
saw	I SAW THE SECRETARY OPEN THE DOOR.
had	I HAD THE BUS DRIVER TURN THE RADIO ON.

1. made	8. expected	15. advised
2. let	9. asked	16. had
3. persuaded	10. made	17. invited
4. ordered	11. told	18. let
5. saw	12. heard	19. helped
6. permitted	13. watched	20. asked
7. wanted	14. forced	

B. Observe the verb forms used after *wish.*

SITUATION	WISH
Tom doesn't live in the city.	I wish that Tom *lived* in the city.

COMMENTS

(1) The verb form (*lived*) used in the subordinate clause after *wish* is identical in form to the past tense form.

(2) The meaning of this verb form is not past. The form *lived* refers here to a present situation.

(3) The situation as expressed in the subordinated clause after *wish* is contrary to the actual truth.

NOTES:

(1) Just as with *think, hear,* etc. the use of the connecting word *that* is optional in *wish* sentences:

I wish Tom lived in the city.

(2)   In *wish* sentences, the verb form of *be* is *were* (or *was*).

> I wish I *were* in Paris. (I wish I *was* in Paris.)
> I wish you *were* in Paris.
> I wish he *were* in Paris. (I wish he *was* in Paris.)
> I wish we *were* all in Paris.

The sentences with "I wish I *was* . . ." and "I wish he *was* . . ." are examples of a less formal style.

(3)   Use *hope* rather than *wish* when the situation or event is possible and not contrary to the real facts:

> I hope you feel better today.
> I hope it rains tomorrow.

ADDITIONAL EXAMPLES

1. My father works in an office all the time. I wish he *worked* outdoors.

2. I wish the other people *spoke* as clearly as you do.

3. My wife is a wonderful dancer. I wish she *were* also a good cook.

4. I wish we *didn't* have to go out tonight.

5. Ann wishes that she *could* drive a tractor. (But she can't, because she doesn't have the skill or strength, or perhaps permission.)

6. We can only get to the stadium on foot. I wish we *could* get there by bus.

7. They won't help us. (They refuse.) I wish they *would* help us. (A wish for willingness.)

8. The weather is awful. I wish the rain *would* stop. (A wish for the coming of an event.)

Exercise 6. Listen to the situation described. Wish for the opposite situation.

The doctor isn't in now.	I WISH THE DOCTOR WERE IN NOW.
It won't rain.	I WISH IT WOULD RAIN.
Your sister doesn't feel well.	I WISH YOUR SISTER FELT WELL.

    1. Alice doesn't live in the city.
    2. Paul can't drive a car.
    3. They don't sell groceries here.
    4. John isn't going with us.
    5. The students don't understand the lesson
    6. I can't play tennis as well as you.
    7. The dentist doesn't work on Sundays
    8. John isn't coming to class today
    9. You don't know the director
   10. Mary doesn't play bridge.

Exercise 7. Form *wish* sentences using an adjective or adverb with the opposite meaning.

I think this pattern is *difficult.*   I WISH IT WERE EASY.

I heard that classes begin *early.*   I WISH THEY BEGAN LATE.

1. I believe that Mrs. Smith is *sick.*
2. I understand that the streets downtown are *narrow.*
3. I discovered that Professor Jones speaks *fast.*
4. I think that John's father is *old and weak.*
5. I imagine that Mary feels *sad.*
6. I heard that the store is *closed.*
7. I believe that the exam is *hard.*
8. I think that John's answer is *wrong.*
9. I think that this tea is *weak.*

Exercise 8. Listen to the situations described. Wish for the opposite situations. Use negative subordinate clauses.

Books are expensive.   I WISH THEY WEREN'T EXPENSIVE.

Mr. Miller is sick.   I WISH HE WEREN'T SICK.

He has a sore throat.   I WISH HE DIDN'T HAVE A SORE THROAT.

1. Books are expensive.
2. You work at night.
3. The children will play in the street.
4. The bus leaves at six a.m.
5. It's going to rain today.
6. There is going to be an examination tomorrow.
7. It's necessary to practice every day.
8. George has to write a lot of letters.

Exercise 9. Make short negative responses.

Joe will help us.   I WISH HE WOULDN'T.

Joe can sing.   I WISH HE COULDN'T.

Joe's a doctor.   I WISH HE WEREN'T.

Joe has a motorcycle.   I WISH HE DIDN'T.

1. Joe will go with you.
2. Joe lives on our street.
3. Joe's a piano player.
4. Joe feels very sad.
5. Joe will lend you money.
6. Joe's hungry.
7. Joe knows your name.
8. Joe will leave tomorrow.
9. Joe can play the violin.
10. Joe has a beautiful secretary.

C. Notice the use of *to* plus a verb with *wh*-expressions.

We decided *where to go.*

We knew *which road to take.*

COMMENTS

(1)   The first sentence means "We decided where we should go." The second sentence means "We knew which road we should take."

(2)   The new pattern expresses the idea of appropriateness or correctness. To know "what things one should buy" is to know "what to buy."

The place one should live	=	where to live.
The time one should leave	=	when to leave.
The people one should invite	=	who to invite.
The way one should park a car	=	how to park a car.
The things one should buy	=	what to buy

ADDITIONAL EXAMPLES

I'd like to find out how to get to Canada.
Can you tell me which provinces to visit?
I haven't decided how long to stay there.
I'm going to ask someone what kind of clothes to wear
I don't even know who to ask.

NOTES:

(1)   In this pattern, the subject of the subordinate verb (after *to*) is understood to be the same person as the main subject. If "we" decide what to do, it is what "we" must do, not some one else.

(2)   After verbs like *advise* and *tell,* the subject of the verb after *to* is understood to be the same as the object, rather than the subject, of the main verb. If we advise "them" where to work, it is advice about the place of "their" work, not ours. The following examples illustrate this sub-pattern:

The lawyer advised us *how much money to send.*
The engineer told us *how to use our new machine.*

Exercise 10. Substitute the words given by the teacher.

He knows where to go.

how	HE KNOWS HOW TO GO.
to drive	HE KNOWS HOW TO DRIVE.
where	HE KNOWS WHERE TO DRIVE.

1. to practice		10. you must know
2. when		11. how
3. what		12. to write
4. I don't know		13. what
5. how long		14. they haven't decided
6. to sleep		15. he knows
7. where		16. how
8. please tell me		17. to drive
9. to park		18. where

Exercise 11. This is a conversation exercise to practice the use of expressions like *where to go.* Listen to the questions and give an answer with "Yes. I told him."

Do you think that he will
   come at the right time?   YES, I TOLD HIM WHAT TIME TO COME.
Do you think that he will
   take the right plane?   YES. I TOLD HIM WHICH PLANE TO TAKE.

1. Do you think he will meet us at the right place?
2. Do you think he will pronounce the word correctly?
3. Do you think he will buy enough bread?
4. Do you think he will find the restaurant?
5. Do you think he will choose the correct answer?
6. Do you think he will take enough money?
7. Do you think he will get up at the right time?
8. Do you think he will give the money to the right man?
9. Do you think he will bring the right books?
10. Do you think he will send the letters to the right address?
11. Do you think he will do what we want him to?
12. Do you think he will make enough ice cubes?
13. Do you think he will use the machine correctly?
14. Do you think he will get enough chairs?
15. Do you think he will address the letter to the right person?

NOTE: *Whether* is also used in the new pattern of Frame C. It usually introduces
alternatives.   *which choice to take*

      I don't know *whether* to go by bus or plane.
      We haven't decided *whether* to visit Chicago or not.

Lesson 22

A. *must have, might have, should have, could have*

B. *must have* with progressive forms:
must have been going

C. Short answers:
Did they go? They *must have.*

D. *Wish* sentences in the past:
I wish you had visited them.

A. Notice the use of *have* to express past time after auxiliaries.

Previous pattern (Lesson 11):	New pattern:
PRESENT OR FUTURE TIME	PAST TIME
1a. They must know him.	1b. They *must have* known him.
2a. They might hear us.	2b. They *might have* heard us.
3a. They should study.	3b. They *should have* studied, (but they didn't).
4a. They could play tennis now, (but maybe they won't).	4b. They *could have* played tennis, (but they didn't).

COMMENTS

(1) The meanings of sentences in the new pattern:

1b. I conclude that they knew him. (The only reasonable conclusion is that they knew him.)

2b. It is possible that they heard us.

3b. It was right and desirable for them to study, but they didn't. (They had an obligation to study, but they didn't.)

4b. They had the capability or opportunity of playing tennis, but they didn't.

(2)   The meanings of the modals + *have:*

1.   *Must have* expresses a conclusion about a past situation.

2.   *Might have* means that the past situation or event is admitted as a possibility.

3.   *Should have* in this lesson is used to express the belief that an event (or situation) was right and desirable. However, the event did not happen (or the situation did not exist).

4.   *Could have* means that the subject had the capability or opportunity of doing something but for some reason did not do it.

NOTES:

(1)   The combination *must have* is used to express suppositions only, never to express obligations or necessity. For past necessity, say *had to* as in "They had to go early."

(2)   To express the possibility that something occurred, *may have* or *could have* are sometimes used in place of *might have.*

> They might have gone.
> They may have gone.
> They could have gone.

All three sentences can be used in the meaning of "It is possible that they went." In this lesson, use *might have* for the idea.

(3)   The conditional *could* as used in this lesson is identical in *form* to the simple past *could* which expresses past ability. (Lesson 11.)

CONDITIONAL

> They could play tennis now,
> (but they won't.)

PAST

> In 1969 they could play tennis
> like professionals.

The conditional *could* implies that something is not the case or that it will not happen. The past *could* has no such implication.

(4)   Negative forms:

must not have	(no contraction)
might not have	(no contraction)
should not have	shouldn't have
could not have	couldn't have

(5)   Negative sentences:

> He must not have known it. =
> I conclude that he didn't know it.
>
> They might not have heard us. =
> It is possible that they didn't hear us.
>
> They shouldn't have studied. =
> It was desirable for them not to study. (However they did study.)
>
> He couldn't have played tennis yesterday. =
> In my opinion, it was not possible for him to play tennis yesterday.

(6)   In normal speech, the word *have* in combinations such as *must have, might have,* etc. is pronounced like the word *of.*

ADDITIONAL EXAMPLES

1. The lake is frozen. It must have been very cold last night.

2. Why didn't the mayor welcome us? I don't know. He might not have received our message. Or he might have forgotten.

3. My friend left for the airport at seven a.m. yesterday, but he missed the plane. He should have left at 6:30.

4. You shouldn't have gone out without your coat. You could have caught a cold.

5. The books we bought last year were very valuable. Without them we couldn't have passed our examinations.

Exercise 1. Repeat the sentence with the substitutions given by the teacher. Change the verb when necessary to agree with the time expression.

We should return the books tomorrow.

yesterday	WE SHOULD HAVE RETURNED THE BOOKS YESTERDAY.
could have	WE COULD HAVE RETURNED THE BOOKS YESTERDAY.
tomorrow	WE COULD RETURN THE BOOKS TOMORROW.
play tennis	WE COULD PLAY TENNIS TOMORROW.

1. yesterday
2. you must have
3. they
4. might have
5. tomorrow
6. go to the bank
7. should
8. yesterday
9. must have
10. heard the news
11. might have
12. gone to Chicago
13. tomorrow
14. help us
15. might not
16. return the books
17. yesterday
18. we
19. should have

Exercise 2. Make a sentence with *must, might, should,* or *could,* according to the situation.

1. Does she live in an apartment now? I suppose she does; it's the only reasonable conclusion.

    SHE MUST LIVE IN AN APARTMENT NOW.

2. Did she live in the dorm last year? I conclude that she did.

    SHE MUST HAVE LIVED IN THE DORM LAST YEAR.

3. Did she decide to get a job? I think it's possible.

    SHE MIGHT HAVE DECIDED TO GET A JOB.

4. Did she save her money? It was desirable, but she didn't.

    SHE SHOULD HAVE SAVED HER MONEY.

5. Did she stay with her sister? She had that opportunity but didn't stay.

    SHE COULD HAVE STAYED WITH HER SISTER.

6. Did she sell her car? I conclude that she did.

7. Does she own a bicycle? I conclude that she does.

8. Did she shop by phone? She had that opportunity but didn't shop by phone.

9. Did she invite her uncle? It was desirable, but she didn't.

10. Did she forget to mail the letter? I think it's possible.

11. Did she hear us come in? I conclude that she did.

12. Did she find your address in the phone book? I think it is possible.

13. Did she look in the wrong book? I think it's possible.

14. Is she a very good dancer? I conclude that she is.

15. Did she help you clean the typewriter? It was desirable, but she didn't.

16. Did she ride in the car with us? She had that opportunity, but she didn't ride with us.

17. Did she tell the children not to sing? I think it's possible.

Exercise 3. Use *must have* in your response to these sentences.

Your sister laughed after she talked with Ralph.	HE MUST HAVE TOLD HER SOMETHING FUNNY.

(or some other original answer)

The doctor had everything ready for us when we arrived.	HE MUST HAVE KNOWN WE WERE COMING.

(or some other original answer)

1. He spoke Italian very well when he came back from Europe.

2. He had to write the check with a pencil.

3. He was very sleepy this morning.

4. He came back from the city with lots of money and no car. What did he do with his car?

5. This morning he left suddenly and went to the dentist's office.

6. He knew English quite well before he entered the university.

7. His music teacher told him he played the piano like an expert.

8. Tom was coughing and sneezing yesterday.

9. He knew what was going to happen every minute during the whole movie.

10. He had souvenirs and photographs of many different cities all over the world.

11. He made a date to meet us at the hotel last night, but he never showed up.

12. His glasses were broken and his nose was bleeding.

Exercise 4. Make sentences with *should have* as shown in the samples given here.

David failed his examination yesterday. —study harder—	HE SHOULD HAVE STUDIED HARDER.
Helen lost her wallet last week. —be more careful—	SHE SHOULD HAVE BEEN MORE CAREFUL.

1. The basketball team lost a game yesterday. —practice more—

2. The students weren't able to find an apartment for this semester. —look earlier—

3. John fell asleep during his last class. —sleep more last night—

4. Mr. Smith was late for work this morning. —get up earlier—

5. Professor Smith didn't give a lecture today. —notify the students—

6. Mrs. Jones wrecked her car last night. —drive more carefully —

   In the following sentences, use the negative
   shouldn't have as shown in the next example.

7. Mary caught a cold yesterday. —go outside without a coat—
   SHE SHOULDN'T HAVE GONE OUTSIDE WITHOUT A COAT.

8. William failed all his exams. —miss so many classes—

9. The thief was sent to prison for two years. —rob the post office—

10. Betty was fined twenty dollars by the judge. —drive without a license—

11. Kermit feels sleepy. —drink wine with his lunch—

12. You can't get your money back now. —throw away the receipt—

B. Notice the progressive verb form used with past modal expressions.

PAST COMPLETE	PAST INCOMPLETE
He *must have washed* the car. (I conclude that he washed it.)	He *must have been washing* the car. (I conclude that he was washing it.)
He *might have traveled* by air.	He *might have been traveling* by air.
He *should have attended* regularly.	He *should have been attending* regularly.
He *could have worked* in the garden.	He *could have been working* in the garden.

COMMENT

The progressive form, made with the auxiliary *be* and the *-ing* form of the main verb, can be used after modal expressions such as *must have* and *might have*. As usual, the progressive form represents an event as incomplete or still in progress at the time indicated by the context.

ADDITIONAL EXAMPLES

1. What was John doing when you saw him in the office? He wasn't doing anything, but he *should have been working*.

2. There was nobody with him, but he was looking at the floor and smiling.

   He *must have been thinking* about something very amusing.

3. I don't know why he was still there at that hour. He *might have been waiting* for somebody.

Exercise 5. Answer with a sentence using *might have* plus a progressive verb with *be* and *-ing*.

Why didn't Paul hear us knock
   on the door? —take a shower— HE MIGHT HAVE BEEN TAKING A SHOWER.
Why was he stopped by the
   police? —go too fast—   HE MIGHT HAVE BEEN GOING TOO FAST.

1. Why was he studying at two a.m.? —prepare for a test—

2. Why were all the women students absent? —attend a meeting—

3. Why didn't Mrs. Johnson answer the telephone? —work in the garden—

4. Why couldn't you see the dog? —hide behind the sofa—

5. Why was it so hot in Mrs. Jones's kitchen? —bake bread—

6. Why was she carrying a bag of corn? —feed the chickens—

   In the following sentences, use the negative
   might not have as shown in the next example.

| She didn't understand anything the professor said. —pay attention— | SHE MIGHT NOT HAVE BEEN PAYING ATTENTION. |

8. Why wasn't she worried about the weather? —travel by air—

9. Why couldn't they understand the explanation? —try very hard—

10. Why did Mike keep his bicycle in the basement? —use it—

11. Why was Mr. Young doing worse than the others? —attend regularly—

12. Why were the students discouraged? —make progress—

13. Why were Donald's hands getting sore? —wear his gloves—

Exercise 6. Give a sentence to fit the situation as illustrated in the first two examples.

| He had a pen in his hand when he came to the door. —must— | HE MUST HAVE BEEN WRITING LETTERS. |
| He still had his lights on at one o'clock in the morning. —might— | HE MIGHT HAVE BEEN PREPARING FOR A TEST. |

1. He wasn't doing anything when I passed by his room this morning. —should—

2. He was talking to Professor Johnson when we entered the classroom, and the professor was laughing. —must—

3. He didn't answer when I called him on the telephone, but I know he was there. —might—

4. We were all working very hard, and Peter was just sitting there watching us. —should—

5. When we went to see Mr. Lands, he had old clothes on and he was carrying some tools. —must—

6. Paul has an examination today, but I saw him at the basketball game last night. —should—

7. I don't know why he had all those maps and airline schedules on his desk. —might—

8. Last Sunday morning I saw Mr. and Mrs. Brown walking down the street, and they were all dressed up. —must—

9. During the lesson, one of the students was looking at a magazine. —should—

10. All during the evening, the people next door were singing and making a lot of noise. —must—

Exercise 7. Form a response with the suggested word. Use the *-ing* form of the main verb if the situation requires it.

George has a test today, but he didn't study for it yesterday. —should—	HE SHOULD HAVE STUDIED.
Alice has a test too, but she wasn't studying when I saw her last night. —should—	SHE SHOULD HAVE BEEN STUDYING.
George had money to buy shoes, but he didn't buy any. —could—	HE COULD HAVE BOUGHT SHOES.

1. Alice got some money from her uncle, but she didn't thank him for it. —should—

2. George was near the bank yesterday, but he didn't cash his check. —could—

3. I don't know what George was doing when I saw him in the bank. —might—

4. George often visits his girlfriend on Saturday. He was home last Saturday when I saw him. —must—

5. Alice sometimes plays tennis on Sunday. She didn't answer the telephone last Sunday. —might—

6. Alice usually plays tennis after supper, but yesterday she had been working very hard and she decided not to play. —must—

7. When the hurricane was announced on the radio, George was the first to learn about it. —must—

8. When we met George, he was not wearing a raincoat, and it was raining very hard. —should—

9. George has a generous roommate who owns two raincoats, but George still didn't have one. —could—

10. Alice doesn't always hear people when she's thinking about something. She didn't answer when I spoke to her yesterday. —must—

11. It's possible she didn't hear me. I don't know. —might not—

12. We couldn't study because the students in the next room were making so much noise. —shouldn't—

C. Notice the shortened form of modal verb phrases.

Did the Johnsons leave early?   Yes, they *must have left early.*
                                 Yes, they *must have.*

We didn't buy it, but we *could have bought it.*
We didn't buy it, but we *could have.*

We weren't working hard, but we *should have been working hard.*
We weren't working hard, but we *should have been.*

COMMENTS

(1)   In short answers and connected sentences the main verb is usually omitted after *must have, could have* and similar modal expressions.

(2)   The use of the auxiliary *been* in the shortened expression (as *should have been* in the example above) makes it clear that the progressive form is intended.

ADDITIONAL EXAMPLES

1. Should I have left earlier? — Yes, you should have.

2. Could he have brought the car? — Yes, he could have.

3. Was it raining? — I don't know; it might have been.

4. Did they hear us? — I'm not sure; they might not have.

5. Did she borrow your umbrella? — No, but she certainly could have.

6. Some of the boys were singing when they shouldn't have been.

7. We didn't give you all the help we should have.

Exercise 8. Give a short answer using *might* or *might have* according to the tense of the question.

Do they make you
    change planes in New York?   I DON'T THINK THEY DO, BUT THEY MIGHT.
Will the doctor
    prescribe some medicine?   I DON'T THINK HE WILL, BUT HE MIGHT.
Did you forget to
    put a stamp on the letter?   I DON'T THINK I DID, BUT I MIGHT HAVE.

         1. Does this train stop in Omaha?
         2. Did the mayor promise to welcome us?
         3. Will you pass all your exams?
         4. Did Alice go to work yesterday?

    5. Do your friends need any ice cubes?
    6. Will the medicine make me feel better?
    7. Did you lose anything at the picnic?
    8. Did Alex leave his keys in the door?

Exercise 9. Listen to the question and give a short answer with *should* or
should have, either affirmative or negative as you prefer.

Did you go to the dentist yesterday?	I SHOULD HAVE, BUT I DIDN'T.
Did you drink a lot last night?	I SHOULDN'T HAVE, BUT I DID.
Are you going to study now?	I SHOULD, BUT I'M NOT GOING TO.

    1. Did you eat a lot last night?
    2. Are you going to help the children now?
    3. Did you play cards last night?
    4. Did you write to your family last night?
    5. Are you going to work hard tonight?
    6. Did you buy a lot of new clothes yesterday?
    7. Did you go to your karate lesson last week?
    8. Are you going to stay up late again tonight?
    9. Did you pay the mechanic for fixing your motorcycle?
   10. Aren't you going to rest a few minutes before you go back?

Exercise 10. Repeat the given statement and add a connected statement with *but.*

I didn't go.	I DIDN'T GO, BUT I COULD HAVE.
He forgot her birthday.	HE FORGOT HER BIRTHDAY, BUT HE SHOULDN'T HAVE.
I thought that she was listening to the radio.	I THOUGHT THAT SHE WAS LISTENING TO THE RADIO, BUT SHE MIGHT NOT HAVE BEEN.
He doesn't think he fell asleep.	HE DOESN'T THINK THAT HE FELL ASLEEP, BUT HE MUST HAVE.

    1. I thought I paid the bill.
    2. I hit him on the nose.
    3. He didn't play the piano when he was here.
    4. It seemed that he wasn't working very hard.
    5. The professor spoke rapidly.
    6. He didn't finish the book last night.
    7. I didn't open the door for her.
    8. We thought he knew English.
    9. He didn't stop for the red light.
   10. I don't think they were sleeping.
   11. We stayed up all night.
   12. It seems that he didn't see me.
   13. They said he had been practicing.
   14. She wasn't speaking English.

D. Notice the use of *had* in wishes referring to the past.

Previous pattern (Lesson 21):

PRESENT SITUATION OR EVENT   WISH

I do not live in a big city now.	I wish I lived in a big city.
The boys are fighting now.	I wish they weren't fighting.

New pattern:

PAST SITUATION OR EVENT   WISH

I did not live there then.	I *wish I had* lived there then.
I broke my window.	I *wish I hadn't* broken it.

COMMENT

After the verb *wish,* a situation or event contrary to the real facts of the past is expressed with *had* and the past participle of the following verb expression.

NOTES:

(1)   If you believe that it might be possible for the desire to be realized, use *hope* rather than *wish:* "I'm sorry you dropped your glasses; I hope they didn't break."

(2)   The verb expression after *had (been)* or *hadn't (been)* is usually omitted if it is identical to what has already been said:

> We didn't go to Moscow. I wish we *had.*
> It was raining when we got off the plane. I wish it *hadn't been.*

ADDITIONAL EXAMPLES

1. I'm sorry you fell in the mud yesterday, but I wish you *hadn't been wearing* my sweater at the time.

2. Alice went shopping after lunch and tonight she has to go to a meeting. Now she wishes that she *had taken* a nap when she had the chance.

3. I borrowed ten dollars from you yesterday and now I wish I *hadn't.* I wish I didn't owe anybody any money.

4. Carol said, "Did you answer all the questions on the test yesterday? I hope you did." And Michael answered, "No, I didn't. I wish I *had.*"

Exercise 11. Change each negative statement to a wish.

The doctor wasn't in his office yesterday.   I WISH THE DOCTOR HAD BEEN
                                               IN HIS OFFICE YESTERDAY.

Helen didn't speak English at that time.   I WISH HELEN HAD SPOKEN
                                             ENGLISH AT THAT TIME.

1. Paul didn't know how to swim last year.
2. Professor Jones's lecture wasn't as interesting as yours.
3. Mr. Smith didn't work in his garden last week.
4. John didn't come to class yesterday.
5. Mr. Peters didn't sell his old car.
6. John didn't speak French last year.
7. He wasn't smiling when I saw him.

   For the following statements, make a negative
   wish, as shown in the next example.

8. Mr. and Mrs. Miller came in at the same time.
                     I WISH MR. AND MRS. MILLER HADN'T
                         COME IN AT THE SAME TIME.

9. Mrs. Smith was sick.
10. Alice broke her leg.
11. The children felt sad.
12. Mr. Miller had to work downtown yesterday.
13. Mary failed all her examinations.
14. Dr. Green lost his notebook.
15. I played tennis all day yesterday.
16. The governor refused to have dinner with us last night.

Exercise 12. Form *wish* sentences using an adjective or adverb with the opposite meaning.

I'm afraid Mary felt *sad*.   I WISH SHE HAD FELT HAPPY.
It's too bad Mrs. Jones was *sick*.   I WISH SHE HAD BEEN WELL.

1. I knew that all the classes began *early*.
2. I found out that the library was *closed*.
3. I thought the tea was *weak*.
4. I discovered that the mayor was *old*.
5. It's too bad the announcer spoke *fast*.
6. I'm sorry the tickets were *expensive*.
7. It's too bad they made the streets *narrow*.
8. I'm sorry they made the exam *easy*.
9. I learned that the shops were *open*.
10. I'm afraid John put down the *wrong* answer.

Exercise 13. This exercise is a review of wishes for the present and future as well as for the past. Make an affirmative wish based on the sentences given. Use the shortened form of the predicate.

Jack doesn't live in the country.	I WISH HE DID.
He won't tell us the truth.	I WISH HE WOULD.
He didn't bring any food.	I WISH HE HAD.
He wasn't carrying his umbrella.	I WISH HE HAD BEEN.

1. He doesn't know the answer.
2. He won't play tennis with us.
3. He can't ride a horse.
4. He isn't listening to the radio.
5. He wasn't listening last night at this hour either.
6. He didn't remind me to get up early.
7. He doesn't like the music they play here.
8. He won't let me use his bicycle.
9. He can't find out what the trouble is.
10. He didn't get off the plane when it landed in Detroit.
11. He wasn't arrested by the State Police.
13. He isn't receiving money from his family.
14. He didn't introduce me to his cousin.
15. He doesn't know how to play the guitar.
16. He can't play any musical instrument at all.

NOTE: In addition to *wish* sentences beginning with *I wish,* we can also use *I wished:*

> All last summer, I wished I *owned* a car.
> During the exam, I wished I *had studied* harder.

In the first sentence, "wishing" and "not owning a car" were at the same time. In such sentences use the forms of Lesson 21.B (*owned, lived, were,* etc.)

In the second sentence, "wishing" and "not studying harder" were not at the same time. The "wishing" took place later. In such sentences, use the forms of 22.D, that is, *had* + past participle.

Lesson 23

A.   Subordinators: *if, unless, because, although, whether, whenever.*

B.   *because of, in spite of, regardless of.*

A.1 Notice the use of the subordinators *if* and *unless.*

> John will stay home *if*   the weather isn't nice.
>
> John will stay home *unless* the weather is   nice.

COMMENTS

(1) *If* and *unless* are used to introduce subordinate clauses, that is, embedded statements. These clauses have a subject, e.g. *the weather,* and a verb phrase.

(2) The essential meaning of *unless* is "if . . . not."

Exercise 1. Change the statements with *if* to corresponding statements with *unless.* Change those with *unless* to statements with *if.*

John will buy a new bicycle unless he can fix his old one today. **JOHN WILL BUY A NEW BICYCLE IF HE CAN'T FIX HIS OLD ONE TODAY.**

John usually goes to the movies on Friday if he doesn't have to study. **JOHN USUALLY GOES TO THE MOVIES ON FRIDAY UNLESS HE HAS TO STUDY.**

1. John might go to New York unless it costs too much.
2. Paul will never know where you live if you don't tell him.
3. I am going to Florida unless I get a good job here.
4. I can't buy any new shoes if you don't give me any money.
5. Joe will take the bus unless he has a date.
6. I can't work these algebra problems if you don't help me.

(Instead of changing the second clause, change the first clause in the following sentences.)

7. John will go swimming if the sun comes out.
    JOHN WON'T GO SWIMMING UNLESS THE SUN COMES OUT.

252

8. John will call Mary if he has time.
9. He won't study unless he has to.
10. I like to go swimming if the water is warm enough.
11. I can't work these algebra problems unless you help me.
12. I'll go to the movies if I finish my homework.

A.2   Notice the use of the subordinators *because* and *although*.

Situation: It was raining.   *(Cause / effect)*

Mary wore a raincoat *because* it was raining.
John wanted to go out *although* it was raining.

COMMENTS

(1)   *Because* introduces a fact or explanation to *support* the idea of the clause.

(2)   A clause introduced by *although* states a contrary fact or an argument *against* the idea of the main clause.

NOTE: *Though* and *even though* are similar in meaning to *although*. Use *even if* to introduce a supposition rather than a fact: "Even if the weather is bad tomorrow, John will want to go out."

ADDITIONAL EXAMPLES

1. Although the traffic held us up, we got to the airport on time. (Even though the traffic held us up.)

2. I forgot my appointment although my secretary reminded me of it. (Even though she reminded me of it.)

3. We don't know who he is, but even if he is the mayor we won't let him talk.

Exercise 2. Make new sentences using *because* or *although*. Use the word which is the most appropriate.

John went to bed early last night. He was tired.	JOHN WENT TO BED EARLY LAST NIGHT BECAUSE HE WAS TIRED.
Mary came to class today. She wasn't feeling well.	MARY CAME TO CLASS TODAY ALTHOUGH SHE WASN'T FEELING WELL.

1. John went swimming yesterday. The weather was nice.
2. Mary stayed at home yesterday. She had a headache.
3. Mr. Miller worked hard. It was very hot.
4. John completed the course. It was difficult.
5. Everyone likes John. He is very friendly.

6. Juan can't go home for two years. He is very homesick.
7. Juan is studying English here. His father wants him to.
8. Juan wrote to the university. It was difficult for him.
9. John helped Mary write the letter. It was easy for him.
10. Susan drove from New York to California. Her car was very old.
11. Mary feeds her cat the best cat food. It is very expensive.
12. Mr. and Mrs. Miller want to sell their furniture. They are moving to New York.
13. Alice is going to Florida. She wants to visit her sister.

A.3 Notice the use of the subordinator *whether or not.*

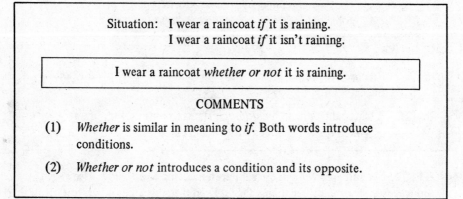

> Situation: I wear a raincoat *if* it is raining.
>   I wear a raincoat *if* it isn't raining.
>
> > I wear a raincoat *whether or not* it is raining.
>
> ### COMMENTS
>
> (1) *Whether* is similar in meaning to *if.* Both words introduce conditions.
>
> (2) *Whether or not* introduces a condition and its opposite.

NOTE: *Whether or not* can be separated.

> I wear a raincoat *whether* it is raining *or not.*

Exercise 3. Answer the questions, using *whether or not.*

Do you study if you are tired?   I STUDY WHETHER OR NOT I AM TIRED.
Are you going to go to   I AM GOING TO GO TO CHICAGO
  Chicago if John goes?   WHETHER OR NOT JOHN GOES.

1. Can John understand Americans when they speak fast?
2. Can you finish your homework before the movies if I help you?
3. Do you like to study before dinner if you are tired?
4. Can you study when your friends are talking?
5. Do you like your friends to visit you when you are studying?
6. Do you continue to study if there is a good television program?
7. Do you want to go to the movies if there is a good television program?
8. Do you want to get something to eat after the movie if it isn't too late?

NOTE: Subordinate clauses may precede the main clause:

> John will call Mary *if he has time.*
> *If he has time,* John will call Mary.

Because it was raining, Mary wore a raincoat [handwritten]

Mary wore a raincoat *because it was raining.*
Because it was raining, Mary wore a raincoat.

John didn't wear a raincoat *although it was raining.*
Although it was raining, John didn't wear a raincoat.

NOTE: *Whenever* means "at any time" or "every time." It is used like the other subordinators. *if* [handwritten]

I go swimming *whenever* the weather is nice.
I wear a rain coat *whenever* it rains.
I read *whenever* I have time.

B. Notice the use of *because of, in spite of, regardless of.*

yesterday, I went to the movie [handwritten]

> Mary wore a raincoat because it was raining.
> Mary wore a raincoat *because of* the rain.
>
> John didn't wear a raincoat although it was raining.
> John didn't wear a raincoat *in spite of* the rain.
>
> I wear a raincoat whether or not the weather is nice.
> I wear a raincoat *regardless of* the weather.

COMMENTS

(1) The meaning of the two members of each pair of sentences is essentially the same.

(2) The subordinators *because, although,* and *whether* introduce clauses that are equivalent to independent statements. On the other hand, *because of, in spite of,* and *regardless of* precede noun phrases (*the rain, the weather*).

Exercise 4. Make sentences with *because of.*

I stayed home because it was raining.	I STAYED HOME BECAUSE OF THE RAIN.
I came here because I wanted to take the English course.	I CAME HERE BECAUSE OF THE ENGLISH COURSE.

1. Mary stayed home yesterday because she had a headache.
2. Mr. Miller is going to move to California because he likes the weather there.
3. George couldn't answer the letter immediately because he had a lot of homework to do.
4. Alice is going to Florida because she wants to visit her sister.
5. John can't go to the movies tonight because he has an exam tomorrow.
6. Mr. Jones moved to Arizona because the state has a dry climate.

7. John got home late because the traffic was heavy.
8. The classes were cancelled because it was a holiday.

Exercise 5. Make sentences with *in spite of.*

We went on a picnic
   although the weather was cool.
	WE WENT ON A PICNIC
	   IN SPITE OF THE COOL WEATHER.

Jack went with us
   although he had a lot of work to do.
	JACK WENT WITH US
	   IN SPITE OF HIS WORK.

Ruth went too although she had a cold.	RUTH WENT TOO IN SPITE OF HER COLD.

1. Betty went too although her mother didn't want her to.
2. George went too although he had a class.
3. We didn't wear coats although the weather was cool.
4. We went in George's car although the engine was in bad condition.
5. We decided to go to Fish Lake although the distance was great.
6. We wanted to go there although the road was not very good.
7. We got there in an hour although George's car was very old.
8. We swam in the lake although the water was cold.
9. We sat on the ground although the grass was wet.
10. We enjoyed our lunch although the coffee was cold.
11. We stayed all afternoon although it began to rain.
12. We started home at 6:00 although Betty wanted to stay longer.

SUMMARY EXERCISE

Consider the following situation. Then complete the statements by continuing the same theme.

> "Oscar is friendly and carefree. He is happy to give everything to
> his friends who spend most of his large amounts of money."

1. Oscar has many friends because —
2. A few of his friends like him only because of —
3. Most of his friends like him because —
4. He likes all of them although —
5. He spends his money freely if —
6. He gives away his books when —
7. He acts like a poor man in spite of —
8. He is still happy at the end of the month although —
9. He is always carefree whether or not —
10. He can't take his friends to parties at the end of the month because —
11. Oscar's uncle should send him clothes in place of the check because —
12. Oscar can't buy any clothes in spite of —
13. He doesn't have any good shirts because —

Lesson 24

A. Conditional Sentences:

> If he knows the answer, he will tell her.
> If he knew the answer, he would tell her.
> If he had known the answer, he would have told her.

A. Compare the conditional sentences, which are parts of possible answers to the question.

QUESTIONS

A	Will he tell Mary the answer?	Maybe.
B	Will he tell Mary the answer?	No, but ...
C	Did he tell Mary the answer?	No, but ...

CONDITIONAL SENTENCES

AA	If he *knows* it,	he *will tell* her.
BB	If he *knew* it,	he *would tell* her.
CC	If he *had known* it,	he *would have told* her.

COMMENTS

(1) Sentence AA describes a possible situation of present or future time. "If he knows" implies "he might know."

(2) Sentence BB describes a hypothetical situation, one that is either contrary to the real facts of the present, or unlikely to occur in the future. "If he knew" implies "he doesn't know."

(3) Sentence CC describes a hypothetical situation of past time, one which did not occur. "If he had known" implies "he didn't know."

(4) Sentences AA and BB both describe situations in the present or future time. However, the *if*-clause of sentence BB contains a verb which is identical in form to a past tense form. The second part of BB (main clause) contains *would* + infinitive.

(5) The *if*-clause of sentence CC contains *had* + past participle. The second part contains *would have* + past participle.

257

NOTE: Some of the above verb forms were introduced in Lessons 21 and 22:

> I wish he *knew* the answer.
> I wish he *would tell* her.
> I wish he *had known* the answer.

ADDITIONAL EXAMPLES

Imagine the following situation:

> I think Mr. Taylor is going to drive to Detroit tomorrow.
> I don't think he is going to go to New York.

The following sentences are based on the above situation.

I *will* go with him	if he *goes* to Detroit.
I *will* ride with him	if he *drives* to Detroit.
I *will* go to Detroit	if he *does*.
I *would* go with him	if he *went* to New York.
I *would* ride with him	if he *drove* to New York.
I *would* go to New York	if he *did*.

Exercise 1. Imagine you are talking to a person who hopes to go to Europe next summer. You want to go also, but you don't have enough money. Respond to his statement as in the examples.

I will go by plane
    if I go to Europe.
I will get there fast
    if I fly.
	I WOULD GO BY PLANE
	    IF I WENT TO EUROPE.
	I WOULD GET THERE FAST
	    IF I FLEW.

1. I will go to London first if I go to England.
2. I will visit Buckingham Palace if I am in England.
3. I will take the train if I decide to go to France.
4. I will spend at least a week in Paris if I go to France.
5. I will see the Eiffel Tower if I am in Paris.
6. I will visit Amsterdam next if my friends invite me.
7. I will rent a car if I decide to go to Sweden.
8. I will see Stockholm if I visit Sweden.
9. I will stop in Germany if I travel to Italy.
10. I will learn a little German if I stay in Germany.
11. I will fly to Berlin if I have time.
12. I will cross the Alps if I go to Italy.
13. I will see many famous museums if I stop in Florence.
14. I will write many postcards if I don't write letters.
15. I will spend a lot of money if I stay in Europe long.

Exercise 2. Give complete answers to the following questions.

What would you do if you were sick?	IF I WERE SICK, I WOULD GO TO A DOCTOR.
What would you do if you were rich?	IF I WERE RICH, I WOULD TRAVEL AROUND THE WORLD.
What would you do if someone stole your car?	IF SOMEONE STOLE MY CAR, I WOULD TELL THE POLICE.

1. What would you do if you were a millionaire?
2. What would you do if you had a car?
3. What would you do if you were president?
4. What would you do if you were ten years younger?
5. What would you do if you had all the money you wanted?
6. What would you do if you discovered a gold mine?
7. What would you do if you found $50 on the street?
8. What would you do if you needed a pencil?
9. What would you do if you were sick?
10. What would you do if you tore your coat?
11. What would you do if you had a vacation next week?
12. What would you do if you were a king?
13. What would you do if you didn't have class today?
14. What would you do if you had an exam today?
15. What would you do if you were in Paris now?
16. What would you do if you thought it was going to rain?

Exercise 3. Imagine a situation where it is *possible* for you to go to New York. Make a series of statements, each of which is based on the preceding one.

First person:	If we receive some money, we will go to New York.
Second person:	If we go to New York, we will go by plane.
Third person:	If we go by plane, we will arrive at Kennedy Airport.
Fourth person:	If we arrive at Kennedy Airport, we will take a bus to Manhattan.
Fifth person:	If we take a bus to Manhattan, we will see the Empire State Building.
Sixth person:	If we see the Empire State Building, we will want to go to the top.
Seventh person:	If we go to the top, we will have a nice view of New York.

(To start a new series, use the following sentence.)

First person:	If I have time, I will take a long vacation next summer.

Exercise 4. Imagine a situation where it is *improbable* that you will go to New York. Make a series of statements, each of which is based on the preceding one.

First person: If we received some money, we would go to New York.
Second person: If we went to New York, we would go by plane.
Third person: If we went by plane, we would arrive at Kennedy Airport.

(Continue as in Exercise 3.)

(To start a new series, use the following sentence.)

First person: If I had time, I would take a long vacation next summer.

Exercise 5. Change the following sentences to past-time statements describing events which did not occur.

I would go to Chicago   I WOULD HAVE GONE TO
   if I had a car.   CHICAGO IF I HAD HAD A CAR.
I would wear my raincoat   I WOULD HAVE WORN MY
   if it were cloudy.   RAINCOAT IF IT HAD BEEN CLOUDY.
I would go to the museum   I WOULD HAVE GONE TO THE
   if it stayed open   MUSEUM IF IT HAD STAYED
   in the evenings.   OPEN IN THE EVENINGS.

1. I would study if I had to.
2. I would visit John if he were home.
3. I would watch television if I didn't have so much homework.
4. Mary would go to the party if you sent her a special invitation.
5. George would bring his friends if you asked him to.
6. I would buy a new car if you lent me the money.
7. Mr. Miller would work in the garden if he needed exercise.
8. I would take an aspirin if I had a headache.
9. I would study the irregular verbs if I didn't know them.
10. I would buy a toothbrush if I needed one.
11. I would throw away my ballpoint pen if it didn't work.
12. George would raise his hand if he didn't understand something.
13. Alfred would get mad if George raised his hand too often.
14. Mary would bring an umbrella if she knew it was going to rain.

Exercise 6. Give complete answers to the following questions.

What would you have done
  if you had
  been sick yesterday?
	IF I HAD BEEN SICK,
	I WOULD HAVE GONE
	TO A DOCTOR.

What would you have done
  if someone had
  stolen your car yesterday?
	IF SOMEONE HAD STOLEN MY CAR,
	I WOULD HAVE
	TOLD THE POLICE.

1. What would you have done if you had stayed in your country?
2. What would you have done if you had gone to France last year?
3. What would you have done if you had found a $50 bill on the street yesterday?
4. What would you have done if you had been Napoleon?
5. What would you have done if you had been born in 1400?
6. What could you have done if you had needed money last week?
7. What could you have done if you had torn your coat yesterday?
8. What could you have done if you had lost all your money last week?
9. What might you have done if you had had a vacation last week?
10. What might you have done if you had been Adam?
11. What might you have done if you had lived 100 years ago?
12. What would you have done if you had been Columbus?

Exercise 7. Imagine a situation where it was *impossible* for you to go to New York. Make a series of statements, each of which is based on the preceding one.

First person:	If we had received some money, we would have gone to New York.
Second person:	If we had gone to New York, we would have gone by plane.
Third person:	If we had gone by plane, we would have arrived at Kennedy airport.

(Continue as in Exercise 3.)

(To start a new series, use the following sentence.)

First person:	If I had had time last summer, I would have taken a long vacation.

10 sentences

261

ADDITIONAL EXAMPLES
OF CONDITIONAL SENTENCES

Notice the words which are used in the same position as *will* and *would.*

I *will*	study algebra next year	*if I have*	time.
I *can*	study algebra next year	*if I have*	time.
I *must*	study algebra next year	*if I have*	time.
I *might*	study algebra next year	*if I have*	time.
I *am going to*	study algebra next year	*if I have*	time.
I *have to*	study algebra next year	*if I have*	time.
I *expect to*	study algebra next year	*if I have*	time.
I *would*	study algebra next year	*if I had*	time.
I *could*	study algebra next year	*if I had*	time.
I *might*	study algebra next year	*if I had*	time.

plan
intend

Notice the words which are used in the same position as *if.*

Juan *would*	enter the university next year	*if*	he *spoke* English well.
He *wouldn't*	enter the university	*unless*	he *spoke* English well.
He *could*	go to a smaller college	*whether or not*	he *spoke* English well.
He *would*	study there	*until*	he *learned* English well.

NOTE TO ADVANCED STUDENTS: Some additional types of conditional sentences are illustrated below. The first group includes possible or likely events and situations. The second group includes the corresponding hypothetical statements.

1. Possible or likely events and states. (These sentences may be thought of as possible answers to the questions, "Was Tom (Is Tom, Will Tom be) happy or sad?")

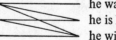

If Mary wrote the letters	he was happy.
If Mary is writing the letters	he is happy.
If Mary writes the letters	he will be happy.

The lines indicate which clauses may be joined. Thus there are six sentences.

2. Hypothetical or contrary-to-fact events and states. ("Tom wasn't (isn't, won't be) happy.")

If Mary had written the letters	he would have been happy.
If Mary were writing the letters	
If Mary wrote the letters	he would be happy.

Lesson 25

A. *so . . . that:* so busy *that* he can't go.
  such . . . that: such a busy man *that* he can't go.

B. Negative questions: Isn't the teacher here?

C. Tag questions: John is here, isn't he?

A. Notice the statements which are connected with *so . . . that* and *such . . . that.*

Previous pattern:

> Mr. Miller is very busy. He can't leave his office.
>
> Mr. Miller is *too busy to* leave his office.
>   ADJ.

New patterns:

> Mr. Miller is *so busy that* he can't leave his office.
>   ADJ.
>
> Mr. Miller is *such a busy man that* he can't leave his office.
>   NOUN PHR.

COMMENTS

(1) The example sentences all have approximately the same meaning.

(2) *So . . . that* is used with adjectives (e.g. *busy*)

(3) *Such . . . that* is used with noun phrases (e.g. *a busy man*).

NOTE:

1. The *so . . . that* pattern also occurs without *that:*

> Mr. Miller is so busy he can't leave his office.

2. The *so . . . that* pattern is used with adverbs as well as adjectives:

> He left so *quickly* that we didn't have time to say goodbye.
>   ADVERB

263

1—5

Exercise 1. Listen to the statements. Make statements with a similar meaning using *so . . . that.*

John is very busy.	JOHN IS SO BUSY THAT
He can't go to Chicago.	HE CAN'T GO TO CHICAGO.
Mary is very homesick.	MARY IS SO HOMESICK
She can't study.	THAT SHE CAN'T STUDY.

1. Bob is very sick. He can't come to class.
2. My chair is very hard. I can't sit comfortably.
3. Mr. Smith is very tired. He won't stay up late tonight.
4. The movie was very interesting. Susan saw it twice.
5. John's car is very old. He can't sell it.
6. Mrs. Taylor is very pleasant. Everyone likes her.
7. Some of the students were very sleepy. They fell asleep during the movie.
8. The new car was very expensive. John couldn't buy it.
9. The ceiling is very high. John can't reach it.
10. Mr. Jones is very lazy. He won't work.
11. Mr. Miller talks very fast. I can't understand him.
12. The students practiced in the lab very often. Their pronunciation improved a lot.
13. John pressed his pencil very hard. The lead broke.
14. Mrs. Smith drove her car very fast. She received a ticket for speeding.

1—5

Exercise 2. Listen to the statements. Make statements with a similar meaning using *such . . . that.*

It was a very cold day.	IT WAS SUCH A COLD DAY
Susan stayed home.	THAT SUSAN STAYED HOME.
A Cadillac is a very expensive car.	A CADILLAC IS SUCH AN EXPENSIVE
John can't buy one.	CAR THAT JOHN CAN'T BUY ONE.

1. The Smiths are very friendly people. Everyone feels welcome at their house.
2. John has a very severe headache. He's going to go to the doctor.
3. John is a very busy student. He sleeps only six hours a night.
4. The football team has very good players. It has never lost a game.
5. Mary is a very good student. She is going to pass all of her exams.
6. San Francisco is a very interesting city to visit. I want to go there as soon as possible.
7. It was a very cold day. Susan stayed home.
8. A Cadillac is a very expensive car. John can't buy one.
9. The museum is a very interesting place. The students want to visit it again.
10. John told a very funny story. Mary wanted to hear it again.

Exercise 3. Listen to the statements with *too . . . to*. Produce similar statements with *so . . . that* and *such . . . that*.

Paul is too short to reach the apple on the tree.	PAUL IS SO SHORT THAT HE CAN'T REACH THE APPLE ON THE TREE. PAUL IS SUCH A SHORT BOY THAT HE CAN'T REACH THE APPLE ON THE TREE.
Peter is too old to become a soldier.	PETER IS SO OLD THAT HE CAN'T BECOME A SOLDIER. PETER IS SUCH AN OLD MAN THAT HE CAN'T BECOME A SOLDIER.
These shoes are too small for me to wear.	THESE SHOES ARE SO SMALL THAT I CAN'T WEAR THEM. THESE ARE SUCH SMALL SHOES THAT I CAN'T WEAR THEM.

1. This book is too difficult for the new students to read.
2. The professor is too busy to leave his office.
3. He is too sick to stand up.
4. This car is too expensive for us to buy.
5. She is too young to go to school.
6. This town is too small to have a fire department.
7. This coat is too long for me to wear.
8. My suitcase is too heavy to carry.
9. This hill is too steep for us to climb.
10. It is too stormy for planes to fly.
11. This lake is too wide for Fred to swim across.

NOTES: In addition to adjectives, the *so . . . that* pattern is also used with adverbs (e.g. *rapidly*) and the quantity expressions *many, much, little,* and *few*.

John spoke *so rapidly that* I couldn't understand him.
Mary had *so much work that* she was busy all day.
John has *so little money that* he can't buy the book.

B. Notice the answers to the negative questions.

Previous pattern:

Is the teacher here today?	Yes, he is.
Is this Lesson 26?	No, it isn't.

New pattern:

Isn't the teacher here today?	Yes, he is.
Isn't this Lesson 26?	No, it isn't.

COMMENT

The answer to a negative question is the same as the answer to the corresponding affirmative question. If the answer to the affirmative question is "yes," the answer to the negative question will be "yes" also. Likewise, if the answer to the affirmative question is "no," the answer to the corresponding negative question will be "no" also.

NOTE: The negative questions above correspond to the following affirmative statements.

The teacher is here today.
This is Lesson 26.

If the speaker has some evidence indicating that these statements might not be true, and if he is surprised at this evidence, he might ask the negative questions. Sometimes the speaker still expects the situations expressed by the affirmative statements to be true, and he asks the questions for confirmation or reassurance.

Exercise 4. Give short answers to the following questions.

Isn't Brazil in South America?	YES, IT IS.
Didn't Columbus discover China?	NO, HE DIDN'T.
Shouldn't we always speak English?	YES, WE SHOULD.

1. Isn't Spain in Europe?
2. Isn't France in South America?
3. Isn't English an easy language?
4. Don't most of the people in the United States speak English?
5. Don't most of the people in Brazil speak Portuguese?
6. Don't most of the students in this class speak English well?
7. Can't a plane go faster than a train can?
8. Can't more people ride in a plane than in a bus?
9. Can't a man work harder than a woman can?
10. Didn't Edison invent the electric light?
11. Didn't Edison invent the automobile?

12. Haven't you learned to speak English perfectly yet?
13. Shouldn't you practice ten hours every day?
14. Don't you expect to speak English perfectly next year?
15. Don't you think the answers to negative questions are easy?

C. Notice the tag questions.

STATEMENT + TAG QUESTION	ANSWERS
John *is* here, *isn't* he?	Yes, he is. No, he isn't.
Mary *isn't* here, *is* she?	No, she isn't. Yes, she is.

COMMENT

Isn't he? and *is she?* are tag questions. Negative tag questions follow affirmative statements. Affirmative tag questions follow negative statements.

ADDITIONAL EXAMPLES

You *can* go, *can't* you?
She *hasn't* gone, *has* she?
John *doesn't* have a TV, *does* he?

They have a car, *don't* they?
Mary speaks Spanish, *doesn't* she?

COMMENT

If a form of *be* or an auxiliary (e.g. *can, has, does*) occurs in the statement part, it is repeated in the tag. If there is no auxiliary in the first part, *do* or *does* (or *don't* or *doesn't*) appears in the tag.

NOTE: A tag question with falling intonation indicates that the speaker thinks his statement is true. He expects the answer to agree with his statement.

	EXPECTED ANSWERS
John is here, isn't he?	Yes, he is.
Mary isn't here, is she?	No, she isn't.

However, if the statement isn't true, the answer will not agree.

John is here, isn't he?	No, he isn't.
Mary isn't here, is she?	Yes, she is.

When rising intonation is used in the tag question, the speaker does not necessarily expect the answer to agree with his statement.

ADDITIONAL EXAMPLES

It's a nice day today, isn't it?	YES, IT IS.
It wasn't very nice yesterday, was it?	NO, IT WASN'T.
There's going to be a football game tomorrow, isn't there?	YES, THERE IS.
There isn't going to be a dance, is there?	NO, THERE ISN'T.
It hasn't been very cold this winter, has it?	NO, IT HASN'T.
It had snowed by this time last winter, hadn't it?	YES, IT HAD.
We should study tonight, shouldn't we?	YES, WE SHOULD.
We shouldn't have gone to the party last night, should we?	NO, WE SHOULDN'T.
You're going to be home tonight, aren't you?	YES, I AM.
We must try to practice more, mustn't we?	YES, WE MUST.
Argentina is the largest country in South America, isn't it?	NO, IT ISN'T.

NOTE: In the last example above, the first speaker expects an answer of *yes* to agree with his statement. But the second speaker thinks the statement is wrong and gives an answer of *no*.

Exercise 5. Repeat the statements and add tag questions.

Mr. Smith is from California.	MR. SMITH IS FROM CALIFORNIA, ISN'T HE?
George wasn't in class yesterday.	GEORGE WASN'T IN CLASS YESTERDAY, WAS HE?
Mr. Smith drives to work.	MR. SMITH DRIVES TO WORK, DOESN'T HE?

1. John can drive a car.
2. Mary speaks Spanish.
3. John lived in New York last year.
4. Mrs. Smith flew to California last week.
5. Bob lost his watch.
6. Dr. Jones has a lot of patients.
7. Mr. Smith doesn't like beer.
8. Mary was at the party last night.
9. There's a party tonight.
10. John won't forget to come.
11. We aren't going to stay very late.
12. We should use English in class.

Lesson 26

A. *Self* pronouns: *myself, yourself,* etc.

B. Verb expressions in *-ing* after other verbs:

I enjoyed singing.

A.1 Notice the use of the reflexive pronoun *himself.*

Previous pattern:

John	sees	*Mary*	in the mirror.
SUBJECT		OBJECT	

New pattern:

John	sees	*himself*	in the mirror.
SUBJECT		OBJECT	

COMMENT

Reflexive pronouns, such as *himself,* are used when the subject and object of a sentence are the same person or thing.

ADDITIONAL EXAMPLES

I see myself.   We see ourselves.
You see yourself.   You see yourselves.
He sees himself.   They see themselves.
She sees herself.
It sees itself.

NOTE: In Lesson 8 it was pointed out that two patterns are possible when a direct object and an indirect object follow certain verbs.

John bought   *a book* for *Mary*.
                      D.O.   I.O.

John bought *Mary a book*.
            I.O.   D.O.

269

Similarly two patterns are possible when the indirect object is a reflexive pronoun.

John bought   *a book* for *himself.*
           D.O.   I.O.

John bought *himself a book.*
     I.O.   D.O.

Exercise 1. Repeat the statements, omitting the prepositions *for* and *to* and making the necessary changes in word order.

John bought a book for himself   JOHN BOUGHT HIMSELF A BOOK.
Mary wrote a note to herself.   MARY WROTE HERSELF A NOTE.

1. George is going to buy a coat for himself.
2. George sent a package to himself.
3. John made a sandwich for himself.
4. Mary is going to bake a cake for herself.
5. George is going to find a job for himself.
6. Bill cut a slice of bread for himself.
7. Mr. and Mrs. Miller are going to build a house for themselves.
8. John ordered a hamburger for himself.
9. George found a chair for himself.
10. Mary sewed a dress for herself.

A.2   Notice the use of *self* words to indicate emphasis.

Previous patterns: *by himself : alone*

John bought *a tie* for *himself.*
     D.O.   I.O.

John bought *himself a tie.*
     I.O.   D.O.

New pattern: *without help assistance*

John bought *a tie himself.*
     D.O.   EMPHASIS

COMMENT

In the new pattern, the subject is emphasized by adding a *self* pronoun. *To emphasize* means "to concentrate or focus attention on something" or "to make something important." In the example sentence above, *John* is emphasized: John — not someone else — bought the tie.

NOTE: *Self* pronouns are also used immediately following the noun phrases they emphasize. This usage is more common in writing than in speech.

John himself bought the tie.

Exercise 2. Add a *self* pronoun to each statement for emphasis.

George bought a car.   GEORGE BOUGHT A CAR HIMSELF.
Mary told the story.   MARY TOLD THE STORY HERSELF.

    1. John is going to make dinner.
    2. George made a sandwich.
    3. Mary is going to bake a cake.
    4. George is going to find a job.
    5. Mr. and Mrs. Miller are going to build a house.
    6. George went to the store.
    7. Alice wrote the letter.

Exercise 3. *By myself, by yourself, by himself,* etc. mean "alone." Substitute *by myself,* etc. in the following statements.

I'm going alone.   I'M GOING BY MYSELF.
Do you live alone?   DO YOU LIVE BY YOURSELF?
John likes to be alone.   JOHN LIKES TO BE BY HIMSELF

    1. You can't play tennis alone.
    2. The children are singing alone.
    3. I don't like to go to the movies alone.
    4. Mary is going alone.
    5. Professor Taylor prefers to work alone.
    6. There was too much work for us to do alone.
    7. Mary is going to go downtown alone.
    8. Do you like to study alone?
    9. John and Mary were alone.
  10. There was so much work that I couldn't do it alone.

B. Notice the use of the *-ing* form of verbs following certain other verbs.

Previous pattern (Lesson 13):

I wanted *to sing.*

New pattern:

I enjoyed *singing.*
I kept on *singing.*
I finished *singing.*

COMMENT

Use the *-ing* form of verbs after *enjoy, keep (on), avoid, finish, consider, get through, insist on.* Do not use *to* + verb after these words.

ADDITIONAL EXAMPLES

I	enjoy	dancing	very much.
I can	keep (on)	dancing	all night.
Paul	avoids	going	to dances whenever he can.
He	insists on	staying	home tonight.
I must	finish	doing	my homework before the dance.
I hope I	get through	working	early tonight.
Will you	consider	helping	me with my work.
George	can't help*	asking	questions.

*Can't help is an idiom which means "can't avoid" or "can't stop."

NOTE: The following examples contain verbs which are followed by either the *-ing* form or the *to* form with approximately the same meaning.

They began	studying	here last year.
They began	to study	here last year.
They started	learning	English immediately.
They started	to learn	English immediately.
They continue	practicing	every day.
They continue	to practice	every day.
They prefer	studying	together.
They prefer	to study	together.
They like	learning	new patterns.
They like	to learn	new patterns.

Exercise 4. Substitute the following words.

Betty considered dancing.

enjoys	BETTY ENJOYS DANCING.
kept on	BETTY KEPT ON DANCING.
working	BETTY KEPT ON WORKING.

1. insisted on	7. enjoy	13. crying
2. the boys	8. I	14. Betty
3. avoided	9. kept on	15. continued
4. studying	10. laughing	16. dancing
5. finished	11. started	17. got through
6. eating	12. the baby	18. considered

NOTE: The following examples contain verbs that are followed by either the *-ing* form or by the *to* form but with different meanings.

> *stop*
>
> John stopped *eating.*
> John stopped *to eat.*

Stopped eating means stopped the activity of eating.

Stopped to eat means stopped some other activity in order to eat. For example:

> John stopped driving (in order) to eat.

> *remember*
>> Mary remembered *writing* to her family.
>> Mary remembered *to write* to her family.

Remembered writing means that she wrote at some time in the past and that she remembered later. Thus the writing was first, the remembering second.

Remembered to write means that she did not forget her intention to write. Thus the remembering was first, and the writing second.

Exercise 5. Combine the words and phrases into sentences. Use the *-ing* or the *to* form of the verb.

Mary enjoys—
  —swim very much—   MARY ENJOYS SWIMMING VERY MUCH.
She likes—
  —swim in the lake—   SHE LIKES SWIMMING IN THE LAKE.
                       or SHE LIKES TO SWIM IN THE LAKE.
She wanted—
  —go there last Saturday—   SHE WANTED TO GO THERE LAST SATURDAY.

1. She decided— —ask Bill and John to go with her—
2. They wanted— —go very much—
3. They considered— —take the bus—
4. John insisted on— —take his car—
5. They needed— —change a tire first—
6. They got through— —change it at ten o'clock—
7. They started— —drive immediately—
8. They enjoyed— —drive through the country—
9. They kept on— —laugh and sing all the way—
10. They learned— —sing some new songs—
11. They stopped— —sing when they got to the lake—
12. They had expected— —swim before lunch—
13. But Bill insisted on— —eat immediately—
14. Mary had remembered— —bring a lunch—
15. They finished— —eat at one o'clock—
16. They began— —swim at one thirty—
17. They avoided— —go into deep water—
18. They continued— —swim all afternoon—
19. John couldn't help— —think about his homework—
20. He had planned— —do it that afternoon—

NOTE TO ADVANCED STUDENTS: Most of the verb expressions in *-ing* presented above are nominalizations. This means they function like nouns. For example, the nominalization *singing* in the first sentence below is equivalent to *what* and *it* in the second and third sentences:

> John enjoyed *singing*.
> *What* did he enjoy?
> He enjoyed *it*.

Some *-ing* forms of verbs, however, are complements of the preceding verbs. For example, the *-ing* form which follows *keep on* is a complement:

> He kept on *singing*.

Singing is not a nominalization. Thus it is not equivalent to *what* or *it*.

He is president (handwritten)
complement (handwritten)

Lesson 27

A. Nouns used as complements after direct objects:

They elected Kennedy *president.*

B. Adjectives used as complements after direct objects:

He pushed the door *open.*

C. Noun + *-ing* verb expressions used as direct objects:

We watched the boys *playing.*

A. Notice the noun used as a complement after the direct object.

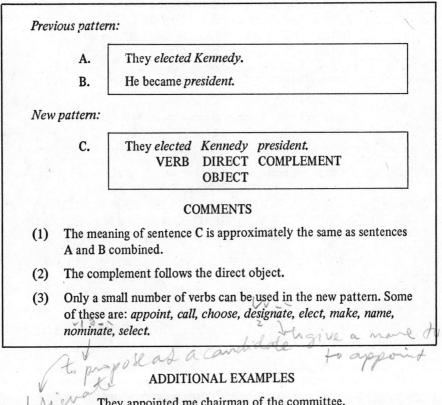

Previous pattern:

| A. | They *elected Kennedy.* |
| B. | He became *president.* |

New pattern:

| C. | They *elected   Kennedy   president.*
VERB   DIRECT   COMPLEMENT
OBJECT |

COMMENTS

(1) The meaning of sentence C is approximately the same as sentences A and B combined.

(2) The complement follows the direct object.

(3) Only a small number of verbs can be used in the new pattern. Some of these are: *appoint, call, choose, designate, elect, make, name, nominate, select.*

designate — to propose as a candidate — to give a name to — to appoint (handwritten annotations)

ADDITIONAL EXAMPLES

They appointed me chairman of the committee.
Do they call William Brown Will?
No, they call him Bill.
They made Mr. Ramsey Director of Courses.
Mr. and Mrs. Clark named their new baby Alice.

275

NOTE: With certain verbs the complement is sometimes preceded by *as*.

> They chose John *as their leader.*
> They selected Mr. Smith *as their representative.*
> Who did they select *as chairman?*

Exercise 1. Practice the use of *name* and *call.*

(Dick) They named their son Richard.	THEY NAMED THEIR SON RICHARD, BUT THEY CALL HIM DICK.
(Betty) They named their daughter Elizabeth.	THEY NAMED THEIR DAUGHTER ELIZABETH, BUT THEY CALL HER BETTY.

1. (Bill) They named their son William.
2. (Ron) They named their son Ronald.
3. (Sue) They named their daughter Susan.
4. (Bob) They named their son Robert.
5. (Jack) They named their son John.
6. (Barb) They named their daughter Barbara.
7. (Al) They named their son Albert.
8. (Jim) They named their son James.
9. (Cathy) They named their daughter Catherine.
10. (Dave) They named their son David.
11. (Tom) They named their son Thomas.
12. (Phil) They named their son Phillip.
13. (Marv) They named their son Marvin.
14. (Joe) They named their son Joseph.

Exercise 2. Substitute the following words. (Keep *Mr. Smith* in each sentence.)

Mr. Smith named John treasurer.

secretary	MR. SMITH NAMED JOHN SECRETARY.
appointed	MR. SMITH APPOINTED JOHN SECRETARY.
him	MR. SMITH APPOINTED HIM SECRETARY.
Jim	MR. SMITH APPOINTED JIM SECRETARY.

1. chairman of the committee
2. made
3. made the younger man
4. treasurer
5. Mary
6. appointed
7. secretary
8. the student
9. Tom
10. manager of the team
11. nominated
12. Jack

Exercise 3. Answer the following questions.

Who did the Americans elect as President in 1960?	THE AMERICANS ELECTED KENNEDY PRESIDENT IN 1960.
Who did Kennedy appoint as Attorney General (Minister of Justice)?	KENNEDY APPOINTED HIS BROTHER ROBERT ATTORNEY GENERAL.

1. Who was elected president in 1964? in 1968?
2. Who did the president appoint Secretary of State?
3. Who did the American people elect in the last election?
4. Who was chosen as the leader of your country?
5. Do you have an advisor? Who was chosen as your advisor?
6. What do you call people from the United States? (Americans, North Americans)
7. What do you call people from Germany? (Germans)
8. What do you call people from France? (Frenchmen)
9. What do you call people from Japan. (Japanese)
10. What do you call people from Spain? (Spaniards)
11. What do you call people from New York? (New Yorkers)
12. What do you call people from Texas? (Texans)
13. Do you have a pet — a dog or cat? What do you call it?

B. Notice the use of an adjective as a complement:

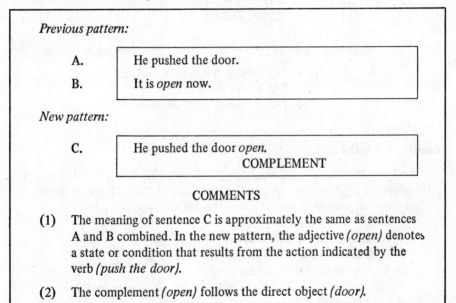

Previous pattern:

A.	He pushed the door.
B.	It is *open* now.

New pattern:

C.	He pushed the door *open*.
	COMPLEMENT

COMMENTS

(1) The meaning of sentence C is approximately the same as sentences A and B combined. In the new pattern, the adjective *(open)* denotes a state or condition that results from the action indicated by the verb *(push the door)*.

(2) The complement *(open)* follows the direct object *(door)*.

ADDITIONAL EXAMPLES

He painted the house. It is *white* now.
He painted the house *white*.

He painted the yellow house. It is *white* now.
He painted the yellow house *white*.

Exercise 4. Make sentences using adjectives (and past participles) as complements.

They painted the house with green paint.   THEY PAINTED THE HOUSE GREEN.
He pushed the door. It is closed now.   HE PUSHED THE DOOR CLOSED.

1. She cut her hair. It is short now.
2. John painted the table. It is blue.
3. The boys washed their shirts until they were clean.
4. The table was wet. Mary wiped it until it was dry.
5. John cracked the nut. It is open now.
6. The windows were dirty. John wiped them. Now they are clean.
7. The cold weather froze the milk. It is solid.

NOTE: There is a related pattern which includes an adjective as a complement. In this pattern the state or condition denoted by the adjective does not result from the action indicated by the verb.

Do you have something wrong

(1)   I found the room *clean*.
                          COMPLEMENT

(2)   I want everything *ready*.
                          COMPLEMENT

The two examples above are more or less identical to the following sentences.

                    (1a) I found that the room was clean.
                    (1b) I found the room to be clean.
                    (2a) I want everything to be ready.

Exercise 5. Practice the use of adjectives as complements.

I found that the lesson was difficult.	I FOUND THE LESSON DIFFICULT.
He wants the window to be open.	HE WANTS THE WINDOW OPEN.
I had someone paint my house.	I HAD MY HOUSE PAINTED.

1. I like my coffee to be black.
2. He found that the movie was interesting.
3. John wants his TV to be fixed.
4. I like my steak to be rare. . . . to be medium. . . . to be well-done.
5. I had someone cut my hair.
6. I prefer the soup to be hot.
7. Mary found that New York is very exciting.
8. John wanted his bread to be toasted.
9. Mr. Miller had someone fix his car.

Exercise 6. Answer the following questions using an adjective (or past participle) as a complement.

How do you like your coffee — strong or weak?	I LIKE IT STRONG.
How do you prefer bread — plain or toasted?	I PREFER IT TOASTED.

1. How do you like tomatoes — cooked or raw?
2. How do you prefer potatoes — baked, fried, or mashed?

3. How do you like your coffee — black or with cream?
4. How do you like steak — rare, medium, or well-done?
5. How do you like tea — iced or hot?
6. How do you have your windows at night — open or closed?
7. Do you prefer girls that wear their hair long or short?

NOTE: The complement in this pattern can consist of either (1) an adjective, (2) a past participle, or (3) a past participle + adjective.

1. I want the house *white.*
2. I want the house *painted.*
3. I want the house *painted white.*

Exercise 7. Make sentences which include past participles as complements.

I want somebody to clean the room.   I WANT THE ROOM CLEANED.
I want somebody to fix the radio.   I WANT THE RADIO FIXED.

1. I want somebody to wash the dishes.
2. I want somebody to fry the potatoes.
3. I want somebody to boil the eggs.
4. I want somebody to heat the water.
5. I want somebody to paint the house.
6. I want somebody to paint the house red.
7. I want somebody to paint the table green.
8. I want somebody to clean the floor.
9. I want somebody to correct the mistake.
10. I want somebody to take the picture.
11. I want somebody to send the books.
12. I want somebody to mash the potatoes.
13. I want somebody to sell the car.

Exercise 8. Continue as in the previous exercise.

I'm going to have
   somebody fix my car.   I'M GOING TO HAVE MY CAR FIXED.
I'm going to have
   somebody clean my coat.   I'M GOING TO HAVE MY COAT CLEANED.

1. I'm going to have somebody paint my house.
2. I'm going to have somebody shine my shoes.
3. I'm going to have somebody wash my shirt.
4. I'm going to have somebody type my letter.
5. I'm going to have somebody dryclean my coat.
6. I'm going to have somebody press my suit.
7. I'm going to have somebody sell my house.
8. I'm going to have the barber cut my hair.

9. I'm going to have the dentist clean my teeth.
10. I'm going to have the photographer take my picture.
11. I'm going to have someone paint my house white.
12. I'm going to have someone paint the yellow house white.

C. Notice the use of the *-ing* form of the verb.

Previous pattern (Lesson 21):

> I heard Mary *sing.*

New pattern:

> I heard Mary *singing.*

COMMENTS

(1) After the verb *hear,* a second verb can be in the simple form *(sing)* or the *-ing* form *(singing).*

(2) Other verbs like *hear* are *see, feel,* and *watch.* These occur in both patterns.

(3) Some additional verbs which occur in the new pattern are: *observe, feel, smell, imagine, find, catch.*

NOTE: Usually there is not much difference in meaning between these two patterns. The *-ing* form, however, sometimes implies continuous activity. Thus the following two sentences are different:

> I saw John *hit* the boy.
> I saw John *hitting* the boy.

> *Hit* suggests one blow.
> *Hitting* implies several.

ADDITIONAL EXAMPLES

You can	hear	the children	playing games.
	see	your friends	waving to you.
	watch	Mr. Smith	painting his house.
	observe	the men	working.
	feel	the toaster	getting hot.
	smell	the fish	frying on the stove.
	imagine	somebody	calling you on the phone.
	find	Paul and me	shoveling the snow.
He will	catch	all of you	throwing chalk.
The boss	keeps	everyone	working very hard.
John	left	his coat	lying on the sofa.

Exercise 9. Combine the statements to make a shorter one.

I saw him.

    He was going to the movies.   I SAW HIM GOING TO THE MOVIES.

You heard us.

    We were singing.   YOU HEARD US SINGING.

We found the boys.

    They were playing baseball.   WE FOUND THE BOYS PLAYING BASEBALL.

   1. We saw you. You were sitting beside the road.
   2. Jim watched the soldiers. They were marching down the street.
   3. I heard the car. It was coming toward me.
   4. Mr. Clark heard Mary. She was speaking.
   5. Larry watched his brother. He was putting stamps in an album.
   6. I heard the leaves. They were moving in the trees.
   7. I could feel my heart. It was beating rapidly.
   8. I saw him. He was standing on the stairs.
   9. He left his coat. It was hanging on a hook.
  10. Jack remembered the book. It was lying open on the desk.
  11. They thought of me. I was studying in my room.
  12. They saw us. We were going into the restaurant.
  13. We saw them. They were falling.
  14. He heard the dog. It was barking.
  15. We can smell the fish. It is frying on the stove.
  16. I saw your friends. They were waving to you.

(handwritten at top:) last night, I watch TV
I watch TV last night

Lesson 28

(handwritten:) Sits in a chair, he watch TV
participial phrase

A. Verb expressions in *-ing* functioning as noun phrases:

Traveling is fun.

B. Verb expressions in *-ing* functioning as subordinate clauses:

Sitting in a chair, he watched TV.

A. Notice the use of an *-ing* form of a verb in subject position.

Previous pattern (14.A.3):

A	It	is fun to travel.
B	*To travel* is fun.	*(handwritten: → not to speak)*

(handwritten: seem to formal)

New pattern:

C	*Traveling* is fun.

COMMENT

Verb expressions in *-ing* can function as noun phrases.

(handwritten: change)

NOTES:

(1) Both *to travel* in B and *traveling* in C are examples of nominalizations.

(2) Patterns A and C are both very common and useful. Pattern B, however, is introduced mainly to make the meaning of C clear.

Exercise 1. Change the statements from Pattern A to Pattern C.

It is necessary to
    practice every day.   PRACTICING EVERY DAY IS NECESSARY.
It makes Jim tired to run.   RUNNING MAKES JIM TIRED.

(handwritten: being on time)

1. It is important to be on time.
2. It makes Jim tired to work all day.
3. It frightens Barbara to be alone.
4. It annoys Mrs. Hastings to hear people argue.
5. It makes me happy to win a contest.
6. It pleases the cat to get fish for dinner.

282

7. It requires time and effort to learn a language.
8. It thrills Alice to get a letter.
9. It is pleasant to go to the lake on a hot day.
10. It makes Sue happy to see her brother.
11. It is interesting to watch cats.
12. It is pleasant to walk in parks.
13. It isn't safe to drive John's car.
14. It is easy to understand this lesson.

Exercise 2. Combine the statements to form a generalization.

Bill teaches English.
     It is hard work.   TEACHING ENGLISH IS HARD WORK.
Ted writes short stories.
     It requires great talent.   WRITING SHORT STORIES REQUIRES
                                   GREAT TALENT.

1. Carlos writes home often. It takes a lot of time.
2. Tom takes pictures. It is a good hobby.
3. Our family plays chess. It provides many hours of entertainment.
4. John sells cars. It is a profitable business.
5. We must take an examination. That means extra hours of study.
6. Mary visited Niagara Falls. It was wonderful.
7. I read the newspaper every day. It helps in learning English.
8. Jerry completed the forms. It fulfilled the requirements.
9. Fred sent a telegram. It was faster than writing a letter.
10. Bob drinks a quart of milk every day. It is healthful.
11. Ted plays baseball. It provides relaxation.
12. Betty learned to speak Chinese. It was difficult.

B. Notice the use of an *-ing* verb phrase to modify a noun.

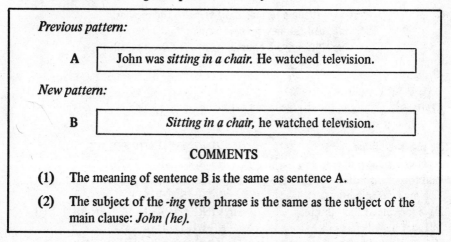

Previous pattern:

     A   John was *sitting in a chair.* He watched television.

New pattern:

     B   *Sitting in a chair,* he watched television.

COMMENTS

(1)   The meaning of sentence B is the same as sentence A.

(2)   The subject of the *-ing* verb phrase is the same as the subject of the main clause: *John (he).*

NOTE: The new pattern is more frequent in writing than in speaking.

Exercise 3. Combine the two sentences to form one with an *-ing* verb phrase at the beginning.

John walked to town. John saw an interesting sight.	WALKING TO TOWN, JOHN SAW AN INTERESTING SIGHT.
John washed his hands. John noticed a cut on his finger.	WASHING HIS HANDS, JOHN NOTICED A CUT ON HIS FINGER.
Mary is intelligent. Mary learned geometry quickly.	BEING INTELLIGENT, MARY LEARNED GEOMETRY QUICKLY.

1. The car turned the corner. The car hit a tree.
2. Jim was feeling sick. Jim called a doctor.
3. The photographer was waving to the child. The photographer took the picture.
4. Mary fell down stairs. Mary broke her arm.
5. John felt tired. John stopped at a hotel to rest.
6. The barber cut John's hair. The barber talked about fishing.
7. Fred had no assignments. Fred went to a movie.
8. Tom expected a call. Tom waited in the dormitory.
9. Dorothy was sick. Dorothy couldn't go to school.
10. The director saw the new student. The director tried to help him.
11. Thomas flew to the United States. Thomas made the trip in one day.

NOTE: In the new pattern above, the action described in the *-ing* verb phrase takes place at the same time as the action of the main clause.

The use of *having* + past participle in the first clause indicates that the action described in this clause precedes the action in the main clause.

> Having written a letter, Mary went to the movies.
> Having read the newspaper, we watched TV.
> Having finished the course, Ann will drive to California.

Exercise 4. Combine the two sentences to form one sentence with *having* + past participle at the beginning.

He saw the police. Then he became worried.	HAVING SEEN THE POLICE, HE BECAME WORRIED.
Paul forgot his notebook. Now he is unhappy.	HAVING FORGOTTEN HIS NOTEBOOK, PAUL IS UNHAPPY.
He is looking at her picture. Later he will feel sad.	HAVING LOOKED AT HER PICTURE, HE WILL FEEL SAD.
He was nominated. Then he began a campaign.	HAVING BEEN NOMINATED, HE BEGAN A CAMPAIGN.

1. He read the newspaper. Later he went to the movie.
2. The firemen put the fire out. Afterwards they investigated the cause.
3. He worked very hard. He became tired.
4. He is working very hard. He will be tired.
5. He will examine the report. Afterwards he is going to write a letter.
6. Tom arrived at the airport. He took a taxi to the dormitory.
7. We are visiting the art gallery. Next we will go through the library.
8. He stayed up all night. The next day he looked weary in his classes.
9. She purchased a stamp. Later she mailed a letter to her family.
10. The boys are playing baseball. They will eat a big lunch.
11. He was worried. Then he went to the doctor.
12. Dave worked all summer. He was able to go to college in the fall.

Exercise 5. (Review of 27.C. and 28.B.)

Combine the statements.

I saw him. He was going to lunch.	I SAW HIM GOING TO LUNCH.
I was going to lunch. I saw him.	GOING TO LUNCH, I SAW HIM.
I saw him. Then I went to lunch.	HAVING SEEN HIM, I WENT TO LUNCH.

1. She smiled at him. He was standing there.
2. She was standing there. She smiled at him.
3. I looked at the leaves. They were blowing in the breeze.
4. Jim wrote a letter. He mailed it on the way to class.
5. He was sailing to Europe. He had a good time.
6. Norman was hurrying home. He met an old friend.
7. Norman met an old friend. The friend was hurrying home.
8. Tom ate breakfast. He walked to school with Jim after breakfast.
9. The ship was tossing in the storm. It creaked noisily.
10. We parked our car. Then we began to do our shopping.
11. Jane heard me. I was laughing loudly.
12. The kitten imitated its mother. Its mother was washing its face.
13. The kitten was washing its face. The kitten imitated its mother.
14. Bob worried about Sue. She was typing too much.
15. He finished his lesson. Later he went to the program.
16. They were shouting his name. They ran through the streets.
17. Dorothy and Helen walked all afternoon. Afterwards they felt hungry.
18. He was driving too fast. He hit the tree.
19. John finished school. He took a vacation in Florida.

to take advacation

Lesson 29

A. Conjunctions: *and, but, or* and sentence connectors: *however, therefore, also,* etc.

B. Adverbial expressions of time and place in sentence initial position: *At nine o'clock* we have class.

C. Summary statements: *In other words, . . .*

A.1 Notice that conjunctions, such as *and, but, or* are used to join sentences as well as parts of sentences.

CONJUNCTIONS THAT JOIN SENTENCES

> George studied in the library, *and* Paul watched a movie.
> Mary went to the picnic, *but* Alice stayed home.
> We can go to the movies, *or* we can watch television.

contrast

gives a choice

CONJUNCTIONS THAT JOIN PARTS OF SENTENCES

> He sat in a chair *and* read a book.
> We were happy *but* tired.
> You can go by bus *or* taxi.

COMMENTS

(1) When conjunctions are used to join sentences, a comma is usually inserted before the conjunction: S, but s

> (Additional patterns: S. But s.
> S; but s.)

(2) When conjunctions are used to join *two* parts of a sentence, usually no comma is used. Some examples of parts of sentences are the following:

> Predicates —
>> sat in a chair
>> read a book
>
> Adjectives —
>> happy
>> tired
>
> Nouns —
>> bus
>> taxi

286

NOTE: Only one style of punctuation has been recommended here. Some writers, however, use other styles.

ADDITIONAL EXAMPLES

He wants to go, but he can't.
He wants to lie down and sleep.
He wrote two weeks ago but hasn't received an answer yet.
Mary bought a new car, and Helen did too.

Three or more items:

He bought a book, two pens, and some paper.
He sat in a chair, read a book, and drank a glass of lemonade.

Exercise 1. Some of the following sentences must be punctuated with a comma. Students may copy each sentence on the blackboard or on a piece of paper and add commas where necessary.

1. Mary was happy but Alice was very sad.
2. George wants to study at Harvard or Princeton.
3. John came in the room and sat down.
4. They want to study but they can't.
5. John is going to drive to California and Bob is too.
6. I saw Mary but not Alice.
7. Do you prefer to eat in a restaurant or at home?
8. Mary wants tea but I'll have coffee.
9. I like my coffee with cream but without sugar.
10. John will arrive next week on Wednesday or Thursday.
11. Mary can read Spanish but she can't speak it.
12. Mr. Miller can speak French German and Spanish.
13. We didn't see the movie but we should have.
14. Mary has a bowl of soup a sandwich and a glass of milk for lunch.
15. John was tired and very hungry.
16. Mary was tired but happy.
17. I like TV but I prefer the movies.
18. Alice laughed but she felt sad.

A.2 Notice the use of the sentence connector *however* to join two sentences.

Previous pattern (conjunction):

> Mary was happy, but Alice was very sad.

New pattern (sentence connector):

> Mary was happy.
> *However,* Alice was very sad.
>
> Mary was happy.
> Alice, *however,* was very sad.
>
> Mary was happy.
> Alice was very sad, *however.*

COMMENTS

(1) When sentence connectors are used to connect two sentences, the first sentence usually ends in a period. A comma is never used between the two sentences. (However, sometimes a semicolon (;) is used in place of a period.)

(2) Sentence connectors occur in the beginning, in the middle, or at the end of the second sentence.

NOTE: The meaning of *however* is similar to the meaning of *but.* Both are used to indicate that the information that follows is contrary to the information that precedes.

Therefore is used to introduce a consequence.

> It's always warm in Hawaii. *Therefore,* there is never any snow there.

Exercise 2. Copy each sentence on the blackboard or on a piece of paper, and add the correct punctuation.

Alice went to the picnic but Mary stayed at home.	ALICE WENT TO THE PICNIC, BUT MARY STAYED AT HOME.
Mary can read Spanish however she can't speak it.	MARY CAN READ SPANISH. HOWEVER, SHE CAN'T SPEAK IT.

1. John was tired however he continued to study for his exam.
2. Mary likes milk but she prefers tea.
3. The water in the lake was very cold yesterday therefore we didn't go swimming.
4. George studied until three o'clock last night therefore he feels very tired today.
5. George studied until three o'clock last night however he is going to bed early tonight.

6. Alice smiled but she felt sad.
7. John wanted to play baseball however it was raining and he stayed at home.
8. Paul wanted to go to the movies however he didn't have any money therefore he stayed home.

Exercise 3. Add an appropriate sentence connector. Use *therefore, however,* or *also.*

He is sick.	HE IS SICK.
He can't come.	THEREFORE, HE CAN'T COME.
He has a cold.	HE HAS A COLD.
He has a cough.	ALSO, HE HAS A COUGH.
He is in bed.	HE IS IN BED.
He can get up tomorrow.	HOWEVER, HE CAN GET UP TOMORROW.

1. We like Mr. Miller as a teacher. We like Miss Smith better.
2. Tom has a good vocabulary. He pronounces well.
3. I don't have a driver's license. I don't drive.
4. We haven't seen the new building. We don't know what it looks like.
5. I can't come today. I'll come tomorrow.
6. She bought her books today. She bought some pencils.
7. The carpenters worked hard. They didn't finish.
8. They are studying hard. They are learning English rapidly.
9. She knows how to play the piano. She can dance.
10. We like potatoes. We like rice.
11. I bought a boat last week. I haven't used it yet.
12. Bill left town. He won't be able to keep his appointment.

A LIST OF CONJUNCTIONS AND SENTENCE CONNECTORS

It is possible to group many of the conjunctions and sentence connectors into three large groups. Although the members of each group are similar in meaning, they are not all completely identical.

The conjunctions and connectors in the first group relate two bits of information that are contrary to each other. The words in the second group relate two bits of information that are similar to each other. The words in the third group indicate a consequence relationship.

CONJUNCTIONS	SENTENCE CONNECTORS
1. but	however
yet	nevertheless
	still
	on the contrary
	on the other hand
	in contrast
	in spite of that
	conversely

289

2.   and

    also
    besides
    moreover
    furthermore
    indeed
    likewise
    similarly
    in addition
    in fact
    as a matter of fact

3.   so

    therefore
    consequently
    thus
    as a result

B. Notice the use of adverbial expressions of time and place to relate two sentences to each other.

1. We have breakfast *at eight o'clock. At nine o'clock* we have class.

2. We have classes *all morning. In the afternoon* there is the laboratory period.

3. Farms are usually small *in the East. Farther west* you will find much larger ones.

4. There are cotton fields *in the South. In the North* there are many cornfields.

COMMENTS

(1)   Each example sentence contains an adverbial expression of time or place. In the second sentence of each pair, the adverbial is in initial position. This adverbial helps relate the second sentence to the first.

(2)   Often (but not always) the word *there* occurs between an adverbial and a form of *be* (or certain other verbs). See Sequences 2 and 4.

ADDITIONAL EXAMPLES

1. We began our practice of English sentence patterns with short sentences.

    Then we practiced long and complex sentences.
    Later we practiced long and complex sentences.
    Next we practiced long and complex sentences.
    Afterwards we practiced long and complex sentences.

2. We are practicing long and complex sentences now.
   Earlier we practiced short sentences.
3. We began practicing intonation the first day in class.
   Before we had never heard of it.
4. It never snows in my country.
   Here it snows a lot.
5. The winter is very cold here.
   There it is warm.
6. I don't like the winter here.
   Elsewhere I have enjoyed it.

Observe the use of *there* in the following sentences. Note that the pattern with *there* is used with certain verbs other than *be* after expressions of time or place.

1. New Mexico and Arizona were the first states we visited. Next there was California.
2. Los Angeles was the first city we visited. Next there came San Francisco.
3. Driving to San Francisco, we had the ocean on our left. On our right there rose high mountains.
4. San Francisco is on the west side of a large bay. On the east side there lies the city of Berkeley.
5. We hadn't seen many forests in Southern California. North of San Francisco there grow large forests of tall trees.

Observe the time and space organization of the following sequences of sentences.

I came here eight weeks ago. Seven weeks ago, I enrolled in this course. Three weeks ago, I took an examination. Last week, I applied for admission to the School of Business Administration. Today, I attended my first class there.

The State of Washington is in the northwest corner of the United States. South of Washington there is Oregon. East of Oregon and Washington there is Idaho. South of Oregon along the Pacific coast, the long state of California extends to the Mexican border. Eastward from California, there lie Nevada and Arizona.

Exercise 4. Change the position of the time or place expression in the second statement in order to relate it more closely to the first.

He gets up at 8:00.
   He eats breakfast at 8:30.

HE GETS UP
   AT 8:00. AT 8:30
   HE EATS BREAKFAST.

They grow cherries in Michigan.
   They grow peaches in Georgia.

THEY GROW CHERRIES
   IN MICHIGAN. IN GEORGIA
   THEY GROW PEACHES.

He studies from six until nine.
   He reads the newspaper from nine until ten.

HE STUDIES FROM SIX
   UNTIL NINE. FROM NINE
   UNTIL TEN
   HE READS THE NEWSPAPER.

1. John started his trip on Tuesday. He was in Chicago on Wednesday.
2. Ted saw an accident. He ran for the police immediately.
3. Mr. Martinez does not like American food. He will get accustomed to it eventually.
4. Bill has one class in the morning. He has three classes in the afternoon.
5. Mary had a headache yesterday. She feels better today.
6. The library has a reading room on the first floor. It has a large reference room on the second floor.
7. We find salt water in the Great Salt Lake. We find fresh water in other lakes.
8. It is 6:30 on my watch. It is 6:40 on Jim's watch.
9. The cold weather lasts four months in Michigan. It lasts three months in Kentucky.
10. Hockey is a favorite sport in Canada. Baseball is a favorite sport in the United States.
11. School begins at 9:00. Classes are over at 3:00, and the children go home.

Exercise 5. Change the position of the time or place expression in the second statement and add the word *there*.

The pronunciation class is in the morning.
   The grammar class is in the afternoon.

THE PRONUNCIATION CLASS IS IN THE MORNING. IN THE AFTERNOON THERE IS THE GRAMMAR CLASS.

The Smiths bought a new house.
   A small garden is behind the house.

THE SMITHS BOUGHT A NEW HOUSE. BEHIND THE HOUSE THERE IS A SMALL GARDEN.

China is situated here on the map.
   Siberia lies to the north.

CHINA IS SITUATED HERE ON THE MAP. TO THE NORTH THERE LIES SIBERIA.

1. Canada is to the north of the United States. Mexico is to the south.
2. Cuba is a large island south of Florida. The Bahamas lie to the east.
3. The church is in the background. A statue in the foreground.
4. The program comes first. The refreshments come afterwards.
5. The paper is in this drawer. Pencils are in that drawer.
6. A large painting hangs above the table. A smaller one hangs by the window.
7. Lake Michigan lies to the west of Michigan. Lake Huron lies to the east.
8. The women sat on the left. The men sat on the right.
9. The holiday comes first. The examinations come later.
10. An elm tree grows on the lawn. An apple tree grows in the garden.
11. There is a book on this desk. Pen and paper are on that desk.
12. The Atlantic Ocean is east of the United States. The Pacific is to the west.

C. Notice the use of the phrase *in other words* to introduce a sentence which summarizes the information that precedes.

> Bob enjoys swimming and playing tennis. He likes to watch football. In the summer, he goes to a baseball game every Saturday. *In other words,* he likes sports.

COMMENT

Some common expressions used to summarize information are the following:

> in other words
> in summary
> in a word
> in brief
> briefly
> in general
> to summarize

There are, however, slight differences in meaning and usage between these expressions.

ADDITIONAL EXAMPLES

New York is famous for its tall buildings. It has a great library and many museums. It is the theatrical center of the United States. Its population includes people from every country in the world. *In other words,* it is a fascinating city.

The three branches of the U.S. Government have considerable control over each other. The President appoints the nine members of the Supreme Court for life and may veto legislation that has been passed by Congress. Congress may, in turn, override the President's veto. The Supreme Court may declare laws that have been passed by Congress and signed by the President to be unconstitutional. *In other words,* we may say that equal distribution of power constitutes an important part of government in this country.

there are 6 chairs and a table
___ is a table and 6 chairs

Exercise 6. Repeat the sentences and add a summarizing statement introduced by the phrase *in other words*.

I like fishing and golf.
    My wife likes tennis.

I LIKE FISHING AND GOLF.
MY WIFE LIKES TENNIS.
IN OTHER WORDS,
WE LIKE SPORTS.

Canada is larger than the United States.
    It is larger than Brazil or Argentina.

CANADA IS LARGER THAN THE
UNITED STATES. IT IS LARGER
THAN BRAZIL OR ARGENTINA.
IN OTHER WORDS, IT IS THE
LARGEST COUNTRY IN
WESTERN HEMISPHERE.

1. Tom reads a book a week. He subscribes to several newspapers and magazines.
2. Mary is having a difficult time with her pronunciation. Her sentence patterns are confused.
3. Thomas does all of his work. He never misses classes, and he studies hard.
4. The play has started. The theater is several blocks away.
5. France has an area of 213,000 square miles. Spain has 195,000 square miles.
6. The weather is warm. The birds are singing. The trees are blooming.
7. The tickets are bought. Our baggage is packed.
8. John has a temperature of 100. His pulse is rapid, and he has a cough.
9. We lost our tickets. Our baggage was stolen, and we ran out of money.
10. The Red Cross gave us money. It provided us with food and shelter.
11. War kills and cripples. It destroys and creates misery.
12. He composes music. He plays the piano and violin.

Lesson 30

REVIEW OF LESSONS 21 – 29*

Exercise 1. (To review answers to negative questions.) Answer the following negative questions with a negative or an affirmative short answer.

Wasn't George Washington born in the nineteenth century?	NO, HE WASN'T.
Isn't her hat unusual?	YES, IT IS.
Can't you take the examination tomorrow?	NO, I CAN'T.

1. Didn't you take English last semester?
2. Couldn't he find the right room?
3. Don't you own a car?
4. Isn't Miss Francisco registered yet?
5. Didn't they go to the program last night?
6. Isn't your cold any better?
7. Doesn't she look pretty in her native costume?
8. Couldn't she have paid her tuition yesterday?
9. Won't you take a plane back to your country?
10. Wasn't he embarrassed?
11. Shouldn't you ask the teacher first?
12. Hadn't they eaten their breakfast?

Exercise 2. (To review tag questions.) Repeat the following statements and add a tag question. Add a negative question if the statement is affirmative, and an affirmative question if the statement is negative.

He isn't sick.	HE ISN'T SICK, IS HE?
They answered all of the questions.	THEY ANSWERED ALL OF THE QUESTIONS, DIDN'T THEY?
They could have taken a later bus.	THEY COULD HAVE TAKEN A LATER BUS, COULDN'T THEY?

1. He is very young.
2. She has her bachelor's degree.
3. He won't return.
4. It's too late to write a letter now.
5. You haven't seen my pencil.
6. He never goes to his office in the morning.
7. They are going to see the play this afternoon.

*NOTE TO THE TEACHER: Each teacher may plan a review lesson suited to the needs of his particular class by making a selection of exercises from the ones included in this lesson. Exercises from previous lessons may also be reviewed.

8. We could have telephoned.
9. They can't see the building from here.
10. His foot looks bad.
11. I didn't get a letter.
12. We always wait for them.

Exercise 3. (To review tag questions.) Convert the following questions into statements with tag questions. Produce two forms of the tag question.

Is John sick?

JOHN IS SICK, ISN'T HE?
JOHN ISN'T SICK, IS HE?

Have they answered your letter?

THEY HAVE ANSWERED YOUR
    LETTER, HAVEN'T THEY?
THEY HAVEN'T ANSWERED YOUR
    LETTER, HAVE THEY?

Has he offered to buy the book?

HE HAS OFFERED TO BUY
    THE BOOK, HASN'T HE?
HE HASN'T OFFERED TO BUY
    THE BOOK, HAS HE?

1. Is he a student?
2. Have you seen Tom?
3. Is she taking a course in biology?
4. Does he work for the government?
5. Can you come to the party?
6. Should I have opened the door?
7. Is she going to the program?
8. Did John promise to come?
9. Will you buy a subscription?
10. Are we going to take a plane?
11. Are they the same?
12. Did you find the correct answer?

Exercise 4. (To review short answers to questions with *could have, should have been, will,* etc.) Produce a negative or affirmative short answer to the following questions.

Should I have written a letter?   YES, YOU SHOULD HAVE.
Won't you have another piece of pie?   YES, I WILL.
Could you have lost the pencil on the way to school? NO, I COULDN'T HAVE.

1. Have you ever been to California?
2. Should I have gone to the picnic?
3. Could he have taken the book with him?
4. Will you be fifty years old this year?
5. Could you pay me for this picture tomorrow?
6. Might he have made a reservation with the travel bureau?
7. Would he have gone if I had asked him?
8. Would you have bought his typewriter from him?
9. Should we take our soccer ball to the picnic?

10. Could he have been talking to Professor Jones?
11. Should you have been taking notes?
12. Has he been studying in the library?

Exercise 5. (To review adjectives (*good, white,* etc.) as complements.) Substitute the following words. Include the adjective after the noun.

They washed the clothes clean.

table	THEY WASHED THE TABLE CLEAN.
painted white	THEY PAINTED THE TABLE WHITE.
blue	THEY PAINTED THE TABLE BLUE.

1. car	14. program	27. tough
2. house	15. interesting	28. wonderful
3. brown	16. found	29. play
4. wanted	17. delightful	30. painting
5. clean	18. movie	31. superb
6. kept	19. funny	32. judged
7. boy	20. thought	33. natural
8. happy	21. good	34. preferred
9. interested	22. food	35. color
10. class	23. delicious	36. red
11. busy	24. considered	37. car
12. lively	25. indigestible	38. painted
13. made	26. steak	

Exercise 6. (To review -*ing* forms.) Listen to the statements. Combine the information so that the second verb ends in -*ing*.

We saw John.	WE SAW JOHN
He was walking to school.	WALKING TO SCHOOL.
They met Mary.	THEY MET MARY
She was hurrying to the concert.	HURRYING TO THE CONCERT.
I found my watch.	I FOUND MY WATCH
It was lying in the street.	LYING IN THE STREET.

1. They found us. We were preparing a program.
2. I can see Tom. He is riding a bicycle.
3. You couldn't have seen us. We were walking in the dark.
4. John heard me. I was talking with Fred.
5. I enjoyed seeing Fred. He was washing his car.
6. He remembers the car. It was going very slowly.
7. Jim had to pay the man. The man was standing by the gate.
8. We watched the cameraman. He was taking a picture of the president.
9. We picked some berries. They were growing in the woods.
10. I discovered the owl. It was sitting on a branch.
11. We noticed Professor Ward. He was eating dinner with some friends.
12. He might have seen me. I was waiting for the bus.

Exercise 7. (To review reflexive pronouns.) Answer the questions. Use a reflexive pronoun.

Who did John see in the mirror?   JOHN SAW HIMSELF IN THE MIRROR.
Who did the students correct?   THEY CORRECTED THEMSELVES.

1. Who did John hurt with the knife?
2. Who did Mary punish for telling a lie?
3. Who did they hear on the tape recorder?
4. Who did the hunter shoot accidentally?
5. Who did the students discuss?
6. Who did the artists draw?
7. Who were they laughing at?
8. Who was she talking about?

Exercise 8. (To review *self* words to emphasize the subject.) Substitute the following words and make the necessary changes in correlation.

We talked to John ourselves.

saw	WE SAW JOHN OURSELVES.
him	WE SAW HIM OURSELVES.
I	I SAW HIM MYSELF.
the book	I SAW THE BOOK MYSELF.

1. it	11. them	21. the money
2. her	12. brought	22. I
3. they	13. the pencils	23. him
4. talked to	14. I	24. them
5. him	15. the apples	25. heard
6. he	16. we	26. her
7. me	17. you	27. she
8. her	18. found	28. me
9. us	19. it	29. saw
10. warned	20. she	30. us

Exercise 9. (To review verb expressions in *-ing* in subject position.) Make statements with verb expressions in *-ing* as the subject.

John has the bad habit
    of wasting time.   WASTING TIME IS A BAD HABIT.
Mary disturbs the teacher   TALKING IN CLASS
    by talking in class.   DISTURBS THE TEACHER.
We work hard when we study.   STUDYING IS HARD WORK.

1. Mary has fun writing letters.
2. Jim has difficulty in pronouncing English.
3. They find it tiresome to study in the evening.
4. I help my pronunciation by listening to the radio.
5. John saves money by taking a bus to work.
6. I find fishing enjoyable.

7. It can be very expensive to go sightseeing.
8. John finds it a nuisance to eat alone.
9. It is dangerous to drive fast.
10. Our goal is to find the correct answer.
11. Fred thinks it is good exercise to play tennis.
12. Jane thinks it is a good hobby to write plays.

Exercise 10. (To review *where to play, how to go,* etc.) Substitute the following words.

I taught John how to play football.

showed	I SHOWED JOHN HOW TO PLAY FOOTBALL.
him	I SHOWED HIM HOW TO PLAY FOOTBALL.
where	I SHOWED HIM WHERE TO PLAY FOOTBALL.
tennis	I SHOWED HIM WHERE TO PLAY TENNIS.
practice	I SHOWED HIM WHERE TO PRACTICE TENNIS.

1. golf	10. baseball	20. buy
2. swimming	11. the program	21. where
3. go	12. prepare	22. find
4. when	13. why	23. how
5. canoeing	14. Mary	24. the elevator
6. told	15. when	25. where
7. where	16. leave	26. the typewriter
8. how	17. book	27. use
9. enjoy	18. where	28. why
	19. for whom	

Exercise 11. (To review *wish* with situations in present time.) Listen to the situation in present time.

Make a wish.

John is sick.	I WISH HE WAS WELL.
They make a lot of noise.	I WISH THEY MADE LESS NOISE.
Jane works slowly.	I WISH JANE WORKED FASTER.

(*were* handwritten above WAS)

1. Mary is tall.	9. I am a student.
2. They are sick.	10. The book is very long.
3. The weather is bad.	11. The movie lasts one hour.
4. He writes small on the blackboard.	12. I read slowly.
5. She talks quietly in the classroom.	13. I talk with an accent.
6. You walk fast.	14. You stay up too late.
7. They are going to the movie.	15. I get a letter every week.
8. He is coming today.	16. He gets to class late.

Exercise 12. (To review *wish* with situations in past time.) Listen to the situations in past time.

Make a wish.

John didn't eat much yesterday.	I WISH HE HAD EATEN MORE.
I studied one hour each day last semester.	I WISH I HAD STUDIED TWO HOURS EACH DAY.
They nominated Jack for president.	I WISH THEY HAD NOMINATED PETER.

1. I didn't see the program last Friday.
2. The newspaperman wrote an article about war.
3. We bought the less expensive rug.
4. All the students went to a movie this afternoon.
5. She sang a selection from an opera.
6. He was careless and lost his money.
7. We could have gone to the concert or the play.
8. I took a ship to Europe.
9. My friend sent me a postcard.
10. I couldn't take Professor Rolo's picture yesterday.
11. We waited for Fred in the corridor.
12. He sold his car to a stranger.

Exercise 13. (To review *must, should*, etc., + *have* + past participle.) Listen to the situations in past time and the words which follow them. Produce comments which explain or elaborate the situation. Use *must, might, could, should* + *have* + past participle.

I worked until ten o'clock yesterday. could have	I COULD HAVE WORKED UNTIL TWELVE.
When I saw Mary, she was crying. must have	SHE MUST HAVE GOTTEN SOME BAD NEWS.
John waited until yesterday to register. should have	HE SHOULD HAVE REGISTERED A WEEK AGO.
He didn't come to the musical program last night. might have	HE MIGHT HAVE BEEN SICK.

1. I saw Mr. Riggs hurrying to the office.   must have
2. John felt sick after dinner.   might have
3. He walked in the rain and got wet.   should have
4. She didn't know what to do with the book she found.   could have
5. The teacher didn't give us a quiz today.   must have
6. I wonder how they found out about my car accident.   might have
7. Fred was supposed to meet me at the snack bar, but didn't.   could have
8. Mary spent three months in Europe last year.   must have
9. I looked for a pencil but couldn't find one.   could have
10. He paid his bill on the third of this month.   should have
11. We didn't see Jane arrive this afternoon.   might have
12. John felt hungry all afternoon.   should have

Exercise 14. (To review *must, should,* etc., + *have been* + the *-ing* form.) Answer the questions using *must, might, should, could* + *have been* + the *-ing* form.

I didn't see John at the party last night.
    What might he have been doing?   HE MIGHT HAVE BEEN STUDYING
Fred says that he didn't hear the
    telephone ring last night
    What could he have been doing?   HE COULD HAVE BEEN SLEEPING.
He was at the movie yesterday afternoon.   HE SHOULD HAVE BEEN
    What should he have been doing?   ATTENDING CLASS.
Paul's clothes are all wet.   HE MUST HAVE BEEN
    What must he have been doing?   WALKING IN THE RAIN.

1. I wonder what John was doing in the language laboratory. What might he have been doing?
2. Paul spent the day talking to his friends. What should he have been doing?
3. They weren't in their room when I knocked. What could they have been doing?
4. We saw John kicking a football on the lawn. What must he have been doing?
5. Mary got arrested for speeding yesterday. What should she have been doing?
6. The worker's face was covered with sweat. What must he have been doing?
7. I saw Fred lying on the couch. What might he have been doing?
8. I wonder why he didn't come to the party yesterday. What could he have been doing?
9. Jim talked over the telephone for two hours last night. What might he have been doing?
10. Mary was busy in the kitchen. What could she have been doing?
11. We missed the bus because we didn't see it arrive. What should we have been doing?

Exercise 15. (To review verbs not followed by *to.*) Listen to the statements and combine them. In some cases, the second verb isn't preceded by *to,* but in other cases it is.

I heard Fred.
    He talked about politics.   I HEARD FRED TALK ABOUT POLITICS
I selected John. He went.   I SELECTED JOHN TO GO.
We saw Mary. She bought a hat.   WE SAW MARY BUY A HAT.

1. They asked me. I took the book.
2. The teacher let him. He spoke to the class.
3. The teacher encouraged him. He spoke to the class.
4. I helped John. He finished his work.
5. We saw the lightning. It struck a tree.
6. We observed the sky. It turned very dark.
7. The policeman told us something. We put on our lights.
8. I felt the toaster. It got hot.
9 I had a tooth pulled. Dr. Todd pulled it.

Exercise 16. (To review verbs followed by an *-ing* form.) Make statements that contain two verbs. The second verb will be either an *-ing* form or an infinitive with *to.*

I enjoyed —
   I watched the movie.   **I ENJOYED WATCHING THE MOVIE.**
I forgot —
   I didn't write to John.   **I FORGOT TO WRITE TO JOHN.**
Fred continued —
   He was walking to town.   **FRED CONTINUED WALKING TO TOWN.**

    1. Jim enjoys — He plays football.
    2. I wanted — read the book.
    3. Mary finished — read the book.
    4. They considered — take a trip.
    5. He began — read the story.
    6. They forgot — cook the potatoes.
    7. He got through — write the paper.
    8. John insists on — walk to class.
    9. I expected — Jim come early.
   10. I remember — see Jim yesterday.
   11. I recall — meet Jim last week.
   12. He likes — drive cars.
   13. She learned — sing a song.
   14. She avoided — talk to him.

Exercise 17. (To review verbs with *-ing,* with *to* and without *to.*) Substitute the following verbs.

I wanted him to buy a car.
   had   **I HAD HIM BUY A CAR.**
   remembered   **I REMEMBERED HIM BUYING A CAR.**
   asked   **I ASKED HIM TO BUY A CAR.**

1. watched	8. helped	15. got
2. told	9. expected	16. begged
3. noticed	10. observed	17. made
4. advised	11. persuaded	18. let
5. encouraged	12. saw	19. permitted
6. insisted on	13. wrote	20. recalled
7. sent	14. found	

Exercise 18. (To review *can, could,* etc., in statements with *if.*) Listen to the situations. Expand the statements given with an *if* clause.

John is probably going to Detroit tomorrow. He is not going to New York. I want to go to Detroit. I want to go to New York.

   I will go with John.   **I WILL GO WITH JOHN**
                            IF HE GOES TO DETROIT.

I would go with him.	I WOULD GO WITH HIM IF HE WENT TO NEW YORK.
I can go with him.	I CAN GO WITH HIM IF HE GOES TO DETROIT.
I could go with him.	I COULD GO WITH HIM IF HE WENT TO NEW YORK.
I might go with him.	I MIGHT GO WITH HIM IF HE GOES TO DETROIT.
I might go with him.	I MIGHT GO WITH HIM IF HE WENT TO NEW YORK.
I expect to go with him.	I EXPECT TO GO WITH HIM IF HE GOES TO DETROIT.
I expected to go with him.	I EXPECTED TO GO WITH HIM IF HE WENT TO NEW YORK.

A. John is probably going to New York next week. He is not going to Detroit. I want to go to Detroit. I don't want to go to New York.

1. I won't go with John if he goes to New York.
2. I would go with John.
3. I could go with John.
4. I can't go with John.
5. I don't plan to go with John.
6. I might go with John.

B. Mary is probably going to the concert. She is not going to the play. I want to go to either the concert or the play.

1. I can go with Mary if she goes to the concert.
2. I could go with Mary.
3. I would go with Mary.
4. Mary won't go with me.
5. Mary wouldn't go with me.
6. I might go with Mary.
7. I will go with Mary.

Exercise 19. (To review *would have, might have, could have* in statements connected with *if.*) Listen to the improbable situations. Change the present time statements into equivalent past time statements.

I would write
   if I knew his address.
	I WOULD HAVE WRITTEN
	   IF I HAD KNOWN HIS ADDRESS.

I might go to Detroit with John
   if he went by train.
	I MIGHT HAVE GONE
	   TO DETROIT WITH JOHN
	   IF HE HAD GONE BY TRAIN.

The director could see you
   if you waited.
	THE DIRECTOR COULD HAVE SEEN YOU
	   IF YOU HAD WAITED.

1. I could go with you if you went early.
2. John would take Mary if she wanted to go.
3. They could come if the program was short.
4. He might buy a raincoat if he needed it.
5. I would go with John if he drove his car.
6. The secretary could take your name if you were leaving.
7. I might buy it if it was for sale.
8. You could buy it if he gave you the money.
9. He would wait for you if you hurried.
10. I might study if I found my book.
11. We could call him if we knew his telephone number.
12. I would take a swim if I had a swim suit.

Exercise 20. (To review the subordinators *if, unless, whenever, although, because, whether or not.*) Listen to the statement and the subordinator which follows. Repeat the statement and use the subordinator to add another statement.

He writes poetry. although   HE WRITES POETRY ALTHOUGH HE NEVER WENT TO COLLEGE.

He writes poetry. whenever   HE WRITES POETRY WHENEVER HE FEELS INSPIRED.

We will go on a picnic this afternoon.
   whether or not   WE WILL GO ON A PICNIC THIS AFTERNOON WHETHER OR NOT IT RAINS.

They won't go to the picnic. unless   THEY WON'T GO TO THE PICNIC UNLESS SOMEONE TAKES THEM.

1. The children get excited. whenever
2. There is no school today. because
3. He can't go to Canada. if
4. She knows her lessons. although
5. The program will go on. whether or not
6. John never hurries. unless
7. The desert cactus blooms. whenever
8. The desert cactus never blooms. unless
9. I have a difficult time with my pronunciation. although
10. He must see a doctor. whether or not
11. I like this city. although
12. I feel happy. whenever

Exercise 21. (To review the use of *because of* . . . and *because* . . .) Answer the following questions. Use the nouns which follow the question in your answer.

Why is he going to the doctor? cold   Stud. A: HE IS GOING TO THE DOCTOR BECAUSE OF HIS COLD.

                        Stud. B: HE IS GOING TO THE DOCTOR BECAUSE HE HAS A COLD.

Why is the teacher angry? John   Stud. A: THE TEACHER IS ANGRY
                                                BECAUSE OF JOHN.
                              Stud. B: THE TEACHER IS ANGRY
                                                BECAUSE JOHN WAS
                                                TALKING IN CLASS.

1. Why couldn't Paul come to class today? toothache
2. Why did he win the election? personality
3. Why did he win the election? hard work
4. Why was John late this morning? watch
5. Why are you carrying an umbrella? rain
6. Why can't Fred walk? knee
7. Why is Tom popular? good nature
8. Why have you stopped writing your letter? pencil
9. Why can't you study tonight? radio
10. Why doesn't your father visit the United States? expense
11. Why can't he sleep at night? noise
12. Why don't you write home more often? time

Exercise 22. (To review *so . . . that, such . . . that*.) Listen to the statements. Compare them with *so . . . that* and *such . . . that*.

His talk was interesting.   HIS TALK WAS SO INTERESTING THAT
   We listened for an hour.   WE LISTENED FOR AN HOUR.
                                 HE GAVE SUCH AN INTERESTING TALK
                                 THAT WE LISTENED FOR AN HOUR.

The problem was easy.   THE PROBLEM WAS SO EASY THAT
   Everybody got the answer   EVERYBODY GOT THE ANSWER.
                                 IT WAS SUCH AN EASY PROBLEM THAT
                                 EVERYBODY GOT THE ANSWER.

1. He is tall. He can't go through the door.
2. Her pronunciation is good. People think she is a native speaker.
3. He talks slowly. The new students can understand him.
4. Her dress was beautiful. All of the girls wanted one like it.
5. The doctor worked hard. He had a heart attack.
6. John's letters are long. It takes fifteen minutes to read them.
7. The clown was funny. We all laughed.
8. The building was huge. We couldn't believe it.
9. The little girl is bright. She talks like an adult.
10. The child is energetic. She runs and jumps all day.
11. The picture is blurred. We can't see it clearly.
12. The professor talks rapidly. We can't take notes.

4/c/ 6 A B C D

= 26 — 29   120
                  100
              ——————
              100 - 120

Final